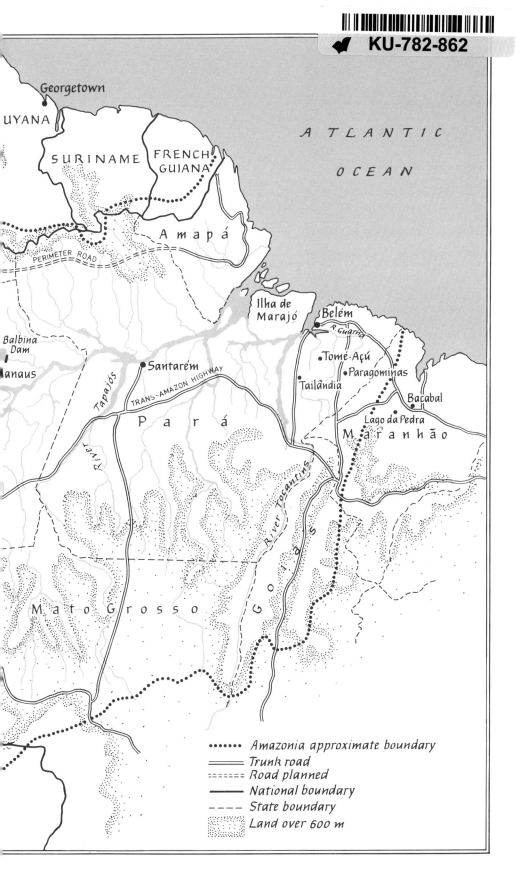

Georgetown

UYANA

SURINAME   FRENCH
            GUIANA

A T L A N T I C

O C E A N

A m a p á

PERIMETER ROAD

Ilha de
Marajó

Belém

Balbina
Dam

R. Guama

anaus

Santarém

Tomé-Açú

Paragominas

Tailândia

TRANS-AMAZON HIGHWAY

Bacabal

River

Tapajós

P a r á

Lago da Pedra

M a r a n h ã o

River Tocantins

G o i a s

M a t o G r o s s o

•••••• Amazonia approximate boundary
═══ Trunk road
====== Road planned
──── National boundary
- - - - State boundary
░░░░ Land over 600 m

AMAZON
WATERSHED

Also by George Monbiot
POISONED ARROWS

THE NCR
BOOK
AWARD

One of the many books entered
for the NCR Book Award for
Non-Fiction and presented
to the Library

Creating value

AMAZON
WATERSHED

The new environmental investigation

GEORGE MONBIOT

London

MICHAEL JOSEPH LTD
Published by the Penguin Group
Penguin Books Ltd, 27 Wrights Lane, London W8 5TZ, England
Viking Penguin, a division of Penguin Books USA Inc.
375 Hudson Street, New York, New York 10014, USA
Penguin Books Australia Ltd, Ringwood, Victoria, Australia
Penguin Books Canada Ltd, 2801 John Street, Markham, Ontario, Canada L3R 1B4
Penguin Books (NZ) Ltd, 182–190 Wairau Road, Auckland 10, New Zealand

Penguin Books Ltd, Registered Offices: Harmondsworth, Middlesex, England

First published in Great Britain 1991

Printed in England by Clays Ltd, St Ives plc
Filmset in Monophoto 11/13 Garamond to 25 ems

A CIP catalogue record for this book is available from the British Library

ISBN 0 7181 3428 1

The moral right of the author has been asserted

CONTENTS

Acknowledgements	vii
List of Illustrations	ix
Chapter 1	1
Chapter 2	12
Chapter 3	21
Chapter 4	44
Chapter 5	61
Chapter 6	103
Chapter 7	123
Chapter 8	130
Chapter 9	167
Chapter 10	195
Chapter 11	230
Chapter 12	258
References	266
Index	273

ACKNOWLEDGEMENTS

My special thanks to Roselis Remor de Souza, Bill Magnusson, Tania Sanaiotti, Anthony and Suely Anderson, Chris Uhl, Milton Monteiro, Maria José, Raimundo Rodrigues, Ilse Walker, Manoel Moura, Sebastião Duarte, Regina Duarte, Frei Adolfo Temme, Domingos Dutra, Regina Pauka, the *barraca* of Chimarão, Antônio Donato Nobre, Helen Lawrence, Ander McIntyre, Sue Branford, Wim Groenveld, Kimo (Langston James Goree VI), Matilde Oliveira de Araujo, Valmir de Souza, Maria Claudia Filipino, David Presswell, Hannah Scrase, Adrian Arbib, Claudia Andujar, Elisabete Monosouki, Christine Hugh-Jones, Barbara Mann, Carlo Zacquini, Tony Gross, Charles Clement, Augusto Pinto da Silveira, Dalila Queiroz Gerolano, Roberto Vancimi da Lima, David Arkcoll, Elisabeth van der Berg, Getulio Kazuyuki Sasaki, Toshihiko Takamatsu, Jan Rocha, Stuart Pim, Charles Secrett, Ju Mallas, Peter Vose, Bruce Nelson, Walter Mors, Sandra Charity, Crispin Jackson, Pat Stocker, Muriel Saragoussi, Chris Cox, Marcus Colchester, Phillipe Lena, Johannes van Leeuwen, José Savio Leopaldi, Jeffrey Richey, Philip Fearnside, Bruce Forsberg, Francisco Bezerra, Alfredo Wagner, Simon Counsell, Anthony Smith, Candy March, Tim Synnott, Guillermo O'Donnell, Alcida Rita Ramos, Dez Weeks, Sharon Pollard, Patricia Feeney, Robert Miller, John Harwood, Chico of CIMI, Lucilene Whitesell, Dave Treece, Anne Askwith, Caradoc King, Mary Loring, William Balée, Alan Poole, Peter Griffie, Oliver Tickell, Irving Foster Brown, Tom Lovejoy, Rubens Born, David Cleary, Pete Henderson, James Shuttleworth, Campbell Plowden, Koy Thomson, Mauro Victor, Eneas Salati, Nigel Sizer, Scott Subler, José Esquinas Alcazar, John Browder, Iara Ferraz, Jean Hebette.

LIST OF ILLUSTRATIONS

A treefrog of the closed canopy forest.
The forest canopy at dawn.
Milton Monteiro, where his father was shot.
Dona Maria José.
The men of São Sebastião.
Houses burnt down by the Barbosas' gunmen.
Manoel Barbosa with his granddaughter.
The third of Barbosa's gunmen.
Flying accident at Jeremias.
Miners working in the valley at Chimarão.
Edilson, one of the men of Chimãraozinho's camp.
Burning off the mercury.
A Yanomami family waiting for food at Jeremias.
An Indian woman bargaining for food.
Barbara Mann and a Yanomami woman.
Miners in Boa Vista.
Forest land cleared and burnt by settlers.
The sixty-four chiefs on the *Santa Marta 3*.
A Tukano woman bathing.
The church in the forest.
Cooking manioc meal in a Tukano kitchen.
A meeting of the Tukano women.
The road the soldiers built at Ipanaré.
Abandoned ranchland.
A logging yard at Paragominas.
Unrolling a log in a plywood mill.
Loading a charcoal lorry.
A bulldozer track through the forest at Paragominas.
Wood bound for Britain in the port of Belém.

Harvesting the fruit of the açaí palm.
Taking açaí fruit to market.
Oscar with the cocoa harvest.
One of the medicine markets in Belém.
Chris Uhl, with a mahogany seedling planted in degraded
    pastureland.
The peasant syndicate's experimental garden.

I

_____

As I sit down to write in the summer of 1990, the story of the Amazon is changing as quickly as ever before. The hopes of the world's conservationists, having risen with the accession of a new Brazilian government, now seem again to be faltering. While the rate at which the forests of the Amazon are disappearing has remained constant, the reasons for the destruction and the means by which it might be stopped have shifted rapidly. It is clear that the future of the greatest living system on earth will be determined in this decade.

Around me in my room in central England are the tokens of this progression, testimony to the means by which one of humanity's most dangerous adventures has governed the most turbulent year of my own life. In a corner beside my desk are the arrows of the Yanomami Indians, traded with an old man whose world was being taken from him. On the windowsill is a clay pot I was given by a woman of the Tukano tribe, while she campaigned to stop one of the most destructive of the new development projects. Inside it is a nugget of gold, a chip of mahogany and some cocoa beans: the last a reminder of the ways in which opinions on how the forest might be saved have changed. Among the piles of paper on my table are the cuttings from Brazilian newspapers reporting my torture, disappearance and possible death. I cannot help feeling that I have witnessed, at times involuntarily, some of the events which will help to shape the future story of mankind.

I set out in the summer of 1989 with the conviction that people in the northern hemisphere were missing the real story of the Amazon. From what I had seen on a previous journey, from what those involved in the events there were telling me, it was clear that we were hearing not about the new Amazon issues, but about the old ones they were supplanting. Most of the reports reaching the North still concentrated on such threats to the forests as cattle-ranching, government-sponsored settlement and dam-building. While these remained important, they were being overtaken by new developments. Settlers were flooding to the forests without government assistance, driven by acquisitive landlords, economic crises and farm technologies they could not afford. A project administered by the Brazilian armed forces had the object of bringing development to 20 per cent of the Brazilian Amazon, opening the regions inhabited only by Indians. Timber-cutting, once an insignificant cause of the Amazon's destruction, was threatening to take over as the economic motor of deforestation.

The best-known ways of preventing the wastage of the Amazon were also beginning to look outdated. The forest's ability to pay for its own upkeep, by means of products whose harvesting did not involve its destruction, was proving to be less promising than scientists had thought; and some of the excitement generated by new agricultural techniques, involving the farming of trees and new crops, was dying down as their problems became apparent. Conservationists had come to appreciate that the most important troubles of the Amazon were human ones, and that no strategy could forestall the destruction of the forests if it did not improve the lives both of the old inhabitants and of the newcomers. Foreign governments were being told, if not yet beginning to accept, that their help for the forests would require not only new environmental policies, but a revision of all the means by which they influenced events in Latin America.

Most importantly, it seemed to me that people were looking in the wrong direction if they wanted to see why the forests of the Amazon Basin were still being destroyed. All I understood of the situation suggested to me that the Amazon's problems were not, as they had repeatedly been portrayed, ecological: that the cutting, burning, flooding or excavation of the forests there were the symptoms, not the causes of the diseases they suffered. The problems, I felt, had their origin not in the Amazon itself, but elsewhere, in the political and economic hinterland of Latin America and the influential nations with which the continent deals. If I was to see why settlers were still streaming into the forests; why the governments of the Amazon continued, despite all the adverse publicity, to devise plans for the destruction of its natural systems; why, whenever one private means of removing the forests was suppressed, another would take its place, I would have to concentrate as much on the situations from which these developments arose, as on the calamities they were precipitating. Never, I felt, had there been so urgent a need to get to the heart of the troubles of the Amazon.

Though the Amazon is divided between the territories of nine Latin American nations – Brazil, Bolivia, Peru, Ecuador, Colombia, Venezuela, Guyana, French Guiana and Suriname – it is Brazil which has the greatest influence over the future of the forests there. This is the nation which possesses 70 per cent of the Amazon Basin, and in which 36 per cent of the world's rainforest destruction is taking place. All I have witnessed in the last year now persuades me that Brazil is also the place in which the victims of ecological destruction seem to have been blamed most comprehensively for the crimes. For the farmers, the miners and the other most visible agents of the Amazon's prostration also suffer from the fundamental problems afflicting the forests. It is these that I shall be investigating in this book, in my attempts to find the real villains of the story of the Amazon, and to see how their destructive power might be restrained.

But to discover why – when so many of those in power acknowledge that the Amazon should be saved – the forests are being cut as fast as ever before, I felt at the outset that a new means of approaching the problems of the Amazon was needed. There had been no rigorous investigations by Northern journalists of the new threats and the deeper troubles which gave rise to them. If I was to come close enough to the issues to understand why the destruction in the Amazon was continuing, and what could be done to stop it, I felt that I would need to launch the sort of voyage of discovery that other writers had been reluctant to contemplate: in which the investigator becomes not only an observer but a potential victim of the troubles.

But my admission to the modern story of the Amazon took place some time before I was shipwrecked, or I was sheltered by a murderer on the most brutal of the forest frontiers, or escaped from the military policeman who tried to kill me. For, just as the Amazon's problems and potential solutions were changing rapidly, new findings were transforming scientific knowledge of the ways in which the natural systems function, and why they might be important to the rest of the world. To understand what the consequences of wrecking the greatest repository of life on earth might be, I needed to look at how the Amazon works.

It is hard to conceive of the size of the River Amazon and the forests and scrublands it drains without a familiar comparison. So I sought, throughout my journeys in the Basin, a river which could be compared to Britain's most celebrated waterway, the Thames. In the far north-west of Brazil, on a journey through the territory of the Tukano Indians, I found one: a tributary called the Rio Tiquié, which is a little longer than the River Thames, but narrower in the lower reaches.

The Tiquié flows into the Uaupés, an unremarkable Amazonian river of around three times the length of the Thames. The Uaupés is itself a tributary of the Rio Negro, a tributary of the Amazon. The Rio Negro is the second largest river in the world, with a discharge slightly greater than that of the Congo, or three times that of the Mississippi, or greater than all the rivers of Europe combined. When it reaches the main river, having travelled 2400 kilometres from Colombia, the Negro, impressive as it is, adds only 15 per cent to the Amazon's volume.

During the wet season as much as one fifth of the world's freshwater may be flowing through the Amazon. Eight hundred kilometres inland it is as wide as the English Channel. In the river's mouth there is an island larger than Denmark, or twice the size of New Hampshire; and the waterflow is such that, at certain times of the year, the river's discharge is visible 300 kilometres out to sea. The Rio Tiquié, a tributary of a tributary of a tributary of the River Amazon, is called a stream by some of the people living there.

The Amazon's great volume is, of course, a product of the basin it drains, and this itself is the result of a convoluted geological history. The rivers of the Basin used to flow from east to west, from close to the Atlantic coast westwards to the Pacific. As the Andes mountains emerged, around forty million years ago, they dammed the westward drainage. The rivers continued at first to flow along their old courses, and the water gathered to become a shallow lake, covering most of the western Basin. But as the land rose further the lake was tipped towards the Atlantic; and the rivers began to flow in the opposite direction. Relief maps of South America show that the Basin is as a result back to front, broadest at its headwaters, narrowest at its mouth. This enables it to capture, in a neat arc, most of the waters of the north and central Andes, as well as the eastern rivers which once fed the original channel. The reversed flow is also responsible for the lack of haste with which the River Amazon descends: in the last 3000 of its 6500 kilometres it falls only 60 metres.

The result is a catchment into which the European Community could fit three times. Twenty-eight Britains could be reproduced in the Basin, and were the United States to fall on top of it, only Alaska, Texas and Florida would hang over the edges. The Amazon Basin, accounting for most of the northern lands of South America, covers 7 per cent of the surface of the earth. More significantly, it contains 40 per cent of its tropical forests.

Over the days I spent with scientists in the rainforests of the Amazon I came to see how little I could hope to know of the animals and plants inhabiting them. Whether foraging over the forest floor at night with a headlight, or climbing up a scaffolding tower into the canopy of the trees, or diving into the streams with a snorkel and a torch, I found that however many times I returned, most of what I saw on each occasion was new to me. Indeed the diversity – of frogs, birds, insects, and of the trees themselves – is such that even the biologists who have worked for several years in the same patch of forest find that they are still encountering new species among the groups of animals and plants they know best.

There may be as many as six million insect species in the Amazon[1], and 10,000 varieties of trees. In the rivers there are said to be 3000 kinds of fish, and we know less of them in total than we do of Britain's 36. I was lucky enough to be among the first outsiders to see a fish species which had recently been discovered. Without eyes or scales, coloured scarlet, the wormfish lived during the dry season not in the water, but in the damp leaves and sand of the forest floor. It seemed to me to epitomize all that is strange and vulnerable about the Amazon, and to hint at the prodigious nature of some of the animals likely to be lost before they are ever found.

That the great tottering pyramids of life in the Basin are built upon sand is now common currency; but in truth the infertility of the forest soils is sometimes exaggerated. While only 7 per cent of the earth in the Amazon could be considered suitable for growing crops, some scientists believe that much of the land is reasonably rich in nutrients; but they are unavailable to any plants except trees. Useful minerals in the soil are bound up by molecules of iron and aluminium, and only trees have the time and the regularity of growth to exploit them as they are steadily released[2].

But once these nutrients have been drawn from the earth, the competition for them becomes intense. Each tree, or piece of a tree, which falls to the floor of the forest is immediately cannibalized by the survivors. For this reason much of the litter which drops from the canopy is caught before it reaches the ground. Rootlets grow not just within the soil, but over its surface, like fur. Sometimes, cutting open a log on the forest floor, you may find that nothing remains of it but bark; the rest is a swarm of vegetable maggots.

This has led scientists to assume that the forest is shallowly rooted. Like the supposed infertility of the soil, this seems to be a misconception. Researchers digging recently in the east of the Amazon found the rootlets of forest trees twelve metres from the surface, and discovered that there was as great a length of roots below the depth of half a metre as above[3]. Deep rooting is likely to be important in the Amazon. Not only can trees by this means probe for more of the sparse available minerals; but the structure of Amazon soils is such that water drains from them quickly, and in the drier season the upper layers can parch. Just as more people in the Sahara die of drowning than of thirst, trees in one of the world's wettest places have evolved a resistance to drought.

Perhaps by contrast to the soils of the Amazon, some of the rivers of the region are poorer in the elements supporting life than rain[4]. The Rio Negro and the other blackwater rivers of the Basin work in terms of their nutrient supplies contrary to nearly all the other rivers of the world. While rivers normally gather minerals on their way downstream, which is why floodplains are fertile and the sea becomes salty, the Rio Negro loses salts as it runs towards its mouth.

Such rivers drain some of the world's most ancient rocks, which, like teabags used too many times, have lost the nutrient minerals they once contained. As the forests, the hoarders of minerals, allow almost nothing they have accumulated to escape into the water, life in the rivers has evolved to survive on a starvation diet. Fungus appears to extract minerals from the water itself, and aquatic animals exploit the opportunities to steal from the forest whenever these arise. When the rivers flood, the fish move into the trees, to pillage what the retreating forest animals have left behind.

The Rio Negro is black – or a deep copper brown – because of the humic acids, released from decomposing leaves, which are dissolved in it. But the River Amazon it flows into and the other rivers springing not from the ancient shields of the nort!. and south but from the Andes in the west are the colour of milky coffee. In these cases the staining acids are mixed with the debris of younger rocks. But because of their peculiar chemistry, and the great distances over which their mineral loads are spread, even the fertility of these rivers and the plains they inundate is limited.

Around 70 per cent of the Amazon Basin is or was covered by dense, closed-canopy rainforests. Here the trees cast shade of such a depth that where the forest is undisturbed it is almost impossible to take photographs, even with a tripod, at midday, close to the Equator. Light penetrating the crowns in the upper layers is intercepted by those below, until the treetops which fill the sky between 15 and 30 metres from the ground prevent any but the slimmest beams from reaching the forest floor. In places where the soils, water or generations of human interference have not permitted the taller trees to grow, they give way to savannahs, scrublands or sparse swamp forests.

The rainforests have been described many times, and quite mistakenly, as the lungs of the world. This concept evolved from a journalist's misquote of a famous Amazon scientist, and soon became popular, amongst Amazonians as well as foreigners. In fact the mature forest neither consumes carbon dioxide nor produces oxygen. Instead, its consumption of gases is in balance. While, during the day, the trees absorb carbon dioxide and release oxygen, using the carbon to make the sugars which build and sustain them; at night this process is shut down and the trees respire, absorbing oxygen and exhaling carbon dioxide. The other organisms of the forest, insects, mammals, birds and microbes, respiring by day and night, settle the balance. If this were not the case, and more carbon dioxide were being destroyed than being produced, solid carbon would necessarily be accumulating somewhere in the system. Either the trees would always be growing, towards an infinity in space; or those that fell would be piling up on the forest floor uneaten. This second situation has in fact occurred, but only on rare occasions in the earth's prehistory, as peculiar conditions have allowed fallen wood to turn to coal.

But while the forest is clearly not, in this sense, the lungs of the world, it is a reservoir of potential carbon dioxide. Trees could be represented as sticks of wet carbon, which, when dried and burnt, returns to the atmosphere as gas. This is the process taking place in Amazonia. Scientists are vigorously debating the extent to which the burning forests might be contributing to the accumulation of the gas in the atmosphere. One estimate suggests that a small farmer in the Amazon, cutting and burning one hectare of forest each year, releases as much carbon dioxide as 30 Americans, 55 Britons or 75 Japanese; while one cattle-rancher incinerating 2000 hectares has the same impact as 60,000 people consuming fossil fuels in America[5], or 115,000 in Great Britain. Burning in the Amazon may be responsible for anywhere between 4 and 25 per cent of the worldwide carbon dioxide emissions now helping to raise the temperature of the planet.

But gases are not the rainforest's only contribution to the atmosphere. The climate of the towns in the Amazon is strikingly different to that of the forest only a few kilometres away. The shade of the forest is several degrees cooler than that of the town, and rain falls more frequently. It is extraordinary to stand on some evenings on a high spot in the central Amazonian city of Manaus, a clear sky above your head, and watch the lightning assault the forest at all points beyond the town's periphery. The city, though a small mark on the map, has altered its own climate sufficiently to receive 25 per cent less rainfall than the forest which surrounds it.

The main reason for this contrast is that the forest, unlike the buildings which have replaced it in Manaus, generates its own rain. In order both to draw minerals from the forest floor and to cool their leaves, the trees pump great quantities of water from their roots to their crowns, and away into the atmosphere. This process, as well as direct evaporation from the leaves, means that around 75 per cent of the rainwater landing on the forest is returned to the atmosphere. The remaining 25 per cent slips away through the earth and percolates into the rivers[6].

The water sustaining the forests of the Amazon comes initially from the Atlantic Ocean. Much of this falls close to the coast, and is pumped back into the air by the forest there. It is only because the trees in the east are in this way recycling the fallen water that it becomes available to those further west. It is carried by westerly winds slowly towards the Andes, passing, as it travels, through several cycles of rainfall, absorption, pumping and evaporation. As it is the forest which generates much of the rain irrigating the west, forest destruction in the east is likely to reduce it. It is in the east that the current deforestation is greatest.

In order to avoid the possibility of parching, the rainforest needs at least 1200 millimetres of rain each year. Most of the Amazon Basin receives between 2000 and 3000 millimetres, but in some parts it is as little as 1700[7]. This means, in raw terms, that a reduction of just over 40 per cent of the water these areas receive will kill the forest growing there.

But the raw figures disguise the more alarming implications. When the rainfall of a region is reduced it tends to diminish unevenly around the year. What often happens is that the dry season becomes longer and drier, while during the wet season the precipitation may scarcely change. In many parts of the Amazon the dry season is already, naturally, of a length which is only just tolerable to rainforest trees, even though the rainfall, if falling regularly throughout the year, would be more than sufficient[8]. The dry season on the central plateau, for example, can last for as long as ninety days, which seems to be more or less the absolute survival limit of the trees there. Were this to be exceeded, two things could happen, with terrible speed.

Under normal circumstances the standing forest is impossible to burn, as the closed canopy of the trees acts as a lid on its saturated atmosphere. When farmers wish to burn the trees, they first have to cut them and then wait for many days for the dead wood to dry. But if the dry season lasts too long, the trees shed their leaves, and the water vapour trapped in the forest escapes. It is then that fires can catch and run in the standing wood.

This nearly happened during the last ninety-day dry, in 1983. Farmers burning their fields on the edge of the trees saw that the flames could travel for up to five kilometres into the forest, before encountering the damper core[9]. Were the dry season to last for more than ninety days, there would be no damper core. The recent history of Borneo provides some indication of what could happen in such conditions. There the dry season of 1982-83 was exceptionally long. Fires started by settlers in the jungle caught amongst the standing trees, and burnt for four months, destroying three and a half million hectares of forest. If the westward drying of the Amazon takes place as a result of cutting in the east, there may be nothing to stop a fire started at the Amazon's mouth traversing much of the Basin.

9

But a serious drought alone, unaccompanied by fire, could kill the forests it afflicted in a single season. In their place, if the drought was repeated, one could expect a thorny scrub to grow, or possibly extensions of the grassland which now covers the drier parts of the Amazon. Slighter effects may be visible already. Rainwater which does not return to the atmosphere creeps through the soil and into the rivers, and the removal of forest which has taken place so far seems to have made the waters less predictable. There is some, equivocal evidence to suggest that wet-season flooding has already become more frequent and more extensive.

The effects of the forests' recycling of rain extend beyond the Amazon. Some of the water vapour from the Basin is exported to other parts of South America[6]. In the important agricultural lands of Paraguay and the centre of Brazil, water is already scarce, and a slight reduction could be critical. Another fraction goes north, and there are scientists who claim that the recent droughts in the American mid-West might have been connected to cutting in the Amazon.

There is another aspect of the cycling of water through the forest which could be of still greater significance. When you step from a shower, even a warm shower, you find that your skin rapidly chills. As the waterdrops evaporate, heat is drawn from your body: the heat is used to transform the drops into vapour. This is what also happens in the Amazon. The shade of the forest is cooler than the shade of the city because, as water evaporates, heat is drawn from the forest and returned to the atmosphere.

If you look at a map of the world you will see that much of the earth's surface around the Equator is covered by ocean. Of the land between the two ten-degree parallels, 50 per cent is or was covered by tropical forests. Thirty per cent is in South America. The band around the Equator produces much of the heat transmitted to other parts of the world by currents in the atmosphere. But it is generated unevenly. While water evaporates from the ocean surface it does not rise, as the temperature at the surface is no greater than the temperature of the air. But as the forest canopy heats during the day, convection currents are generated, which lift the water vapour it loses into the atmosphere.

Air moves globally, just as it does locally, from hot places to cool ones. As it moves from the tropics towards the poles, it carries some of its water vapour with it. As the vapour reaches colder climates it condenses, and the latent heat it stores is released. Some scientists have suggested that it is this, the water from tropical rainforests, which is partly responsible for keeping the ice at the ends of the earth from spreading[8]. This suggests that the absence of tropical forests could provoke not only an acceleration of global warming, by means of the greenhouse effect; but also a profound polar cooling, caused by the reduced transfer of latent heat. The effect, if it occurs, is likely to be more powerful in some areas than in others. Europe, on the same latitude as some of the world's coldest regions, is kept warm by currents in the ocean and the air. They come from the tropics, from the south-west, the continent of South America.

2

———————

PERHAPS THE MOST EXCITING of the scientific work in Amazonia involves the people who were once its only inhabitants. The Indians are believed to have arrived in the Basin between 12,000 and 10,000 years ago, having travelled from Siberia, over the Aleutian islands or landbridge, through the lands which are now Alaska, Canada, North America and Mexico, across the Darien Peninsula and into the mountains of the South American north-west. Arriving in the Amazon, these Chinese-Siberian-Inuit-Redskin-Maya-type people had to adapt yet again to an unfamiliar environment. They shed the conventions and the clothes of their northern ancestors, and became the apprentices of the forest.

The extent to which these strangers adjusted their lives to the natural systems which were there already, or altered the systems to suit themselves, is subject to a scientific debate of great practical importance. On the basis of several new discoveries, some scientists have entirely revised their understanding of the ways in which the forest systems can be changed without destroying them, and how the existing destruction might best be contained without harming the Basin's more recent arrivals. No means of assessing the new developments in the Amazon, I felt, would be more useful than an attempt to understand the practices of the forests' first inhabitants.

Until recently anthropologists were tending towards the opinion that the lives of tribal people are the products of their environment: that they adapt their lifestyle and even their population to the requirements of the natural world. It is the view I tendered in my last book, *Poisoned Arrows*, about the people and the problems of Irian Jaya, the Indonesian half of New Guinea. But researchers working in Amazonia in the last few years have begun, independently, to come to a different conclusion: that the Amazon may be as much the product of the Indians as the Indians are the product of the Amazon.

Earlier work in the Amazon suggested that the Indian societies there had characteristically been simple ones: small in scale, without big chiefs or a distinct division of labour. Those communities differing from this rule, some of which were encountered by the first Europeans to invade the Basin, were simply groups of Indians from the Andes, who had recently transferred themselves, their culture and their social hierarchy down from the mountains into the plains, and had little to tell us about the society of Amazonia. But what are to my mind the most intriguing – if among the least celebrated – archaeological discoveries since the tombs of the pharaohs were opened suggest that the cultural pattern may have been just the other way around. Small scattered settlements may have accounted for fewest of the Indians; for it was in cities that Amazonian culture had its heart.

The American Anna Roosevelt is the pioneer of this greatest archaeological frontier. She has been able to do what was open not even to the Victorian explorers of Egypt – to clear a field in a scientific wilderness – and to do it moreover with modern analytical techniques. Her findings have overturned all but the most prescient thinking on how the Amazon must have been before the Europeans arrived[1].

Along the big whitewater rivers of Amazonia were closely spaced settlements, each of several thousand people. The modern town of Santarém, where 200,000 Brazilians of European blood now live, sits on the site of an older, more extensive one. Around this and the other pre-European towns of the Amazon are earthworks covering thousands of square kilometres.

Among them Anna Roosevelt has found the burial chambers of Indian leaders, whose mummified bodies are surrounded by the images of gods. They and a class of managers who served them seem not only to have been honoured in death, but privileged throughout life: analysis of their skeletons shows that they had access to foods unavailable to their minions. This suggests a ranked society, like the traditional states of Europe or the Middle East, but quite distinct from those of the modern Amazonian Indians. There is evidence that Indian leaders ruled over areas greater than the ancient British kingdoms. Pottery depicting human figures suggests that the Indians had turned away from their beliefs in animal spirits, towards the possible worship of other human beings.

The development of these stratified societies appears to have accompanied changes in Indian agriculture, made necessary by growing population pressure. The first arrivals seem to have exhausted the big game and shellfish they first exploited, before turning to the cultivation of manioc: the root known outside South America as cassava. As the population expanded further and the remaining wild foods of the forest failed to provide it with all the protein it required, the people turned towards the more proteinous seed-crops, such as maize and grasses, as their main means of subsistence.

The cultivation of seeds allows a population to store the surplus food it produces. Stocks of food enable a community to remain in one place, and release some people from the need to farm. The stratification of society might have occurred when some citizens began to turn from agriculture to trade or administration. The high productivity the Indians achieved appears to testify to agricultural techniques the modern world has yet to master.

The *conquistadores* destroyed the urban civilization of the Amazon just as, had they arrived among the ancient Egyptians, they might have destroyed theirs. But in the case of South America the Spanish and the Portuguese brought a particularly potent means of conquering the people of another time: their biological weaponry. It would seem reasonable to suppose that the invaders of the sixteenth century saw only fragments of the society which must have existed before their arrival, because the diseases they imported marched ahead of them. As Indians fled into the interior, they carried their new infections with them. These are believed to have spread along the trade routes[2], and smallpox, tuberculosis, flu, measles and common colds were exchanged for the Amazonian diseases which Indians could resist and Europeans could not. The Amazon's armies were routed before the Europeans raised a sword. Lacking stone, the Indians of the Amazon floodplains, unlike those of the Andes or Central America, left nothing but mounds of earth to remind us of their obliteration.

The Europeans conquered and settled the floodplains before the rest of the Amazon, as these were the lands most likely to sustain the farming and the commerce they were used to. The floodplains Indians died or scattered, destroyed by war, disease and slavery, and the fragments of their nascent civilization disintegrated on the plateaus they fled to. The diseases they carried and the slaving raids which followed them introduced their troubles to the upland Indians. Until the late 1970s there were fewer people in the Amazon than there were before the invasions of the 1500s.

While the riverine Indians were obliterated, a small proportion of those living in other parts of the Basin, in the forests and savannahs of the plateaus, survived. Anthropologists working with their descendants are now trying to determine the extent to which they restrain their lifestyles to fit the existing environment, or alter the environment to suit their lives.

Much of the anthropological theory of the later years of this century has been built around the supposition that forest people, like animals, are limited to what the natural habitat can provide. Aware that if their numbers become excessive they will exhaust the soils, the wild plants or the game on which they depend, they have been supposed to practise various forms of population control: contraception, infanticide or bloody warfare.

Such practices do indeed seem to take place among some Indian groups. The women of the Yanomami tribe, for instance, are known to kill some of their newborn babies, particularly females. But there are now suggestions that this might have less to do with controlling of the population in order to preserve a pristine environment than with the reduction of a family's size to suit the parents. Even if the numbers of people in a community are being deliberately limited, there is no reason to suppose that the cause is necessarily environmental. A small, mobile population with a greater number of males than females, for instance, could make a community less vulnerable to attack.

Most importantly, several anthropologists have shown that certain Indian tribes deliberately alter the forest they live in, managing it to support a higher population. What might seem to outsiders to be a pristine forest may in fact be the tended garden of the tribe that lives there.

While anthropologists have long been aware that most tribes in the Amazon farm small patches of their territory, their assessment of Indian agriculture has tended to underestimate its scale and its complexity. Traditional forest farming anywhere in the tropics involves the cutting and burning of trees to make a clearing, in which crops are raised for a few years, before the forest is allowed to repair the hole. It looks crude and untidy. But studies of the

Kayapó[3,4], one of the most robust tribes still to inhabit the southern Amazon, now hint at an astonishing precision.

To earlier observers, among them Brazilian developers, Kayapó fields were a mess that lazy farmers make. In the patch they cut from the forest they plant several crops at once, scattered among the tree trunks which are left on the ground. Weeds are allowed to grow with them, and parts of the clearing are on occasions burnt. In this disorder the anthropologist Darrel Posey and his colleagues have found a science of tropical agriculture far more sophisticated than our own.

Among the most striking of the Kayapó's crop developments are fire-resistant varieties of sweet potatoes. By planting these breeds before the felled vegetation is burnt, the Indians avoid the most pressing of the problems suffered by the colonists of Amazonia: that of the loss of the nutrients released by the burning of the trees. The sweet potatoes, having established themselves before the burn, are ready to catch these minerals as they are washed into the soil.

Each of the many different crop species is planted in the patches of the field which suit it best: some favour the direct sunlight of the centre, others the partial shade of the forest edge. The dead trees left on the ground release the nutrients they had accumulated steadily, offer partial shade and trap moisture. Among the many plants producing foods, medicines, poisons and fibres, manioc is cultivated as the principal staple crop; in my estimation the world's most sophisticated. Some of the manioc varieties developed by the Amazonian Indians are so toxic that people eating the unprepared roots die within a few hours. The poison is cyanide, which can be processed out of a root by soaking, grating and squeezing. This means that while the crop is edible to humans, it will kill the other animals which try to eat it. The plant also secretes sugar from nodules on the stem. The sugar is eaten by ants which, in return, cut off any vines entangling the plant. So manioc not only provides its own pesticide, but also weeds itself. It is adapted too to thrive in soils which are deficient in nutrients, seasonally parched and poisoned by aluminium: the soils which many Indians have little choice but to farm.

The Kayapó believe that different crops require different preparations of fertilizer, and take pains to apply what they consider to be the correct type of ash. They also pile the nests of termites and biting ants onto the fields, not only because these are high in certain nutrients, but also because the biting ants are believed to drive away leafcutter ants, which might otherwise destroy the crops[2]. The weeds growing amongst the favoured plants also seem to have a purpose. They shade the bare soil from the sun and rain, and trap nutrients which might otherwise be washed away.

By contrast to most modern Amazonian agriculture, Kayapó farming seems to improve the soil. The Kayapó aerate the earth with machetes, and as a result it never loses its friability. As large quantities of food are not, or traditionally were not, exported from their communities, there is no loss of nutrients. Crop wastes are returned to the soil, as are scraps, excrement, animal bones and even human corpses. As organic refuse accumulates around Kayapó settlements the soil becomes deep and black; while the earth farmed by colonists loses its nutrients within a few years.

As the field ages, the forest begins to reclaim it. Since Kayapó clearings are small, the gap closes rapidly. But the Indians also manage the returning trees. They plant or favour those species which will produce food, fibres or medicines[5]. The forest, when it regenerates, may be as diverse and structurally complex as that which grew there before; but it now contains a different assemblage of trees, many of which are useful to the Indians.

It is mainly the women of the Kayapó who manage the clearings; the men of the tribe manipulate the wilderness around them. In the savannahs covering parts of their territory, the men plant copses of the useful trees they would otherwise have to search for in the forest[4]. Researchers have found 120 species in these forest islands, of which 98 per cent are useful, providing food, medicines, magical preparations, drinking gourds, firewood and insect repellents.

Kayapó men may trek for several weeks across their territory. To avoid the trouble of carrying the quantities of food, medicines or weapons they need, they plant the raw materials throughout the wilderness. They establish groves in the forest, cultivate crops beside the trails, or encourage the growth of certain wild trees at the expense of others. The land they wander is a jungle only to Northern eyes; to the Kayapó it is a rambling forest garden.

Not all the surviving Indians of the Amazon farm their lands as the Kayapó do. Some do not appear to farm at all, while some groups are careless of their resources, and seem to overexploit their soils. Like us the Indians may on occasions be destructive or cruel: one tribe has been reported to use fish poisons repeatedly, until all the animals of a stream have been killed; and the Kayapó, while planting trees in some places, may burn them in others, among other reasons to produce 'beautiful effects in the sky'. But in general the Indians have learnt to work beside nature, to subvert the natural processes into providing for themselves. Whilst in temperate countries we can wipe the slate of nature clean before sketching in our agricultural designs, the tropical world is harder to suppress. Farming which makes use of wildlife, rather than confronting it as an enemy, is likely to demand less effort and to be more sustainable.

The science of the Amazon Indians is not a formal process of deductions and decisions. A variety of manioc is selected not for its resistance to aluminium toxicity, but because it happens to do well in a soil type the Indians recognize. Theirs is a process of experience and learning through watching, or through examples encoded in traditional fables[6]. The relationship they have with the forest and their fields goes beyond understanding, and into the realm of sensation. In many tribes there are deliberate efforts to use resources sparingly, to conserve certain assets which might otherwise be exhausted: the Tukano Indians, for instance, protect the flooded forests where the fish they catch feed; while a Kayapó legend warns that if part of a raided bees' nest is not left behind for the bees to rebuild, the spirit of a shaman will punish them with thunderstorms. But walking lightly on the earth is only one of several means of living from the forests.

There is no doubt that even the forests of the plateaus once supported many more tribal people than they do today. Some historical reports suggest that there may have been several million. In 1599, for instance, the Jivaroan Indians of a part of the Upper Amazon rose against the Europeans. They mustered 25,000 warriors, half as many active men as all the tribes of the Brazilian Amazon could now supply. There is evidence that some of the Kayapó settlements each contained several thousand people. It seems reasonable to suggest that the low population in the Amazon uplands is a result of the European conquest, not of the poverty of the forests.

If then there were some millions of Indians living on the Amazon plateaus, as well as some millions more in the floodplains, and if most of the groups were farming much as the Kayapó do today, then they must have had a profound effect upon what we have taken to be a wilderness. There is evidence to suggest that much of the Amazon forest has, over the millennia, been remodelled by the hands of man.

When I had spent several days and nights in a nature reserve to the north of Manaus, and had marvelled at the diversity of the plants and the animals of the forest, I was taken to a hole dug in the sand and clay it was founded on. Some centimetres from the surface, cutting through the earth, was a layer of dark particles. Most were small flecks, but among them were blackened twigs and pieces of heartwood: it was charcoal. Not long, in geological time, before I had stepped among that multiplicity of trees, the forest had been burnt to the ground.

Charcoal is found to underlie three quarters of the Amazon[7]. Some scientists believe that this is the product of man, others of natural fires started in times of drought. Just a few kilometres from the reserve I stayed in, the carbon layers are found in association with pieces of clay pot, and griddles for preparing manioc. Radiocarbon dating suggests that this forest was burnt between 800 and 1100 years ago[8]. Yet the trees now growing there are among the most diverse in the central Amazon.

The implications are astonishing. Not only might much of the Amazon rainforest, patch by garden patch, have been burnt down by the Indians who lived there, but those Indians appear to have preserved, possibly even enhanced, the natural systems' diversity. By altering the composition of the forest, either as it regenerated or as it stood, the people could have acquainted species which would never otherwise have been found together. Certain useful trees, such as oranges, avocados and papayas, entered the Amazon and spread from tribe to tribe before the white man arrived, and there are some plants which seem to have accompanied the Indians all the way from Asia to Argentina. Others might have been traded from tribe to tribe within the Basin, and introduced to forests in which they had not grown before.

There are some trees which, though at first assumed by outsiders to be wild, show all the signs of selective breeding by humans: a palmtree, for instance, bearing fruits the size of grapes in some places and fruits the size of apples elsewhere. As the patches the Indians cut and burnt were small enough to have been easily recolonized by forest, as the nutrients were carefully conserved and no chemical pesticides were applied, as their manipulation of the forest might have delayed the maturity which could have allowed

19

certain species to become dominant, Indian farming might in some places have made the environment more complex than it was before. There are some parts of the Amazon, by contrast, which bear the marks of overexploitation by Indians: forests dominated by vines or by a single tree species, or replaced by sparse scrub.

There are no more than 650,000 Indians in the Amazon today, many still suffering the diseases, slavery and war with which the white man first persecuted them. Along the floodplains of the whitewater rivers, where Indian kings were once buried with their gods, the only fragments of surviving tribal culture are found amongst the *caboclos*. These are the peasants of mixed indigenous and Portuguese blood, descended from the Indians corralled, in the seventeenth and eighteenth centuries, by Jesuit priests and the Portuguese crown.

The caboclos have scattered along the riverbanks in response to the demands of the export economy, extracting forest products such as brazilnuts, rubber, chewing-gum resin and jute, not only for their own use but also for sale originally to Portuguese traders, now to other Brazilians. Like the Indians of the plateau they also grow manioc in forest clearings. They are inventive and skilful cultivators, often experimenting with new crops. But the farming techniques of the old kingdoms have been lost; they disappeared with the culture which gave rise to them. The big farmers of the floodplains now raise cattle or buffalo, an inefficient use of land. There is no greater indictment of the Amazon's development than that for all the technology applied, all the pesticides, the fertilizers, the learning and advice, the people now living there rely on imported food.

3

To FIND OUT WHERE the responsibility for the despoliation of the Amazon lies, I felt I should look first at the most numerous of its new inhabitants: the peasant colonists. If I was to see why small farmers from other parts of Brazil are continuing to move into the Amazon, I believed that I should first examine not the places in which they arrive but the regions from which they come.

It seemed to me that I should start at this point because, of all the perceived aggressors of the Amazon, it is the colonists who are most often blamed for the destruction there. In the newspapers and on television, in Brazil and in the North, we see pictures in which the agents of destruction are closely linked to the mess they make: smallholders cutting fields from the forest, or goldminers destroying the Indians' habitat. We see less of those with long levers – absentee landlords, corporate executives, development consultants, government policy makers – as they are seldom found close to the forests destroyed by their decisions.

As human rights groups have made clear, but a regrettably small number of politicians have chosen to acknowledge, hundreds of thousands of the colonists arriving in the Amazon and destroying the natural systems there are not doing so through choice. The briefest examination of the patterns of migration shows that the movement is not simply that of hordes of peasants decamping to the forests to improve their lives.

The states the settlers are coming from all have better soils than they will find in the Amazon. Most of these states, including those sending most of the settlers, are underpopulated in terms of their farming potential. Brazil is a nation thirty-five times the size of Great Britain, with a little over twice its population. If, in some disastrous collectivist enterprise, all the land outside the Amazon were divided equally between its inhabitants, then every man, woman and child, whether living in the countryside or the town, would be entitled to two and a half hectares: enough, in most places, to support one person indefinitely. The fact that people are fleeing from fertile but empty farmland to grow crops on a barren and increasingly competitive frontier suggests that many of them are being driven by something other than volition.

Peasants are being dislodged from the south of Brazil partly by the intensification of agriculture. As new technologies and the export crops the government supports favour those farmers who have capital to invest, and exclude those too poor to buy new equipment or chemicals, the peasants there find themselves unable to compete. But in the North East region of Brazil, which lies in fact just to the south-east of the Amazon, small farmers are leaving their land because the big landowners are forcing them to do so.

Land and power in the North East of Brazil are indivisible. The political control of the countryside has always been the privilege of the people who own the most land. Many of the biggest landowners in the North East and the rest of Brazil are the senators, ministers and army chiefs who govern the nation. Their power indeed is often rooted in their landholdings, the local political bases from which they established their national influence.

The peasants living in or beside these estates have traditionally been treated as the chattels of the landlords. Into the second half of this century they were still marketable in some areas, and the owners took for themselves the peasant women they wanted. On a few farms this continues, and there are slaves in Brazil living in worse conditions than the African plantation workers of previous centuries.

While in most regions unpaid labour has ceased – though the equally pernicious debt slavery is still widespread – the lives of the peasants in the North East have if anything deteriorated. Thousands of legitimate peasant properties have been handed over to large landowners by the authorities, even though the peasants depended on these smallholdings for survival. Partly as a result of these acquisitions, landownership in the North East, and in Brazil as a whole, is among the most uneven in the world. Less than 1 per cent of the landowners in the nation possess 43 per cent of the land, while, in this republic of empty spaces, 35 million rural peasants are landless. Some landlords own properties of several hundred thousand hectares, much of which may be entirely unproductive. An area larger than India is used, like paper investments, for nothing but financial speculation.

But through their trades unions, aided by radical priests and human rights lawyers, the peasants have been fighting not only for the right to retain the lands they own, but also for agrarian reform: the redistribution of some of the properties owned yet unused by the biggest of the landlords. Since Brazil's military leaders began to be eased out of office, being replaced by civilians in 1985, government in Brazil has become less repressive, if not necessarily more representative; and the peasants' voice has gradually become louder.

In 1989, for instance, in the first direct presidential elections for twenty-eight years, the Workers' Party candidate, representing the small farmers and the urban poor, was only narrowly defeated. The increasing visibility of the peasants and the stirrings of social conscience in the urban middle class have prompted the last three governments to promise a widespread agrarian reform. The promises have never been fulfilled, but they have provoked two conflicting effects: they have raised the hopes of the peasants and they have frightened many of the landowners. With the possibilities of reform the landlords began to see in the peasant movements serious threats to their traditional hegemony. For this reason among others they have, in the last and this present decade, been expelling the peasants of the North East from their own lands.

Between 1980 and 1990 over 1000 peasants and the priests, lawyers and union leaders trying to help them have been murdered, to silence them and to persuade others to flee. To this end the landlords and the gunmen they hire have also burnt tens of thousands of peasant homes, poisoned the small farmers' crops and taken many of the people from their villages for torture. In these operations the landlords act with the approval of the authorities. State governors depend on the support of the local mayors, who are characteristically landlords. The police and the judiciary are controlled by the governors, so, in practice, work to uphold the interests of the landowners, against those of the peasants. Members of the federal government, who might have been expected to overrule the corrupt authority of the states, are often themselves the biggest landowners of all, and will do little to hinder the privileged minority to which they belong.

There is little recourse for the peasants being persecuted, so they flee. When the land or the livelihood has been taken from people in the North East of Brazil there are only two places to go. Some move to the shanty towns around the big cities, where they find theft, prostitution and social dismemberment. Tens of thousands flee to the Amazon. Many of them go because it is the best alternative to being murdered.

The state which both kills more peasants and, for reasons not unconnected to this record, probably sends more to the forests than any other, is Maranhão, the North Eastern territory whose northern border touches Amazonia. It was there that I had decided to begin my research.

I had collected, over the course of several months in Britain and Brazil, many case histories of the expulsions from that state, most of which seemed worthy of investigation. In the middle of September 1989 when I, through choice, was living in the Amazon, I heard of a situation which impressed me with its urgency. The village of Centro dos Aguiar, close to the town of Bacabal in the centre of Maranhão, seemed, on the day I first received news of it, to be on the point of forcible abandonment and migration.

Centro dos Aguiar had been founded thirty-five years before by refugees from droughts in the southerly state of Ceará. When they had arrived on what was then the agricultural frontier, they chose to live in an area whose land had no owners. It was fertile, the rainfall was good, and the people, caboclos who farmed using some of the skills of their Indian ancestors, ranged freely across several thousand hectares, cutting clearings in the forest, taking crops for a year or two, then allowing the land to recover for twenty or twenty-five years before returning to the same plot.

But as Maranhão began to attract roads and investments, landowners from other states saw in it opportunities to expand their holdings. They began to buy, from government agencies, much of the unclaimed land. Though by Brazilian law the people of Centro dos Aguiar had, by then, full rights to possession of the land they had occupied, in 1960 it was sold, ironically by the Brazilian Institute for Land Reform. The thousands of hectares they were farming were handed over to two cattle-ranchers, and the 700 people of the village were left with a 100-hectare common.

Evidently only a few of them could survive on such a holding, and over 300 people followed the many thousands dispossessed from

Maranhão to the inferior soils and difficult conditions of the Amazon. The two ranchers erected fences and cut and cleared all the forest they had bought, as this, though it destroyed for ever the natural resources the people had protected, was the most effective means of securing their dubious purchase of the land.

For the people who stayed in Centro dos Aguiar, survival ceased to be a certainty. They used the common to graze their cattle and donkeys and rented some arable land from the ranchers, which allowed these new barons to consolidate their power. In 1964 a coup, backed by the United States, replaced Brazil's weak democracy with a military government, which was nowhere more repressive than in the North East. Peasants demanding their rights were tortured to death in police stations: for twenty-one years discontent was gagged. But by 1985, when nominal democracy returned to Brazil, villagers all over Maranhão had come to believe that the time of silence was ending. In Centro dos Aguiar they began to lobby the state authorities for the return of some of the lands which had been taken from them.

Threatened with the loss of a few hundred of their thousands of hectares, the ranchers of Centro dos Aguiar took recourse to the law they knew best: the law of guns. One of the two, Adelino Barbosa, hired a team of gunmen which he sent to threaten the villagers. On his instructions they expelled the community leaders in 1986; when they returned to the village one of them was shot dead. The peasants continued to resist without violence, helped by the Franciscan priests of a nearby parish. In May 1989 the two ranchers seized their 100-hectare common and sold it to a third landowner, who drove off the villagers' animals. The peasants still would not leave their village, and the police moved in to help the ranchers to expel them. By 16 September when, in Manaus, I was told of the case by a human rights group, the police were destroying the peasants' possessions, and it was clear that the future of Centro dos Aguiar would be determined in the days to come. I flew to the eastern town of Belém that day, and by the evening of 17 September I was on the night bus to Bacabal, not a day too early to witness the turning of a page in the history of the Amazon.

The breeze tugged at the curtains and cooled me as I tried to sleep. At times it lifted through the window a smell of woodsmoke or cows. When I opened my eyes I saw through the gap in the curtains a vast empty land over which the moon played. Palmtrees like ragged men stood and waved in the pastures. Along the road were dark caboclo huts, and a ranch lit up like a backlands motel.

Waking at dawn I saw a fenced-in land, of treestumps and sedges. Rarely, like antelopes glimpsed in a safari park, there were cows. As the bus approached the centre of Maranhão, the toothless, wooden-skinned old man beside me began to point out the places he knew.

In the bus station at Bacabal the daily pantomime played at the strangely irregular pace of life in the Brazilian boondocks, shifting between energy and stasis. A grey-haired porter, hat turned sideways for comic effect, pretended to wrestle a man half his age, wheezing with laughter. Boys of seven or eight jostled between the parked buses, hissing between their teeth, pushing oranges on forked sticks through the windows. Peasants from the countryside sat on the benches, waiting for buses, still but for blinking; the softness of old age in their eyes, faces as hard as crumpled paper. They wore their Sunday clothes, shirts patched and stiffly clean, buttoned at the neck and cuffs. Hands like rootstocks were curled on their faded trousers.

Taking a minibus into the interior, I travelled through a land of low hills and plaster churches. Graven brown men walking on the roads stepped onto the verges and stared as we passed. The minibus shuddered into the village of Lago da Pedra, and stopped in the square.

Men sat beneath a tree, flicking their boots with whips, their horses tied to the low wall of the inner square. Oxcarts passed by, loaded with timber, bricks or churns of milk. A watermelon seller cut a melon slowly in two, then in two again, and began to eat. I was directed up a hill, and climbed streets paved with iron ore, the sun on my neck as hard as a hoof. At the top was a church being built by men on wooden scaffolding. I paused, then knocked at the door of the friary beside it.

The man who opened the door was blond, and taller than the people I had travelled with. I remembered, late, that some of the priests helping the villagers were German. He looked at me from one side, apprehensive.

'Yes?'

I explained who I was.

'A journalist. A journalist indeed. You were sent? You were not?' He watched me a second longer, then smiled. 'This is a good thing.' He invited me to lunch, and I followed into a cool, echoing building with a courtyard and wild doves, sedative after the iron and the sun outside.

The friary was crowded with peasants. They sat in the corridors and talked, or shelled peas with the housekeeper in the garden. One man sat on a wall and wept into his hands. Frei Adolfo, the blond priest, introduced me to the men and women of several families who were eating with us. Adolfo had been a little suspicious of me at the door because the friary had that morning received a death threat on the telephone, assumed to have come from the local Ranchers' Union.

The reason given was that the priests were sheltering the peasant leaders and their families who had fled the night before from two of the villages close to Centro dos Aguiar. While I had been sleeping in the bus from Belém, Manoel Barbosa, the brother of the rancher Adelino Barbosa, one of the two who had annexed the common, had led a party of military police into the two villages, to serve an illegal warrant signed by a state judge. They had tied and beaten all the men they could find, captured and tortured three of those on the warrant, and had now imprisoned them in the local military police station. Their crime was to have sheltered the men of Centro dos Aguiar, who had all been expelled from the village by Adelino Barbosa on pain of death. The Ranchers' Union had already decided, at a meeting ten days before, to kill Frei Adolfo, as well as a nun at the friary and the Bishop of Bacabal, and the phone call suggested that they might make an attempt that day.

The village leaders had difficulty eating their lunch. Afterwards they showed me the marks the police had made: rope marks around their wrists, burns where they had been dragged on the ground, and the suppurating bruises made by rifle butts. They had fled as soon as the police had left, and walked the forty kilometres to the friary. Some of the women, and occasionally the men, cried when they told me what had been done to the people taken prisoner.

Frei Adolfo, who was calm, asked me if I knew how dangerous the situation was, and whether I had experience of similar troubles. I told him briefly of my hazardous travels in Indonesia and he nodded and thought for a while. He walked over to two of the men and spoke to them quietly, out of my hearing. Then he called me over.

'They are returning to their village this evening and they say you can go with them. Don't go to Centro dos Aguiar or you'll be shot. The police might be in the villages so they'll be taking the back route. Do everything they say, and don't be seen. *Vai com Deus.*'

He shook my hand and left me. I looked at the two short brown men and grinned, a little foolishly.

'Let's go then,' said the smaller of the two.

By the time we reached the thin and roundabout path which approached the men's village from the back, and would afford us a view of the houses before we arrived, our shadows were already long on the path in front of us. We crossed the lands of some of the ranchers that other communities had battled with, ranches with names such as 'High Happiness' and 'Christ the King'. There were few cows, as the speculative value of the land rose faster than the value of production. The ground we walked on was equity, a 10,000-hectare share certificate.

Palmtrees grew from the grasslands, or thorn bushes where the land had been long ungrazed. The men pulled down a bunch of palmfruit, nuts the size of lemons and carved, it seemed, from wood. The *babaçu* fruits had become an economic staple, though the work their processing required was long and the reward was small. We passed firepits beside the path, in which the husks of the fruit were baked for charcoal; the seeds, piled beside them, were sold for oil and cattle-cake.

Every kilometre or so along the path was one house or two, peasant homes with chickens and piglets. Over one a flowering vine had sprawled, and in its bower, hanging beside the door, a girl was sitting sewing. A householder invited us in, and offered us bananas. When we had eaten I tried to pay, and she said, 'You've come to help us, have you?'

'I would like to ...'

She waved me away with her hand.

Our shadows lengthened until they overreached themselves and dissipated. The flies which had sprung from the path at our approach were replaced by nightjars, jerking up to take the insects we disturbed. At times we passed into a gout of cool air, trapped in a declivity of the path, and smelt on it the breath of cows. The babaçu palms hung like crucifixes on the sky.

As we came close to the village we were joined by other peasant men returning from their work in the fields, carrying sickles or mattocks. They were small, brown, work-cut, with palms which felt like polished timber, splayed feet, wide hips, and arms and legs like knotted driftwood. Their faces were graven, with stubble, small moustaches and few teeth. The skin on their shoulders felt like suede or crêpe paper, rubbed by the sun a size too large.

Like the two men I walked with they were returning to their village of Pau Santo, The Holy Tree. This settlement was not directly involved in the current land dispute, but several of the people of Centro dos Aguiar had fled there. The police, hunting these fugitives, had beaten up some of the men of Pau Santo the night before; but, the returning people told us, they had not reappeared. We came to the crest of a hill, looked down upon the huts, crossed a small valley and walked up into the village.

Only the church in Pau Santo was built of bricks and tiled. The other houses were of wattle and red clay, thatched with palmleaves. They huddled about a laterite arena, over which dogs and donkeys strolled. A thin man with gentle movements came from his doorway to greet us. Milton Monteiro had seen me in the friary at lunch, and had left for Pau Santo before us. He was the community's catechist and leader, and had as a result been badly beaten by the police. He took me to see the cross marking the place where, in 1985, his father had been killed.

As Amnesty International has recorded, Pau Santo had once been involved in a land dispute of its own, under circumstances similar to those now afflicting Centro dos Aguiar. In 1985 the villagers there and in the nearby settlement of Aldeias had been lobbying the government's land reform agency for the return of some of their lands. Their petitions, backed by lawyers and the church, were by the autumn of that year being considered by the agency. Having been settled for fifty years, they had, like all the villages of the region, full entitlement to their lands, legally theirs after five years of settlement and cultivation. The chances of these two villages setting a regional precedent for success in a land dispute seemed good.

The state authorities came out in force. In November a state judge signed an eviction order for Pau Santo, in favour of the local rancher; and the police wrote themselves a warrant to investigate the people of Aldeias. On 23 November 1985, 115 policemen arrived in Aldeias, led by no less than the State Superintendent and his Security Secretary. The Security Secretary assembled the villagers of Aldeias and announced that he had come to investigate allegations of subversion. The doors of the houses were broken down, the money in the village was taken, and anything resembling a weapon, kitchen knives and sickles included, was confiscated. Two men were taken away and tortured until they signed statements saying the local priests had organized their subversion and supplied them with arms.

The police moved on to Pau Santo, to evict the eighty-two families living there. By the time they arrived the men were out working in the fields. They ransacked the village. Under the guidance of the State Superintendent they broke down the doors, windows and some of the walls, and fired into the houses they couldn't destroy. In one of them Milton's father, Manoel Monteiro, seventy-six years old, had been sleeping. Awoken by the gunfire, he stumbled out of his house, confused and frightened, and tried to run. The police shot him, and left him on the path for the labourers to find when they returned.

The next day the peasants quietly killed the rancher's goats, and distributed the meat among all the villages of the county. The Bishop of Bacabal travelled to the federal capital, Brasília, to speak to the Ministry of Justice. The commotion he caused, telegraphed in the national press, ensured that these two villages, Pau Santo and Aldeias, won their land disputes, and became examples the other peasants of the region would try to follow. The villagers were granted 950 hectares of the land the rancher had taken from them, on which 110 families now farm.

In Pau Santo I was to stay in the house of Maria José, the oldest woman of the village, strong-armed, steel-haired, her face a sunburst of wrinkles, ever on the point of twitching into a laugh. She would stand on her clay floor, leaning her elbows on a hammock and swinging the top half of her body as she teased the people who came into her house. She worked with vigour, pounding maize, breaking babaçu nuts, cooking, chasing donkeys, herding her chickens and, in such a way that it never seemed to need an explanation, laughing.

After supper I sat on a log on the brown village green and talked with Milton and other people, about the troubles of Centro dos Aguiar and the police raids. The sky was an hallucination of light, the Milky Way glowing in purple and red, stars so round and warm that all seven of the Pleiades shone as clearly as a cluster of near planets. Shooting stars swung across the night in leisurely arcs. In the light of these flames I watched the women: dumpy, capable, beauty short-lived as fireflies; soon crumpled up by work and childbirth. One was the mother of fourteen; I had taken her to be their grandmother.

30

By nine o'clock the people were becoming tense, and Milton suggested that the whole village assemble in the church. At midnight of the night before the police had broken into Pau Santo with their illegal warrant, failed to find the men on the list, and beaten the community leaders to try to extract information. The villagers feared they might return that night, and whenever the dogs barked the men would jump to their feet.

Milton led a service in church, the men sitting on one side of the hall, the women on the other. They sang hymns they had composed themselves, printed in books the priests had produced, which had once been rounded up by the police as evidence of subversion.

'O *companheiro* why are you so sad?
Tell me, what has happened?
You have no land to plant your crops
When it was God who gave the land to us.

'Come *companheiro*
Come my brother
Don't be sad,
This land is all yours.
Let us have land reform,
Let us continue the fight.'

Afterwards Milton spoke, building up the people's courage. He was a gentle and inspiring leader, opening his talk into a discussion on what should best be done. Whenever the church door opened, people turned sharply.

In the morning I walked with Milton to São Sebastião, half an hour away, in the direction of Centro dos Aguiar. Like Pau Santo, São Sebastião had been sheltering the men of that village, and had been raided by the police while I was asleep in the bus from Belém.

As I had learnt from documents compiled by the priests[1,2], the men had fled from Centro dos Aguiar two months after the ranchers Adelino Barbosa and Rubens Jorge de Melo had enclosed and sold the common on which they grazed their animals. In May 1989, the lawyers defending the villagers there told them that the ranchers' sale of their land had been illegal, and they would fight it on their behalf. The peasants, whose animals were starving, tore down the fences around the common and part of the ranch. Adelino Barbosa, feeling threatened, fled to Bacabal, and sent his gunmen in to frighten them away.

The gunmen were joined on 22 June by a man named José Almeida, who came dressed as Adelino's new cowboy, but armed with a rifle, two revolvers and a shotgun. He was known from other parts of Maranhão as the killer of several peasants. He arrived at the common, caught one of the villagers' donkeys and mutilated it with a knife. The next day the people ambushed him, and killed him with a shotgun. The day after that the chief of the nearest police station, Sergeant Vidal da Costa, led a posse of twenty policemen into the area. They caught an old man returning to his village from the fields, and Sergeant Vidal had him held while he beat him to the ground with his submachine-gun. He marched to the nearby Pau Santo, caught another old farmer and shouted, 'There's going to be some killing today, and we're starting with this one.'

In the following month Sergeant Vidal and his policemen twice raided Centro dos Aguiar, damaging houses, killing livestock, threatening the men with death and the women with sexual assault. With the blessing of the state governor eight military policemen were installed in Adelino Barbosa's ranchhouse. The police armed Barbosa's seven hired gunmen with automatic rifles and short-barrelled shotguns. Among them were the two men who, in 1986, had shot dead one of the village's leaders. In late July a local judge granted an expulsion order to the two ranchers, and the men of Centro dos Aguiar were ordered by the police to leave on pain of death.

But rather than fleeing, as had thousands before them, to the Amazon frontier, the peasants, encouraged by the church and the people of the other communities, took refuge in neighbouring villages, among them Pau Santo and São Sebastião. They were hoping to gain time while the lawyers fought the expulsion order in the courts.

At the end of July Sergeant Vidal heard that five of the leaders of these communities were to come to his town the next day for a meeting in the council chambers, to discuss with other councillors the problems of Centro dos Aguiar. Vidal illegally invested Adelino Barbosa's brother with police powers. The next day Manoel Barbosa arrived at the council chambers with two military policemen and arrested the five old men. They were marched down the streets to the police station, outside which Adelino Barbosa was waiting on the pavement. As they passed him they were beaten with rifle butts.

Inside the police station the old men were stripped naked and forced to walk around their cell on their knees. They were kicked and beaten with rifles, then they were held down in turn while the policemen passed faeces into their mouths. The police kept beating them and seemed prepared to torture them to death. But as a cell door was opened, one of the men slipped out, reached the street, stopped a minibus and, still naked, arrived at the friary in Lago da Pedra before the police caught up with him. The priests called a lawyer, who telephoned the police station. The men were released; but one of them had by then been partially blinded by being beaten round the head.

At the beginning of September the local judge issued a warrant for the preventive detention of seven community leaders, some of whom had been residents of Centro dos Aguiar, others the people who had protected them. On 17 September Vidal extended Manoel Barbosa's police powers, and at around midnight Barbosa arrived in Pau Santo and São Sebastião with eleven policemen, to serve the warrant. In Pau Santo he had failed to capture any of the listed men, and he was angry when he arrived in São Sebastião. The men there showed me what had happened then.

Half the men pretended to be police, while the others, the real victims of two nights before, reconstructed what had been done to them. The victims were pushed out of their houses at gunpoint – stick-point in this case – and were forced to stand against the walls while their hands were tied behind their backs. Then they were thrown to the ground in a circle, faces down. The police pointed their guns, and Manoel Barbosa walked around the circle, lifting the heads by the hair to identify them. Three of the men were on the list, and they were dragged away and forced into the mayor's car, which was waiting near by. Barbosa asked where the remaining four were. No one would tell him, so he stepped back and let the police work.

They pulled up the men's heads by their hair and banged their faces into the dust. Then they walked around the ring and drove their rifle butts into the men's backs; one boy of seventeen, lying on the ground to show me, had been hit so hard that he now had difficulty walking. Several men were dragged over the ground, and had burns on their chins and shoulders.

The three men in the car were driven out of earshot of the village.

The car stopped and they were pulled out and beaten to the ground, picked up and beaten to the ground again. They were taken to Vidal's police station and imprisoned.

Milton had a copy of the judge's warrant. It was illegal in several respects. A mandate for preventive detention can be issued only if the indicted people are known to be of no fixed address and no employment. All had union cards to show that they were agricultural labourers, and the police went to their houses to collect them; indeed they were being persecuted for trying to keep their addresses fixed. The seven named men were charged, astonishingly, with land invasion.

That afternoon Milton took me to see a small plant the villagers had installed in Pau Santo for processing manioc meal. Men were bringing in sacks of manioc roots from their fields and adding them to a pile, and women were peeling, soaking and grating them. I asked Milton how each man knew how much manioc he had brought, and therefore how much of the profit was due to him. Milton seemed at first not to understand. He explained to me that everyone contributed equally, and the profits were shared by all the villagers.

'But how do you know that everyone brings an equal share?'

Milton merely looked at me, shook his head and laughed. I learnt later that the peasants of Maranhão hold, or held, their land much as their Indian ancestors had done, in Ceará or other parts of the North East. That land could be bought and sold was to them sacrilege: it belonged to the community, and the communities of the future. Each farmer would have rights of use – but not of ownership – over the portion which he happened to be cultivating. As the community owned the land, and the land was the basis of its economy, production and profits were also shared.

I stayed in Pau Santo for the rest of that day and the next, listening at night to the crickets that sung from the crevices in Maria José's walls. On the afternoon of my third day in the village I wanted to return to the friary to continue my research. I was given a mule and rode back to the road, leaving it, as instructed, to return to Pau Santo by itself.

Soon after I arrived at the friary Frei Adolfo was taking the wives of the three imprisoned men to Sergeant Vidal's jail in the nearby town of Lago do Rodrigues, to see their husbands. I washed and changed hurriedly and climbed into Adolfo's truck with them.

34

The military police, neat, muscular, secure, lounged about curiously in Bermuda shorts and surfshirts. An eighteen-year-old, fresh from the Higher College of War, with ginger hair and a squint, was on duty, and paced, self-aware, up and down behind us, in high boots and military uniform, stroking the butt of his revolver. Sergeant Vidal was away.

The three men held hands with their wives through the bars. Their cell was without beds or hammocks, with just a blanket for each to lie on, and a communal pot. The prison was as hot as an airing cupboard. The three wives were crying, and one of the men could stand at the bars no longer, let go of the hands and hid his face in a corner of the cell. After fifteen minutes the eighteen-year-old, steadying his voice, told us the visit was over.

That evening Frei Adolfo held a service in a hall in the friary. Several people from Pau Santo and São Sebastião had arrived, and he preached a sermon on the Biblical rights of all people to food, which for peasant farmers meant the rights to land. Some of the villagers spoke from the floor about unity and agrarian reform, then they held up their hands, palms open to the sky, and prayed. After the service Adolfo took my arm.

'I bet you never knew the Bible could be so revolutionary.'

For Adolfo the duties of the church extended far beyond administering the sacraments. The people were poor, uneducated, suffered avoidable diseases and at times came close to starvation. In response he and the other priests and nuns had each studied to teach a different discipline: community medicine, literacy, nutrition, childcare or mechanics. They were training instructors in the villages, who would themselves then train the next generation of teachers.

But the priests had seen that these efforts would be rendered worthless if the people lost their land, and were driven to the disruption and poverty of the shanty towns or the Amazon. So they had been reading too from the gospel of the Brazilian Constitution, showing the peasants how its laws affected them and what they were entitled to. They preached a casting-off of the traditional deference to authority, and a need for political literacy; they taught them to assess the choice of leaders the elections offered, and use their votes wisely. The priests, while addressing the physical welfare of the people, had come without premeditation to preach a social revolution: the theology of liberation.

Liberation theology was a practice long before it became a philosophy. By the time it came to be a written doctrine, peasant movements in Latin America had already overtaken it. In Maranhão the priests had stepped back and the peasants now studied their rights without guidance. Working through the rural trades unions, they were confronting their oppressors with the laws which they themselves had drafted: the Constitution which is now among the most advanced in the world, but as yet little more than a theory of good government. Peasants unable to sign their names were outwitting mayors in public discussions, and it was this inversion of the power of knowledge which was winning some of the battles over land. But though the welfare of the communities which had succeeded in their land disputes was clearly far greater than the welfare of those which had lost, Pope John Paul II has condemned liberation theology, and imposed a silence on its leading advocate.

I was woken at dawn by the church proclaiming its strength, broadcasting music and parables from the tower being built beside the friary. All that day men came in from the villages, to meet in the courtyard and discuss strategy. In the afternoon three lawyers arrived from the state capital and set up office in a room in the friary.

Lawyers are often the first to be assassinated, now that the Brazilian ranchers have become better organized and have identified as the greater threat the legal and political support on which the peasants depend. One of the three, Dutra, the man who had rescued the elders being tortured in Vidal's police station, had survived an attempt on his life. A colleague of his had been killed and another had a chain of bullet scars across his belly. While company lawyers were among the best paid people in Brazil, these three, though they had qualified well, lived on what human rights charities could afford to pay; one had been without wages for five months, and was supported by the other two. Through the afternoon and when I woke at night I could hear the clatter of their typewriters, echoing in the corridors.

I had intended to travel the same morning to the police station in the nearby town of Lago do Rodrigues, to interview Sergeant Vidal about the torture he was said to have supervised, and his apparent support for the illegal activities of the ranchers. I had wanted to move from there to Centro dos Aguiar, to see for myself what had happened to the village. But at breakfast Adolfo told me that the situation had become critical. The lawyers had drafted applications of habeas corpus, which they were to take back to the state capital that morning. If they succeeded, the three men could be released that day; if they failed, the land dispute could be lost. An inquisitive journalist could be seen by the state authorities as a threat sufficient to warrant the final slamming of the door of justice. He wanted me to leave the area for a few days, and suggested I travel to the capital with the three lawyers and try to obtain permission from the police headquarters there to continue my work; so distancing myself from the work of the priests. This sounded impossible to me, but I left with the lawyers as he had advised.

On the way to São Luís, the capital, the three men were to stop at the town of São Luís Gonzaga, thirty kilometres from Bacabal. The leader of a rural union had been murdered there by gunmen in July, shot in the head while he slept between his wife and two children. As we travelled they pointed out to me the landmarks in a history of repression. In that thin strip of land, the thirty kilometres of road and the several hundred metres either side of it, Dutra showed me two crosses where peasant leaders had been killed, and the stumps of twenty-eight incinerated houses. As we left the car in São Luís Gonzaga we were told that just the night before a seventeen-year-old boy had been stabbed to death there by a hired killer, in front of his friends. The various assassins had made no attempt to hide themselves, and still lived among the people they persecuted. The story of Centro dos Aguiar and the villages which surrounded it was unexceptional.

For the one thousand murders of peasants, priests and lawyers during the 1980s in Brazil, only three men have been brought to justice. The three were gunmen; the law has yet to touch any of the people who commissioned them. There is no lack of evidence, indeed there has been no effort to hide what has been done. The killers rely upon an ethic of government summarized in the Brazilian proverb: 'for our friends everything; for our enemies the Law'.

Many of the cases, documented by Brazilian human rights groups and by Amnesty International[3], demonstrate a disregard for the law nowhere so blatant as among the judiciary, a criminality introduced to communities only with the arrival of the police, an anarchy engineered by government. While Maranhão, as I write, is most afflicted, in all the states of the North East and the southern Amazon there have been killings in the last decade, and the uprooting of settled farmers and their propulsion to the forest frontier. The

37

authorities appear to have done their best to protect those least in need of protection, and persecute those who are most vulnerable.

The village of Aldeias, for example, which had been attacked with Pau Santo by police in 1985, was, in February three years later, celebrating carnival. Two cars filled with ranchers arrived, and sprayed bullets over the celebrating villagers. They fled into their houses and the men left their cars and threw lighted torches onto the roofs. As the villagers ran from their houses they were shot down. In Rio Maria in Pará, a peasant was shot dead by a landowner while he was harvesting his crops. Though several other peasants were present, they were not interviewed by police. The police chief accepted the landowner's claim of self-defence – though the peasant was unarmed – and closed the case, destroying all records.

Near by in Goianésia a man was shot in the back by three gunmen while his child was riding on his shoulders. The local police chief told his widow that he couldn't register the crime, as he had no pen and paper. Human rights lawyers, however, forced a police enquiry and then a hearing. At the hearing the clerk of the court was reluctant to record the widow's statement, and when the gunmen were released they were driven away in his car. In Imperatríz in Maranhão, peasants were beaten by police to force them to implicate a priest in the murder of a landowner. A delegation of bishops, knowing the priest was in danger, applied to President Sarney for his protection. There was no response. Eleven days later the priest was shot dead on the stairs to his office, reportedly by police officers. When the case came to court, the federal attorneys said the priest's death was brought about by his bad attitude.

While tens of thousands of peasants were expelled, through such violence, from their home states during the 1980s, still more have left through a lack of land and a lack of infrastructure. The land of course is unavailable to them: peasants in Brazil own only 3 per cent of the agricultural space, with many communities possessing too little to sustain their farming. The infrastructure tends to serve not the villages but the ranches: nearly all the ranchhouses in the area of Bacabal are reached by roads, even though their owners might not inhabit them, while most of the villages, though they may house 300 families, are accessible only on foot or horseback. This means that the marketing of any surpluses the village produces is difficult and slow. Schools and hospitals are so few and so poorly supplied that many people mature and die without once having visited either. As the ranchers in Maranhão characteristically live in the cities, where their children are educated, there is little incentive for the authorities to improve this situation.

Whereas at the beginning of the 1980s the killings the ranchers commissioned were haphazard, by 1990 they had become more disciplined. Now when a public figure needs to be killed in Maranhão, the murder is likely to be commissioned jointly by the local members of one of two societies: the Union of Democratic Ruralists, or Ranchers' Union; and Tradition, Family and Property. As there are mayors and judges in both associations, this pooled responsibility serves to institutionalize the crime. The Ranchers' Union runs cattle auctions to raise money for arms. The gunmen too have become more professional, and now have a scale of charges, depending upon the importance of the target. They are sometimes paid for their services on receipt of the victim's ears.

The police in most cases have avoided investigating these crimes[3]. They have failed to collect evidence, interview witnesses or conduct post mortems, and records of any enquiries they do make disappear. When obliged to enquire, they have intimidated witnesses, or forced them to sign false statements. But when the police themselves are involved in a murder, or the hired assassins are issued with police uniforms or arms, investigations are unnecessary, as the survivors will not register the crime.

The ranchers prefer, if they can, to use the police to evict or intimidate the peasants, as this removes all likelihood of an enquiry. Peasants are arrested and questioned about their political beliefs. If they admit to belonging to a union or to the Workers' Party, both legal organizations, they are likely to be tortured. The police, like those portrayed in *The Grapes of Wrath*, often seem to believe that the peasants belong to an underground movement of subversives, organizing to overthrow the state.

Torture, by contrast to the science of agony once perfected in the south of Brazil, is crude. Peasants are held down repeatedly in water tanks, or have electric shocks applied to their genitals, pieces of wood pushed up the anus, bottles, thorns or lighted cigarettes forced down the throat. 'Telephone torture', beating the victim's ears with cupped hands, is common. Women and sometimes young girls are raped; in one incident a child was suspended by the hair from a beam to persuade her to reveal the whereabouts of her father.

39

Sometimes, despite the efforts of priests and community leaders to restrain them, peasants use the law of the backlands to settle their disputes, and kill the landowners or gunmen who have killed their own people. It is then that the police force is transformed. Post-mortems are conducted with diligence, the most detailed evidence is collected, and witnesses are interviewed with such enthusiasm that some do not survive the experience.

When the police are forced, by legal pressure or a public outcry, to arrest or charge the gunmen, the gunmen have demonstrated a supernatural ability to escape from police cells, and they return to live among the people they have terrorized. When a series of jailbreaks begins to seem suspicious, the killers have been known to commit suicide in their cells, managing to shoot themselves several times through the head.

The involvement of the federal government in the exacerbation of Maranhão's problems, while often subtle, has on occasions been overt. One of Maranhão's landowners is José Sarney, the man who in 1969 became the state's governor, and in 1985 President of the Republic. It was he who did most to take land away from the poor, to give to the people who could develop it as the government thought fit.

When Mr Sarney became governor of Maranhão, much of the state was still forested, and farmed traditionally by peasant communities. While it exported little, it supported its people adequately, as most of the peasant farmers still had sufficient land. Sarney put Maranhão up for sale. His agriculture minister and treasurer travelled through Brazil, offering land at risible prices, informing big businesses that for the price of one hectare in São Paulo state they could buy 1000 in Maranhão[4]. His government provided tax breaks and subsidies to investors, and allowed them to defer payment for several years, with no interest and no correction for inflation; which meant that the land cost the investors approximately nothing. Though it was disbursed in lots of 3000 hectares, there was no limit to the number of subsidiaries a company could register, and some speculators received as many as 80,000 hectares.

The investors, unlike the citizens of the state, were guaranteed roads and electricity, and an absence of competing landclaims. Regrettably the land they were sold was owned already. Thousands of peasants were farming the two million hectares Sarney had

40

dispensed, and the government had to fulfil its guarantees. The peasants were expelled, and they moved to the cities or the Amazon.

José Sarney, once he became President, did little to redress the inverse agrarian reform he had instituted. As I write, the succeeding government seems to be doing no better. President Collor's Agriculture Minister, Antônio Cabrera, is one of the biggest landowners of Brazil[5]. The fact that on all his 200,000 hectares he runs only 41,000 head of cattle suggests that he may also be a land speculator. He was reported by a Brazilian newspaper as having helped organize auctions to raise money for the Ranchers' Union, the body responsible for the majority of the political killings in the Brazilian countryside. His brothers were campaign managers for the bid made by the President of the Ranchers' Union to become President of the Republic. Fernando Collor has entrusted Mr Cabrera with the agrarian reform programme he promised would be the 'biggest in the world'.

The Ministry of Justice refuses to assist the state courts to prosecute gunmen. When an Amnesty International delegation complained to the last Minister of Justice about the torture of peasants in police stations, he replied that the delegates had 'omitted any reference to the criminal backgrounds of the accused'; the accused being the people being tortured[3]. This suggests that he not only presumed the untried men to be guilty; but also condoned the torture of criminals. But despite the overwhelming support for the landowners and big investors at most levels of the legislature and the judiciary, there are, both in Maranhão and in the national capital Brasília, some brave and compassionate civil servants and policemen. They have the voice of a lark in a tempest.

In some parts of Brazil, especially in the south, the peasants without land, tired of waiting for the promised reforms, have attempted to redistribute the unproductive ranchlands themselves. They have organized night caravans of lorries carrying thousands of peasants into a ranch, to establish themselves before they can be stopped. The police have done all they can to prevent them; but if the peasants succeed, as occasionally they have, the result is a benefit to the nation, as unused land becomes productive. It is indeed on peasant agriculture that Brazil depends. Though farms of less than 100 hectares occupy only 3 per cent of the land, they grow 82 per cent of the manioc, 79 per cent of the beans, 68 per cent of the maize and 37 per cent of the rice the country produces, Brazil's principal staple foods. They account for 82 per cent of rural employment, sustaining 35 million people. Yet while the farmland is kept out of the hands of the peasants, 50 million Brazilians are undernourished.

In some regions local agrarian reform has taken place, often with the help of the enlightened politicians whose voices are slowly and erratically beginning to be heard. But the promises successive governments have made of a significant nationwide land reform have repeatedly been broken, as these threaten the interests not only of the legislators themselves but of the privileged minority most of them were drawn from. Instead governments have chosen to give peasants not the land in their home states, but land in the Amazon. This solves neither the problems of the peasants nor those of production. Amazonians consume more food than they produce; and the peasants' land disputes tend only to be transferred to another place or another generation, as ranchers move into the settlement schemes, expanding their properties in the Amazon just as they did in the North East. The last government's land agency – the Institute for Colonization and Agrarian Reform – was a contradiction in terms.

President Collor's Agriculture Minister has endorsed colonization in the Amazon, but has also promised to reform some of the properties already in the possession of ranchers. He claims he will do this under the terms of the new Constitution, drafted in 1988. But as a result of the lobbying activities of the Ranchers' Union, a society which Mr Cabrera himself is said to support, a widespread constitutional reform of the big estates has been rendered impossible. The new Constitution obliges the government to buy land for more than its market value, at a price so high that one state governor has been using land reform to grant political favours, purchasing land from ranchers who pledge their support in forthcoming elections. Not only are Cabrera's plans for reform impossible to finance, they would also, were they to occur, be rewarding the theft through which many investors became landlords.

There is one way in which reform could be legally effected. Farmers are supposed to pay a land tax reflecting the size of their properties. In practice only the small farmers are caught, the big landlords being equipped to evade it. In 1988 only 30 per cent of the tax was collected. Were they charged as they should be, many of the landlords would no longer be able to afford their rambling properties. As agrarian reform would seek to appropriate unproductive land, the owners could forfeit the difference between the productive land they declare for tax purposes and the land they claim is productive to avoid reform. The extra tax revenues could be used to finance the redistribution of the land.

But the mechanics of reform are a secondary problem. While landowners retain their political power nothing of substance can be done. Full and successful land reform has taken place in only three nations, Japan, Taiwan and South Korea, in each case as a result of the disabling of the traditional landed class by war[6]. In these places reform has brought prosperity to the countryside, and a firm agrarian base on which industry has been built. Japan has some of the highest yields in the world, and as the landholdings are small, mechanization has boosted rather than diminished agricultural employment.

Elsewhere, however, where partial agrarian reform has taken place, productivity has often been disappointing. It needs to be accompanied by education, road-building and the development of markets. Many of the peasants with small plots in Brazil have financial problems, partly as they have no access to or understanding of investment. They sell two crops a year, each sale followed by six months in which inflation corrodes the money they make. Without instruction in such things, agrarian reform could serve only to delay their economic failure and flight. Agrarian reform is difficult, politically and practically. It is the only way to save the peasants, and the Amazon, from ruin.

4

WE CROSSED THE CAUSEWAY onto the island of São Luís, and the
lawyers took me to the diocese, where I was to stay. The priests
there were struggling with the results of the land disputes. Many of
the peasants leaving the interior of Maranhão move to the capital,
looking for work. Instead of waged labour they find the only
employment which does not cease with oversupply: theft and
prostitution. The peasants, self-respecting, generous in the
countryside, discover that in the town these qualities distinguish
them as bumpkins, and compromise their chances of survival.
Without a place in society, detached from the community which
gave them meaning and respect, they tend to become reckless;
among the lowest of criminals are the men least suited to the
challenges of the town.

As we had arrived on a weekend I could not visit the police
offices, so I spent the two days swimming with Dutra or wandering
the city. São Luís had been a slaving town, built in the eighteenth
century, and it was now a refulgent monument to evil. Yachts
rocked at anchor where the galleons once moored.

Surrounded by beauty and decay it was impossible not to be
happy. As the mansions of the slavers rotted, they lost their
impressiveness and became intimate, weeds winking from the lintels,
the open-toothed grin of loose tiles on the roofs. Where houses had
collapsed they achieved a complexity of design cleverer by far than
any seen through the drafting spectacles of their progenitors; walls
freestanding amongst rubble still bore their painted tiles. The men
who had traded in black, red and gold had coloured their town pink
and blue. In the slavers' houses still standing the descendants of the
slaves now lived. On the second evening the western sky burnt
yellow, and a twin-towered church stood black against it, trees

sprouting from the battlements, the sun cutting through the windows with the tinge of blood. In black, red and gold I saw the cruelty of a European god, and the numinous city his people built.

Dutra had introduced me to Célia, the capable, energetic woman who ran the human rights foundation in São Luís. On Monday morning she took me to the police offices to meet Colonel Francisco Xâvier, the State Secretary of Security, to obtain permission to work in Maranhão.

He was a man of striking colours, black hair, a white beard, raw blue eyes latticed with red. He had the broken face of an old soldier, a drinker and a glutton. He carried his belly like the prow of a battleship. At the time I did not realize that it was he who had helped supervise the sacking of Aldeias and Pau Santo, and the murder of Manoel Monteiro.

Xâvier was gruffly polite and uncooperative. His power was limited, Maranhão was full of criminals, and he did not want the responsibility of letting me wander about unguided, getting myself into trouble. As I interpreted this, his power was excessive, Maranhão was full of criminals, and he didn't want me to wander about unguided getting them into trouble. I blustered a little. Célia cut me short.

'This man is a brilliant and famous foreign correspondent, and a friend of the Minister of Justice.'

Xâvier's raw eyes watched her for a second, looked at me, I nodded, then he grunted and pressed a bell on his desk. The colonel's assistant entered.

'I've got a letter for you to type.'

When the letter had been dictated and signed I asked Colonel Xâvier if I could interview him about the situation in Centro dos Aguiar.

'What situation?'

'The trouble with the land and things. The gunmen —'

'What gunmen?'

'I was wondering, Colonel, if I could possibly seek your opinion on some of the disputes in the villages of the interior. I understand that quite a few people have been killed.'

He stood up without speaking, pulled out a drawer of a filing cabinet and threw a dossier onto his desk. It was marked 'Unsolved'. He sat, opened it and flicked through some pages.

'Look at all these murders. I don't know why these people were killed. Are you telling me you do? Most of it is family feuds. These villagers of yours, they get fighting, and who knows how many people are killed?'

Célia pointed to an entry in the dossier. 'His killing was commissioned by a rancher. Everyone saw the gunman do it. Everyone knows who it is and where he lives. He's never even been questioned.'

The colonel snapped into anger. 'Are you suggesting I don't know my job? Are you suggesting it's easy to investigate these murders?'

'Yes, when it's the police who commit them.'

Xâvier was furious. He stood up, pointing his finger into Célia's face, cheeks red above his white beard, shouting spittle and cigarette breath from a few centimetres. I failed to understand the insults he used. Célia, her lip trembling, stayed where she was for a few seconds, then took my arm and we walked out. The door was slammed behind us, but the letter was in my pocket.

I moved quickly back to the countryside, anxious lest Xâvier should ring ahead and tell the police there to look out for me. I hired a car in Lago da Pedra and drove to Sergeant Vidal's station in Lago do Rodrigues. He was just emerging from his siesta.

Vidal was short and fat, with a moustache and a forehead puckered into worms. He was bad-tempered on waking. He pulled a Hawaii shirt over his breasts and gold medallion, and rummaged the drawers of his desk to find his sunglasses. He waved me curtly into his office. I handed over the letter of permission. He read it several times, then wrote over the top 'Received', and put it into one of a heap of untidy files.

'I'm sorry, could I have that back? It's addressed to any policeman in the interior.'

He told me it was confiscated. I argued for a while without success; but it had served its purpose, dissociating me from the priests. I took out my tape recorder and asked his permission for an interview.

Vidal denied all the reports I put to him. He had no connection with the Barbosas, he had been quite entitled to make Manoel Barbosa a policeman, for the protection of his brother against criminals. He had beaten no one, had never entered Centro dos

Aguiar, and on the day on which the old men claimed to have been tortured in his police station he was out of the state. It was not his responsibility to investigate the death of the murdered village leader, as cases of that nature came under the jurisdiction of the state. He was anxious to know who had given me my information. We shook hands politely and I returned to Lago da Pedra.

The three men imprisoned by Vidal were yet to be released; their habeas corpus application was being contested. But Frei Adolfo had news of the four wanted men who had escaped Manoel Barbosa's raid on the villages. They were now living in a safe house in São Luís, after narrowly escaping from Barbosa's police. In Pau Santo, while I had been travelling from the Amazon to Maranhão, the police had been looking for one of the four, a man named Chicuta. When he left his house with his hands in the air, they pulled him onto the village green, encircled him and discussed how best he should be killed, whether he should be shot, stabbed or hanged from a tree. The police often played such games with the people they captured.

They decided on hanging, and wondered where they might find a rope. As they debated this, Chicuta judged which of the policemen were standing furthest apart. He prayed to Saint Francis, then thrust his hands in the air and shouted, 'I know I have to die.' As the policemen started he dived, slipped beneath the elbows of two men, and threw himself towards the barbed-wire fence separating the village from the ranchlands. The police ran after him and began to shoot. The fence was close to two metres high; but suddenly he found himself on the other side. He could not remember how, and later said, 'São Francisco must have lifted me over it.' He escaped, unwounded, into the scrubland. When Barbosa's men had gone the villagers went in to call for him, and he stayed in hiding, in touch with them for several days.

The second man being hunted in Pau Santo was Newton, who was sleeping in another house when the police arrived at his door. They asked his family where he was, and the family told them he had gone away on a journey. But his eleven-year-old brother, who knew he was in the village, was still asleep, and the police decided to test the story. They woke him up and questioned him. The people were terrified. 'He's gone away,' said the boy, understanding the situation, 'on a journey.'

When they had finished with the men of São Sebastião, the police

47

moved on to São Paulo village. They caught a woman and told her to take them to the house of a man named Antônio. She came close to Antônio's house, then pointed, up a hill, to the house furthest from them. 'He's in there,' she said, 'but I can't walk any further.' While the police ran up to the house on the hill, she slipped round to the back of Antônio's house, called him out, and the two of them ran into the scrub.

The fourth man was simply missed. All four made contact in the scrublands, and the villagers supplied them with food and news of their families. While I was in São Luís, the priests sent a message to them. They had arranged an escape route through the Franciscan network, speaking in German on the telephone as they suspected it was tapped. One night past midnight the four fugitives assembled in the bushes close to a road. A jeep without lights arrived and they climbed in and were driven away. Beyond Bacabal they swapped vehicles, as jeeps are rare in São Luís, and they were driven to a safe house in a saloon car. The people told the police they had gone to the goldmines.

I walked quickly to Pau Santo, by way of the village of Zé Machado, where a missionary lived. In Pau Santo I was welcomed warmly and prayed for. I set off for Centro dos Aguiar, to meet the ranchers and the men they had hired.

It is hard to know whether or not you are frightened in the tropics, for they replicate the symptoms of dread: the sweat, the loose bowels, the shakes caused by fever or salt deficiency. I felt a little cold, and shivers ran along the muscles of my legs. An hour or two up the track, which was sunken between banks of scrub, I stopped under a cashew tree and ate some of the fruit. I lingered a little, not wanting to go on. Butterflies bounced giddily in the sunshine. When some minutes had passed I continued. Three hours after leaving Pau Santo I knew I was coming close to Centro dos Aguiar, as the outlying houses had been burnt down.

The people must have been in the fields when the houses were burnt, or they might have fled in a hurry, for scattered in the ruins were the remains of their few possessions: hammocks, reed mats, baskets, exploded oil lamps. I walked on, into the village. Apart from some men building a brick house the settlement was empty, and most of the huts were boarded up. Following Milton's directions, I passed the church, with its three bullet holes in the door, where one of the gunmen had fired in frustration while Frei Adolfo held a service inside. I came to a blue plaster-fronted house, as Milton had described, with the words 'House of Saint Manoel' painted above the door. A fat, gentle-looking man was sitting beside a table on the verandah with his daughter and granddaughter. It was Manoel Barbosa.

I had decided to be brisk and professional. I had already taken out my camera, and while I asked his permission I took three photographs. He remained calm, watching me, half-smiling. I told him who I was and asked if I could record an interview. I pulled my tape machine out of my rucksack. He shook his head, so I put it away and opened my notebook. I was nervous, and stumbled on the first question.

'I'd like to ask, please, where were you on the first of August?'

Barbosa laughed, leant across to the table and took a handful of popcorn from a plate there.

I waited, then repeated the question. 'Five men say that on the first of August you were torturing them in Sergeant Vidal's police station. Is that true?'

He pointed to his mouth. 'I'm eating.'

I waited, then asked again.

'Where was I? I don't know where I was.' His wife, a plain, pleasant-faced woman, had come out of the house. He turned to her. 'Where was I?' She shrugged and shook her head.'I was here, here in my house. That's where I was.'

'Why do these men say you were in Lago do Rodrigues, torturing them?'

He looked away and laughed, then stopped and looked at me steadily. 'There are a lot of liars here. A lot of criminals.'

The sun was hot on my neck. Barbosa was in control, leaning back benignly in his chair.

'Could you tell me where you were on the night of the seventeenth of September?'

'How should I know these things?'

'A lot of other people seem to know.'

'In Bacabal. I was travelling in Bacabal.'

He was too calm, and I began to feel scared. I felt I was being neither assertive nor polite.

'To do what?'

'Buy some things, go to the bank.'

'At night?'

He raised his arms into the air and threw them down as if to shake me off. He looked away and patted his granddaughter on the head.

'Why are so many of the houses boarded up here?'

'The people left.'

'Why?'

'Because they're thieves and they know they'll be arrested if they come back here. The greater part of them are thieves. Listen. I have nothing to do with all this. You don't see the situation very well, do you? I like to live in peace.'

As he uttered these words, three men stepped up onto the verandah behind him. The first was armed with a rifle, with a revolver in his belt; the second carried two revolvers and a pair of handcuffs; the third had a pump-action short-barrelled shotgun and a machete. They wore shorts, loose shirts and flipflops. They were insubstantial-looking men. Two of them nodded to Manoel and walked indoors. As the third, a man with bushy hair, approached the door, I raised my camera and took a photograph. He put up his hand to stop me, and half raised his gun.

'It's all right,' I said. 'I'm meant to be here.'

He stared at me, then followed the other men into the house. I took a shot of his back. I was later told that he was one of the two killers of the dead village leader.

'Who are those men?' I asked Manoel.

'Police.'

'Why aren't they in uniform?'

'They've been fishing.'

'With guns?'

He stood up suddenly. 'Why don't you go away?'

'I have permission to be here, from Colonel Francisco Xâvier, the State Secretary for Security.'

This time he kept his eyes on me, and smiled. 'Well, well, Colonel Xâvier. That's something.' He laughed, pushed away the chair he had been leaning on and walked into the house. I could see him through the window talking to the gunmen. His wife was still standing on the verandah. I turned to her. My lips were trembling.

'What does he mean by that?'

She pointed in the direction of Adelino Barbosa's ranchhouse. 'Xâvier. He lives there.'

'Colonel Xâvier lives in Adelino's house?'

'No, Moises Xâvier, Captain Moises, his son.'

A gust of fear and understanding blew over me. Colonel Xâvier, who had denied knowledge of the situation, had appointed his own son to protect the ranchers. I had stepped into the engine room of the destroyer.

The three gunmen, having conferred with Manoel, came to the door of the house. I raised my camera as the first man stepped out. He lifted his rifle and pointed it at my head.

'Don't play with me. Don't play with your camera here.'

I lowered the camera. The three men padded away towards Adelino's ranchhouse. Manoel Barbosa came to the door and watched them go.

'Captain Xâvier is Colonel Xâvier's son?' I asked, a tremble in my smile.

'That's right.' He opened his broken-toothed mouth, full of food, in a grin. 'That's right. I wonder what he'll make of you, eh?' He shambled back into his house.

I picked up a chair, moved it against the wall of the house and sat on it, to cover my back. I wanted to run, but I reasoned that the police or gunmen would then follow me, and possibly shoot me in the back. It would be harder to shoot a man, especially a foreigner, who faced them. The sun made me feel sick. I tried to find something to say to Mrs Barbosa, but nothing came. I half stood, sat again, then stood up.

'I think I'll go and meet the police.'

'They're coming,' she said.

Eight men had emerged from Adelino's ranchhouse, in the blue uniform of the military police. All but one were armed with rifles, which they held, half-raised, in both hands as they approached me. The man in the centre, big, good-looking, swung a shotgun loosely at his thigh.

I pulled on my rucksack and walked out to meet them. As I reached them I put out my hand to the captain. He did not take it, but nodded; and my arms were seized. The police pulled my rucksack from my back, lifted my arms in the air, pulled up my shirt and emptied my pockets. My possessions were passed to Xâvier, who inspected them with curiosity. He let me retrieve them and return them to my rucksack.

'Wait here,' he said.

The police walked on to where Manoel was now sitting on the

verandah, watching. Xâvier conferred with him. Manoel, still seated, pointed in my direction, explaining something to the captain and giving instructions. I stood in the sun. If I ran they would pursue me. A policeman in sunglasses returned and took my arm.

'Come on.'

As I approached the police beside the verandah two or three guns were raised. I thought they might shoot me then, and I felt the strange passivity of helplessness. I had no desire to fight, I would do what they told me, acquiescing in my own death. Xâvier said, 'Give me your film and tapes.' I said nothing, and shook my head uncertainly. The films and tapes must be kept. They were the story.

'The film and tapes, please.'

Looking at Xâvier I saw he lacked a certain confidence. I was a foreigner. If he killed me, outsiders would hear, and he could be brought to account. My resolve returned and I refused. I felt I could take control ...

The rucksack was pulled from my back and emptied on the ground, and the police started foraging through the pockets. They pulled out my camera and tape recorder. They handed the films and cassettes they found to Xâvier. As they inspected the rucksack I recognized the trouble stored in a hidden pocket inside. I had interviewed the leaders of Pau Santo earlier in the week, hidden the tape and forgotten to remove it. The policemen were examining the inner lining. I shouted at Xâvier, hoping to distract them.

'You've no right to do this. Those are my films and tapes. I am a friend of the Head of the Security Council. I'm going to complain to the British Ambassador.'

Xâvier watched me with a faint smile. 'Where is your permission to be here?'

'It's with Vidal. He took it.'

'Well, if you had a letter of permission you could have your films and tapes back. But without permission you have no right to be here.' He was beginning to find this assignment amusing; it was a diversion for his men. The police found the hidden pocket.

I pushed them aside, opened the cache and snatched out the tape, which I moved in a flash to the zipped pocket of my trousers. I sealed it and held my hand over the outside. I backed away from them. They would need to use violence to retrieve it. I gambled that they were unprepared, that they were now less certain of the situation than I was.

'Give me that tape,' said Xâvier.

'No. Stay off me. I'm going to the Minister of Justice.'

'Give me that tape.'

I shook my head. I was seized from behind. I smashed an elbow into what I took to be a throat, and stamped on an instep. Seven policemen landed on top of me. I thrashed with my fists and feet, then fell to the ground, on top of the tape. I was immobilized. My body was lifted from the dust and my arms were wrenched behind my back. They goose-necked my thumbs, and I tried not to shout out in pain. I was thrown to the ground and kicked. The tape was taken from me.

I stood up, shaking with fear, angry. The policemen were panting. They let me snatch up my rucksack and pull my possessions back into it. They had not taken my camera or my recorder; they knew, I reasoned, that I could then accuse them of theft. They pushed and kicked me down to the path to Pau Santo. Xâvier kicked me in the back.

'Go home, gringo.'

I ran, past the burnt houses, along the sunken track and on and on, until I had passed the cashew tree, halfway to Pau Santo. I stopped, panting and shaking, and heard men running only in my ears, the footsteps in my heart. I realized they had missed the film they most wanted: the one in my camera.

A friend from Pau Santo, Raimundo, met me on the path as I entered the village. I told him in a babble what had happened. He took me back to his house. Some men had bought a bottle of cane rum, and they came in and made me drink some. The village assembled around the house. Haltingly I recounted what had happened. Dona Maria shook her head slowly, the lights in her eyes glowing with sympathy. 'The criminals, the beasts.' I told them about the tape. The men said this worried them a little. The police already knew who the spokesmen were, and approximately what they thought, but the tape afforded them certainty, the most valued weapon in this battle of confidence. Raimundo, however, was excited. He said there could be no better publicity for their cause than the ill-treatment of a foreign journalist, and suggested we exploited the incident as quickly and as thoroughly as we could. The conflict had broadened.

Night came down like a hand over a candle, and I walked with the men to the well, to draw up the bucket and wash. As we stood and poured water over ourselves, I realized that the fences there had been between us had fallen. Now that I had seen a little of what had afflicted them I found that my self-consciousness had evaporated. They too had relaxed with me, and I was no longer Senhor, but Jorge.

Raimundo had asked me to stay in his house. When the village fell quiet I lay in the dark, listening, rehearsing my flight. My notebooks and remaining film were in the corner. If the police came to the front door I would leave through the window, and I could be into the scrub in ten or fifteen seconds. When the dogs barked I tensed, hands on the sides of the hammock, waiting for the sound of boots. I slept for two hours, my ears open. A cat jumped onto the roof, and I was onto the floor and picking up my books before I was fully awake. Raimundo later told me that he too had lain planning, measuring in his mind the distance to his baby, whom he, in like manner, would rescue. We would have jammed together in the window.

At dawn we left for Lago da Pedra, striding swiftly over the pastures. Raimundo walked easily, joking, pointing out houses. We stopped in Zé Machado, and the priest gave us a breakfast of maizecakes, honey, papayas and hot milk. When we reached Lago da Pedra I telephoned, at Raimundo's insistence, the British Embassy, and registered a complaint, which the consul told me would be passed to the police. I then spoke to the national newspapers. Within an hour I was on the road to Lago do Rodrigues.

I had determined to retrieve the tapes before the police found a recorder and listened to them. I told Vidal I wanted to speak to him, immediately. My tone frightened him, he became small and obsequious. If the tapes and films were not returned to me that evening I would fly to Brasília the following day and meet my friend the Minister of the Interior. Vidal was to travel to Centro dos Aguiar and retrieve them for me, or he was likely to lose his job.

'Senhor Jorge, I don't have the authority. I cannot tell them what to do.'

I remembered that Xâvier had told me I could have the tapes and films if I could show him my permission. I asked Vidal to return the letter to me. He said that this was impossible, it was police property, addressed only to himself. I asked him to show me the letter, whereupon I could prove it was addressed to any policeman in Maranhão. He dumped the untidy pile of folders on his desk without grace, and I sat down opposite him.

Vidal had filed the letter in a blue folder, which was now halfway down the pile. Forgetting this, he had picked up one of another colour from the top, and slowly began flicking through the pages. I feigned impatience. I leant across the desk as if to take the next file, knocked the heap onto the floor, apologized, and picked the files up. I returned all to the desktop except the blue one. I opened it under his desk, took out the letter and held it between my knees. I returned the file to the heap. As Vidal continued to search I folded the letter and slipped it into my pocket.

Half an hour later Vidal was sweating. He had hunted through all the files. His secretary had entered the room and he was admonishing her, suggesting she had misplaced it. She insisted she had never seen it. The other policemen were pulling out drawers around his office.

'You've lost my letter, haven't you?'

'No, no, Senhor Jorge. It's here, it's right here. We just have to find it.'

'This is ridiculous. Tomorrow I go to the Minister of the Interior. And you are finished.'

I stormed from the police station, the letter crackling in my pocket, Vidal's pleading voice raised behind me.

It was too late that day to return to Centro dos Aguiar. In the evening Frei Adolfo took me to a church festival close to Lago do Rodrigues. Before the service there was a crude funfair, men drinking beer and throwing horseshoes, bunting flapping from long poles. In the shooting gallery I met the eighteen-year-old policeman with the ginger hair and the squint, who had been guarding the prisoners when we had visited them. I asked him if the letter had been found.

'Vidal was really sorry. He reckoned it must have been dumped with the rubbish. We spent eight hours looking for it. We turned the whole station upside down.'

A thunderstorm extinguished the party. I huddled with many others in the porch of the church, and watched the bunting flutter down, and lightning which lit the countryside with the colours of the day. In church the hard voices of the peasants strained into harmony; they sang the sounds of parched earth and stones. At the end of the service they hugged each other.

I slept at the back of the church and in the morning returned to Lago da Pedra, where I hired a jeep from an old bear-faced caboclo who on occasions helped at the friary. We would travel to Centro dos Aguiar, where I hoped to retrieve the tapes, along the road built for the rancher, entering the village by the far side. Antônio, a church worker, came with us, as an extra witness.

The track had suffered from the thunderstorm, and was submerged in places. The jeep, of dented metal and torn canvas, skidded on the mud, and water sprayed through the covers. The stubbled old driver became irritated, and after fifteen kilometres we stopped at the house of a peasant, who was sitting outside carving a maize pounder. His wife prepared coffee and hot milk. The old man told the peasant where we were going.

'Don't go there, it's dangerous.'

'Ah,' the driver winked, 'I've got a gun.'

'You've got what?' I asked.

'Look.'

He proudly lifted the seat of his jeep to expose a shotgun he had made himself. The barrel, cut from part of a car, was bound to the stock with wire.

'This'll look after us.' He patted it.

'That gun is staying here.'

'It mightn't look much to you, but I'm telling you, if there's any trouble ...'

He lifted it and swung as if shooting at a bird.

As we rode on to Centro dos Aguiar he repeated, 'I tell you, we should have brought the gun.'

We drove past the House of Saint Manoel and the church with three bullet holes in the door, and up to the gates of Adelino's ranchhouse. It was a low, wide, tiled house, on a hill, surrounded by a wire fence. Trees and bushes had been cleared from the field it stood in. In a tackhouse beside the fence was a cowboy, dressed in leathers, watching us steadily. A policeman stood on guard on the verandah.

Antônio and the driver stayed in the jeep. I opened the gate of the ranch and stepped up to the policeman. He recognized me and shifted his feet. I smiled, took his hand and asked him his name. I wanted the moral advantage. I asked for Xâvier, and showed him the letter from the captain's father. He told me he was out in the fields training, but as we spoke he pointed and I turned. I was suddenly frightened. Xâvier, followed by three other men, was running towards us across the fields, gripping his gun. He was dressed only in sports shorts, and I saw he was elaborately muscled. The way he ran, the way he held his gun, told me that the situation had changed. Before he had been casual, uncertain; now he was convinced.

He threw open the gate and strode to the verandah. I held out my hand.

'What are you doing here?' He held his gun like a weapon. Before it had been a decoration.

'I have the letter you wanted to see.' I thrust it at him. 'Could I have the tapes and films back, please?'

He pushed my hand away. 'That is worth nothing.'

'Could I have the films and tapes back, please?'

He nodded at the other men. I was seized with a cold strength, greater than they had exercised before. They propelled me to the gate. I tried to resist, I half turned and saw a gun being raised. They threw me through the gate and tied it behind me. The driver had started the engine. 'Let's go. Come on. Let's go,' he hissed in a voice calm with suppressed urgency. I stood at the fence and shouted.

'The problem is your problem, Captain Xâvier. The tapes and films are mine. I'm going to the Minister of Jus—'

The jeep had reversed down the track and was trying to turn. Xâvier had broken his shotgun and was pulling two cartridges from his belt. I ran. As I reached the jeep I saw the barrels snapping up. I ducked beneath the bodywork, ran alongside it as it accelerated, then jumped in under the canopy. The jeep bounced through sumps and fords, skidding then jolting forward on wet mud, the driver's head rigid on his neck. As we approached the peasant's house he said, 'Shotguns, shotguns and rifles. They had shotguns.' He kept the engine running, scrambled into the house, looking up the track behind us, picked up his own gun and jumped back into the jeep. We skidded back to Lago da Pedra.

I was not aware of how frightened I had been until I walked into the friary. There I found myself depressed and unwilling to say what had happened. I saw with clarity how terrifying the situation of the peasants must have been. When my work was finished I could go home. My life was invested elsewhere. I had access to consulates, publicity, to the sympathy of all the social classes of my own country. I could have my revenge in print. Yet despite this I was frightened. All the peasants had was in their homes.

Antônio took me to the mayor's office in Lago do Rodrigues. Outside the building was a group of prosperous-looking men, in white shirts, sunglasses and gold chains, leaning on their cars.

'Ranchers' Union,' said Antônio.

The mayor was away, but his secretary left the other men and invited me into his office. He was polite, trim, bearded, with oiled hair and gold teeth and rings. He was the model of a reasonable man, turning up his palms in generous gestures, holding my gaze with profound black eyes.

'What we have to distinguish are the rights to the land. There are two sides to this question and the Brazilian Constitution is clear about it. When a man, such as Adelino Barbosa, has certificates for the land, then that land is his. He and Rubens are the owners of the common, as they have the titles, granted by the state government. As the owners they have to be respected. The people of Centro dos Aguiar are land invaders.'

'Why are they frightened to return to their village?'

'It is their own guilt which keeps them from returning. They know they are land invaders and they feel ashamed.'

'Don't you think the gunmen there have something to do with it?'

'Who is a gunman? I know nothing of any gunmen. Everyone in this county has guns. Does that make them all gunmen? If people know who the gunmen are why don't they denounce them to the police? They could take it to the top if they wanted to, to the Secretary of Security.'

'I heard that the prisoners arrested in São Sebastião were driven away in the mayor's car. Why was that?'

'The police are short of cars. Any citizen should lend his car to the police if necessary, to help them maintain the peace.'

When I returned to the friary I was told that the British consul had registered my complaint with the federal police. I was advised to leave early the next morning, for if the local police found me I might be killed.

At dawn I lay awake listening to the music broadcast from the church tower. To my surprise I started to cry. I felt hopeless, exhausted. I had lost the battle of confidence. My clever words, the science, the literature, the politics I had read, the subtleties I had cultivated in my life, had broken and fallen against the brick wall of Captain Xâvier and his gun. With dread I saw that there was nothing corrupt about Xâvier. He was doing as his state had bidden, and was committed to it with all he knew as integrity and uprightness. I cried because I felt that as I had lost, and Xâvier and the system he defended had won, because he was upright and consistent, he must have been right and I must have been wrong. Looking down the mighty barrel of the gun of state, you lose confidence in your convictions.

I left the friary and travelled to Bacabal, where I wrote a report for Dutra to use as evidence. I found it hard to believe I was leaving Maranhão. In the bus station I sat beside a travelling salesman, who traded in winding sheets.

'Yes, it's a great business,' he said, 'expanding all the time.'

I took the bus to Belém and moved north, into the Amazon, along the route so many had taken before me.

My friends in Manaus were surprised to see me alive. The reports in the national newspapers had been a little embroidered. Dutra had apparently tried to contact me after I had left Maranhão, without success. The newspapers had connected this disappearance to my troubles with the police, and by the time I had dallied for a festival in Belém and visited some forestry projects near by, I had been beaten, imprisoned and lost, believed dead.

The three prisoners in Vidal's station, and the four men captured when a safe house was raided in São Luís, were released from jail on 29 December, three months after their arrest. The rains arrived in Maranhão on the same day. As the freed men walked back towards their villages they shouted for happiness and let off firecrackers. Frei Adolfo wrote: 'When the Lord changed the luck of His people it seemed a dream, a marvellous dream. Someone in the village recognized the shouts. "It is Chicuta and Newton!" Our mouths were filled with happiness. The people said, "But how wonderful!"'

The villagers held a party in the rain: it seemed to them that the drought of justice was over.

Vidal was dismissed from his post, after the state governor had received repeated complaints of torture, illegal imprisonment and other abuses, culminating in the mistreatment of a British journalist. Manoel Barbosa was relieved of his powers of arrest; the police left Centro dos Aguiar in January and the people moved back in. They were granted 200 hectares of Adelino Barbosa's land, with more promised in the future. They had won their war.

Eight months after I left Maranhão I was sitting in my room in England, working through a pile of papers about agrarian reform. Among them was a cutting from a Maranhão state newspaper, from October 1989. It told the story of a foreign journalist investigating land disputes, who, despite having special permission from his friend the President of the Republic, was captured by police. He was imprisoned and tortured, and the police held a revolver to his ear and threatened to kill him. It was not until I reached the end of the article that I realized I was reading about myself.

5

FROM THE SHADOWLANDS of Maranhão the dispossessed stream north, into the Amazon. They are joined by the peasant armies from south and south-east Brazil, people not formally expelled from their holdings, but wrung out, no less surely, by the concentration of land in the hands of a few. These people have started upon a journey with no foreseeable end, moving through the southern states of Brazil, settling for a while, being rooted out, moving on, finding one season of labour, being expelled once more; and they make their tortuous way to the shanty towns or to the Amazon.

Amazon settlement, for most, is not a destination but an interlude. The expulsions, the concentration of resources the colonists fled from in the other states follow them inexorably, as the same caucus of businessmen and politicians, Brazil's plutocracy, moves its own operations northwards, driving the peasants still further into the wilderness. Some settlers do succeed, and find a patch of fertile land to farm, secure their title, and become small and stable landowners. Some find a permanent job in the expanding cities, a toehold on the glass cliff of prosperity. Most follow no more than a promise of wealth, becoming poorer the further they search, the pioneers of the unmapped frontier of poverty.

But the migrants are both the slaves and the masters of opportunity. They respond immediately to the possibilities of wealth, however precarious these might be. The great opportunity of the 1980s and 1990s in Amazonia is gold.

For several decades men in the Amazon had taken up picks and pans and spread across the Basin as unauthorized freelance miners. In 1980 a seam of extraordinary value was discovered in the south of the Amazon, and, rather than passing into the hands of a big company, was invaded and annexed by thousands of peasant opportunists. Their numbers enabled them to stay, and the great Amazon goldrush began.

The Amazon's colonists found that not only were they able, through the force of thousands, to defy the companies which owned concessions they invaded, but that in some places they were welcomed by local governments. State governors or the administrations of secluded territories were anxious to increase the numbers of people under their authority, being able in this way to command greater funds from the federal government, and to increase the numbers of loyal voters. Cooperatives of freelance miners, working in public lands, were legalized, and gold digging and the services which supported it became the erratic profession of 600,000 people in the Amazon[1].

But the miners, or *garimpeiros*, as they are called in Brazil, were not satisfied with the deposits under public lands. In the ring of mountains around the Amazon and in the rivers draining from them were lodes of greater promise. But the nature of these territories determined that more was hidden there than gold. Where both distance and mountains had hindered the advance of the white man, preventing cattle ranching and the cutting of timber, providing barriers to introduced disease, the Indians still lived, in lands now being demarcated as reserves, from which all but they were excluded. The government's own laws, protecting the last of the Amazon tribes from the devastation which had eliminated the majority, constrained it to resist the economic and political pressure to let the garimpeiros in.

Among the indigenous people of the mountains was the biggest undisturbed tribe remaining in the Americas. The Yanomami Indians, through lack of contact and their own traditionalism, were believed to have changed little in the 3000 years they had inhabited the remotest covert of Brazil. In the north-west of Roraima, the northernmost territory of the Republic, 9000–10,000 survived as their hunting, gathering, sensitively farming ancestors had done, part of a tribe which bestrode the border with Venezuela, where a further 12,000 lived. There had been no contact between them and the developed world before 1950, and since then it had been meagre: sparse missionary groups, health teams, and a disastrous and locally destructive attempt by the army to force a road through part of their territory. The majority of the Indians were said never to have seen a white man.

In the 1970s diamonds and tin ore were found in their territory by government surveys, and small groups of miners invaded the heart of the Yanomami lands, and were expelled by the government. In 1985 some of the big financial interests supporting the garimpeiros, working with the owner of an air transport company, tried to stage an invasion of the Yanomami lands, to fly in sufficient numbers to frustrate any attempts to stop them. The invasion failed, but by then prospectors, walking undetected for months through the territories of the Indians, had begun to spread reports of an extraordinary richness of gold.

In 1986 the health teams and campaigners working to protect the Yanomami warned the government repeatedly that the lands were being invaded, first by hundreds, then thousands of garimpeiros. In the middle of 1987 the government responded, and expelled not the miners but the campaigners trying to keep them out. In 1988 FUNAI, the government's Indian protection agency, an institution said by its critics to represent the interests not of the Indians but of the administration, collaborated with the National Security Council to reduce the legal lands of the Yanomami by 76 per cent, leaving the remainder open to exploitation. As the government removed its officials from the region, the garimpeiros were allowed to spread even into the fragments of land which had been decreed still to belong to the Yanomami.

The Indians, like the tribes whose lands were invaded by the first European conquerors, were felled by epidemics of disease to which they had no resistance: plagues of influenza, mumps, tuberculosis and malaria. Others died in conflicts with the goldminers, as they tried to protect their lands. By 1989 there were perhaps 40,000 miners in the territory, and many of the Indians could no longer survive on the resources which had supported them for 3000 years. Their gardens had been destroyed by hungry miners, the game had been driven away, and the rivers which supplied most of their animal protein – in the form of fish – had been polluted by mud beyond the point at which most life could survive. They became dependent upon the garimpeiros for food and, in the absence of the health teams which had been expelled by the government at the time of their greatest need, for medicine. The Yanomami turned for help to the only outsiders there, the people who were destroying them. They began to die in such numbers that the survival of the tribe became a matter of speculation.

The world was dismayed. As Brazilian campaigners worked to expose what was happening to the Indians, and the horrors of the situation became a feature of news bulletins both in Brazil and abroad, a federal judge, in October 1989, ruled that the presence of the miners was illegal, and that the government was obliged by the Constitution to remove them. By then, however, many of the most powerful businessmen and politicians had invested in the invasion, and the government procrastinated. On 9 January 1990 it chose a compromise with the law, and declared that the garimpeiros would be removed from all but three parts of the territory of Roraima, two of which were inside the traditional Yanomami lands. The campaigners trying to protect the Indians condemned this as unenforceable: there were no realistic provisions for preventing the miners from spreading back into the remainder of the Indian lands.

On 10 January, when I flew to Roraima, the northernmost province, the police were mustering to move the garimpeiros into the three declared reserves; the government was still deliberating about whether even this relocation should take place; the campaigners were trying to start a health programme; and the Yanomami were dying in hundreds. In the mountains of the north was another of the Amazon's watersheds.

I arrived at night in Boa Vista, the capital of Roraima, and the station from which the miners flew into the Indian lands. It was a city of crapulence. Never since the music festivals of western Ireland had I seen so many drunks. They fell over in the grand plaza, slept on the plinth of the Post-Art statue of a goldminer with his pan, swore in the mean streets made gaudy by goldshops and tinsel hotels. It was a city of illusion, an unreal city, of inhuman monuments and human dissolution, of brave visions and cramped reality; it bore all the signs of money spent on pomp and not on welfare. I met a drunken Macuxí Indian, whose tribe, from the east of Roraima, had been overrun long before the Yanomami, and he showed me to a cheap hotel, where miners vomited in the corridors or tried to pull the clothes off girls before they reached their rooms.

I had arranged to travel with a friend I had made in Manaus, a Canadian biologist who had lived in Brazil for two years and, being for a while out of work, was anxious to expand her knowledge of the Basin. I met Barbara Mann in the morning, and we drove to the airport. We had heard that the head of a garimpeiros' union was organizing authorized tours for journalists, of just half an hour in the mines, to show the hardships the miners would suffer if they were expelled. Our intention was to join one of the tours and escape from it when we arrived, to spend, if we succeeded, two or three weeks in the mines.

Our first sight of the problem was inauspicious. We made friends with a pilot, who took us onto the airport balcony to show us what was happening. Though it served a town of less than 200,000, Boa Vista airport was the second busiest in Brazil. Each day 300 small planes took off for or arrived from the goldmines, and on the aerodrome used also by transnational flights there was always the hazard of accidents. On that day, however, federal police were keeping watch over every fleet of parked planes. The police had told the pilot that they were checking that miners and supplies were to enter only the three reserves, and that they were closing the remainder of the Indian territories to all but people the government had authorized. Every plane was to carry a policeman, and there were police on all the airstrips of the interior. They would surely prevent our escape.

We visited the head of the garimpeiros' union offering the tours, in his office beside the airfield. José Altino was neither a garimpeiro nor a trades unionist. He ran an air-taxi company and represented the big business interests now surrounding the miners – the financiers who hired them, the owners of the airstrips, the suppliers of their provisions: the people into whose hands most of the gold the miners found would fall. Altino was a lion-headed man, his green eyes glinting from crevices, proud outcrops of bone and beard proclaiming power and impunity. He spoke with gravel in his chest, chopping the air with thick hands, slowly, softly, knowing his gallery would fall silent to listen.

He was the man who had organized the initial invasion of the Yanomami lands, in 1985. In the days leading up to the Carnival of that year he had assembled in secret 3000 garimpeiros around airports in the northern Amazon. On the first day of Carnival, when government offices were shut and most people, police and soldiers included, would be taking leave, he had planned to land with his gunmen at the one government post inside the Yanomami territory, in uniform, with machine-guns, to take over the airstrip there and knock out the two-way radio. Over the next three days, the garimpeiros would fly into the region, unreported by the officials being held captive in their post. By the time Carnival was over, and the authorities had realized what had happened, mining in the Indian territories would have become irremediable.

He was thwarted by a resentful colleague, who alerted the military police. They arrived on the government airstrip at the same time as Altino, and the two forces faced off over machine guns. At length Altino surrendered. The brevity of his prison sentence, for what was effectively a local *coup d'état*, bore testimony to his influence in government.

Altino said we could take one of his tours, but that we were too late to fly that day. We returned to Boa Vista, pessimistic, unable to see how we could break the police cordon, resigned to seeing nothing but what Altino and the local government wanted to show us. We had seen other journalists in town, so I walked around the expensive hotels, hoping, in vain, to find and join a television crew rich enough to bribe the authorities into allowing them to stay in the mines for longer. I stopped in the lobby of the grandest, where big rich men with rings – mine owners and gold traders – swapped improbable stories over cocktails. On the television was a news report about the goldmines, which showed first a demonstration by Survival International outside the Brazilian Embassy in London. I stared, astonished, at several friends of mine, holding banners and reading speeches denouncing the invasion of the Indian lands, while the mine owners drowned out their voices with shouts of *'comunistas! americanos!'*. I sank into the shadows, dejected.

In the morning, we sat on our rucksacks outside Altino's office, trying to decide what to do. With a frail hope we had noticed that the police, by contrast to what they had told the pilot we befriended, were checking but not boarding the aeroplanes. A television crew and a team of newspaper reporters were haggling with Altino over the price of a tour, the pilot standing by patiently. Barbara in turn bargained with the journalists, negotiating the contribution we might make if they took us. I wandered forlornly onto the airstrip. I could see little point in joining the tour, to learn nothing we could not be told in Boa Vista. I saw the television crew and the reporters leave Altino's office, drive across the airfield and board a propeller plane. Their task was so easy, I felt, reporting what they had been told to see, reinforcing the preconceptions of their audience with material which needed be neither true nor original, simply available, moving on the next day to another story of which they knew little. The police counted them onto the aeroplane, filled in a form on a clipboard, and walked away across the airstrip to where another plane was soon to take off. I slid into reflection.

I was startled by a shout. Barbara was running out from behind Altino's office carrying both our rucksacks. 'Stop that bloody truck!'

A pick-up truck was about to pass me, carrying the film cameras of the crew about to taxi. I jumped in front of it. 'Er, wait, could you just wait a moment,' still uncertain of why, and Barbara ran up and threw the packs into the back.

'Let's go.'

We jumped in and the truck drove up to the plane. We boarded with the equipment. Barbara grinned.

'The police ... don't know we're on,' she panted.

We soared across the savannah plains of eastern Roraima, the mountains of the Guiana Shield blue in the northern distance. As the grasslands gave way to forest, clouds blinded us, and we travelled without sensation for an hour, as one of the last great wildernesses passed by below. We lurched and came through the clouds, and small sharp mountains rushed at the plane. For one or two minutes I saw nothing but forest, uncharted, scarcely inhabited. Then the plane fell, like a starling tilting down to its roost, and there was a gash between the mountains, and a river of orange blood. We banked and I saw a battleground of the same weeping wounds, blue tarpaulins, dead trees, and then men, hundreds of men, crawling like flies on the flesh of the earth. The forest was sodden with mist and rain. We dropped, skidding on the air, then bounced and slid on a wet clay airstrip, almost to the end. The door opened and I saw a world of gypsy men, small and dark, in a scrapyard of trees and broken machinery.

The rain and – we were told – the police had stopped supplies of diesel from reaching the airstrip; so the men, without their machines, had to act out the process of goldmining for the television cameras. They found this hilarious, killing themselves with laughter as they invented activities of no relevance to mining. The cameramen filmed everything, and the journalists leapt among the mines, trying to catch people unawares, who would only turn and laugh at them. I stood behind the huts beside the airstrip and watched. The land in front of me resembled a beach which had suffered a naval bombardment. Some craters were empty, others had filled with orange water. Around them were tumps of gravel and mud. Machines, some broken, some awaiting diesel, were scattered among the shingle banks like unexploded bombs. Beyond were dead trees, their roots undermined by excavations or drowned by repeated flooding; beyond them, when I raised my eyes to exclude the war zone below, was forest, which looked unaltered.

The garimpeiros' operation was a mechanized amplification of the gold-panning process. The strip in front of me, perhaps 300 metres wide, surrounded what had once been a small forest stream. The miners had dug up first the bed of the stream itself, then the surrounding deposits, spreading out until they reached the edges of its valley. Having excavated the sediments they would grade them to extract the gold laid down among the stones, and the mud and rubble would slide back into the stream, or accumulate in mounds. The same process followed this river from its source to the point at which it became deep enough to navigate, whereupon rafts with pumps attached would continue the work downstream. Only the forests of the valley floors had been destroyed, for only the deposits of the rivers, old or new, held gold.

Around the beach the garimpeiros had assembled their huts, which were simply frames of sticks supporting tarpaulins, with hammocks slung from the roof poles. Above them, on a terrace overlooking the river, was the airstrip, of clay, potholed in places, and beside that was a cluster of houses built of planks, where the owner and his associates lived, the helicopter pilots, engineers, mechanics and managers. This makeshift world had alighted in one of the remotest parts of Roraima, the hills of the furthest west, just eleven kilometres from the Venezuelan border, in the middle of what had once been an Indian reserve shared by both nations. The airstrip, named Jeremias, was one of 270 in the Brazilian Yanomami lands, many of them, itself included, within the 24 per cent of the former Indian territory decreed still to be reserved exclusively for the Indians.

There were no police at Jeremias, there had never been, and we could see no reason why we should not be able to stay. The television crew finished its filming of the miners' pantomime, then interviewed the owner of the airstrip, amid a circle of smirking garimpeiros. He told the camera, with compassion, how the police had cut off the necessary supplies, and the garimpeiros were on the point of starvation. The circus of journalists rounded itself up and pranced back into the plane. They seemed not to miss us. The garimpeiros waved them away with decorous smiles and two minutes later a supply plane landed on the strip and started unloading sacks of food. We had arrived, thanks to Barbara's quick wits, in the land of false promises.

Without diesel to drive their machines, the men sat idly around the canteen and the control shed, short, brown skinned peasants, some with black blood, like the people I had seen in the North East of Brazil, now far to the south of where we were. They had an idle, vagabond charm. They had abandoned the ordinance of the societies they had come from – even their names had been replaced with imaginative epithets – and they were free, friendly and volatile. Many of them wore gold chains around their necks, on which were hung nuggets they had found; on others gold capped their ever-flashing smiles.

They were watching the sky for a DC3, which had been due to deliver their fuel for the last four days. They said that at first the police had held it up, to assuage world opinion. Now the police had liberated it again, but the strip had been too wet for the heavy plane to land. It had dried a little since the day before, and they were anxious to get back to work. As the airstrip was short and slippery there were many accidents; and planes were scattered in the forest like spent moths beneath a candle. A DC3 without wings was upended in the trees; another, which had lost an engine, was being repaired by men on scaffolding; two smaller craft, 210s, lay decapitated amongst the huts. One pilot flying to Jeremias had arrived three days late, having walked through the forest after crashing.

I asked if anyone there came from Maranhão. Gold sparkled as the men laughed.

'What's funny about that?'

'Well,' said a man beside me, 'he's not, and ... over there, he's not.'

I looked around at the twenty or thirty people I was talking to. 'And all the rest of you ...'

They nodded. I was later to find, surveying the strips I walked to, that 80 per cent of the goldminers had come from that single state.

Indeed, many of the people who did not come from Maranhão carried as their nicknames, their distinguishing feature, the name of their state. In the group I sat with there were several men from the district of Bacabal; later I was to meet people from Lago da Pedra, São Sebastião and Lago do Rodrigues, where Vidal had his police station, and the brother of the housekeeper who was working in the friary. The state which held the record for the torture of rural workers was also the principal supplier of the men now plundering the Yanomami lands. The two facts were not unassociated.

Some of the men had left Maranhão because they had been expelled. Among them were people who had moved first to the shanty towns of that state, found little work, then continued towards the Amazon, some joining settlement schemes in the forests as farmers, which they had abandoned either for a while or permanently, as the soil could not support them. Others had not been expelled from their villages, but had found the combination of economic hardship – in a land managed for the prosperity of a few – and political repression unendurable, and had fled.

Most left with the consent of their wives, who agreed that sending their men to the mines was their best chance of providing for their children; but the priests of Maranhão had told me that some, especially young men, two or three years into marriage, finding their first children difficult to support, afraid of the landowners who often selected men of such an age for persecution, chose the coward's remittance. Groups of smallholders in Maranhão had been known to stay up drinking at night and to decide, on the spot, to abscond to the mines, leaving behind still greater poverty for their wives and children. Of those who returned many would be chronically sick, dependants on a family already destitute.

These men, around me at Jeremias, up and down the whole long river, in every part of the Yanomami reserve, swarming on the bounty of the forest's unguarded larder, were not gold prospectors. This was not a gold rush. This was an exodus, and Roraima was one of its terminals. They had rushed, but rushed away, away from their problems, into the arms of the only solution which presented itself. Their fever was not the fever of gold, but the fever of poverty. One evil, the injustice of Maranhão, had given rise congenitally to another, the destruction of Roraima.

There were, too, Klondikers among them – professional people, the sons of rich families, foreigners – but these were hundreds among the tens of thousands, the few for whom gold, not survival, was the final objective. The majority were no less the victims of development than the Indians.

These facts had not, in January 1990, been reported before. Though journalists had poured into the lands of the Indians for months, to film the spectacular mess the miners had made, not one of them had asked the fundamental question, not one of them had had the pertinence to wonder who these human beings were, and why they had come. Instead they had promulgated the accepted falsehoods, which might most conveniently accompany their pictures, or be most entertaining in the breakfast newspapers. They had spread their lies of negligence among people who wanted to understand why the invasion had happened and how it could be stopped, and as a result the world was ill-equipped to respond to the event. It did not know what it was fighting.

The men told me that several foreigners were known to be at work in the mines, and when I asked if any were at Jeremias, someone called out, 'Get Papillon.' A youth ran off and returned with an extraordinary curio, a man of six feet three inches, blond-grey with blue eyes, big bones and a long moustache, striding past the small dark men from Maranhão. He introduced himself as Henri, a Frenchman who was born just north of Paris, about forty years before. After graduating he had emigrated to the south of Brazil, where he had worked in vineyards and wheatfields as an agricultural technician. After fourteen years he became bored, left on an impulse and appeared in the goldmines. He was a calm, gentle, charming man. There were deep cuts in his fingers, filled with dirt, and mud in his tousled hair. He described himself as 'only a little bit French' and said, 'Any place is good, once you are there.' He was finding no gold but enjoying himself. I was told there was also a Scotsman working as a goldminer, two Japanese from Japan, some women, and one Yanomami Indian. This was the goldrush, the tail of the exodus.

Barbara had met some people from an adjoining airstrip and went to stay with them. I was to spend the night at the owner's house in Jeremias. I spoke to the boss, Lauro, over supper. The strip had been built in 1987, during the first wave of the successful invasion. Before it existed, goldminers had come to the area on foot or in helicopters. Jeremias had become the first airstrip in the far west, the starting-point for the subsequent invasions up and down the Rio

Mucujaí. As a result Lauro had been able to monopolize much of the air transport entering the region. Each plane landing at Jeremias paid him fifteen grams of gold, except for his own growing fleet, which made substantial profits by selling supplies to the minor bosses and middlemen. He owned several of the mining enterprises at Jeremias, which he described as cooperatives, though in reality he paid each team of miners 30 per cent of the gold they produced and kept the rest. I liked him, and trusted not an atom of his being. He was thirty-five or so, wore a dirty baseball hat and a frayed shirt, and had engine oil on his face and hands. He was probably one of the richest men in Brazil.

Lauro told me that ten or fifteen supply planes were arriving at Jeremias each day. Only diesel deliveries had been delayed, and those were due as soon as the DC3 could land. The men were under orders to leave the region within sixty days, and move either to one of the three miners' reserves or to another part of Brazil. He told me that if, indeed, the expulsion order were to be enforced, the men would not resist; but they would be difficult to extract. There were 5000 miners within a six-kilometre radius of the strip, and he doubted whether the federal police, not famed for their efficiency when pursuing anything other than their own financial interests, would be able to shift them in time.

He told me that his airstrip was well known for being free from fighting, as he had banned the principal agents of trouble: prostitutes, drink and guns. I was a little less credulous when, the next day, I saw a man slouching past with a rifle on his shoulder, drinking from a bottle of rum, his free arm around the waist of one of the attractive 'cooks' at Jeremias; though there was no doubt that this airstrip was less troubled in these ways than others I was to see.

In the morning I was watching the supply planes unloading, when three tiny figures stepped shyly out of the forest and walked up the airstrip towards the huts. They were two women and a man. The women were bare-chested but wore shorts the garimpeiros must have given them. The man carried a bow and two arrows, fifty centimetres taller than himself. As they approached I saw that they had pudding-bowl haircuts, large bellies but fine hands and feet, and that one of the women was suffering an eruptive disease, which might have been chickenpox or syphilis. They wore bunches of leaves tucked into bands on their arms, and the women had pulled tufts of dried grass into holes in their earlobes. The garimpeiros gathered round them, and the Indians started asking for food. I was called in to speak to them.

The miners clearly knew the three Indians well, and spoke to them in Portuguese with a few words of their own language. The Indians seemed timid but not uncomfortable. The small men from Maranhão towered over them.

'Go on,' someone said, 'ask him some questions.'

I asked the Yanomami man in Portuguese if I could speak to him. He seemed not to understand, but nodded and grinned, looking round to the miners for approval.

'What is your name?'

'Yanomami garimpeiro friend.'

'He's called João,' the garimpeiros said.

'What do you think of the garimpeiros?'

'Garimpeiro friend,' the garimpeiros said.

'Garimpeiro friend.'

'Why are they friends?'

'Garimpeiro friend.'

'Clothes, food,' said the garimpeiros.

'Clothes, food.'

'Shoes.'

'Shoes.'

'Garimpeiros go, *brokay*, police come, *brokay*,' said the miners, *brokay*, I assumed, being Yanomami for bad. The Indian repeated the mantra. I began to feel uncomfortable; 'João' was smiling but seemed not to be enjoying himself.

'Garimpeiro *sharami*,' said the garimpeiros.

'Garimpeiro *sharami*.'

'Garimpeiro goes, Yanomami die.'

'Garimpeiro die,' said the Indian, mistaking his prompt, and the miners hooted with laughter. The indian lowered his head and pushed through the crowd to get away.

The two women began bargaining for food, though they had nothing to barter. The miners gave them eggs, manioc meal, sugar and biscuits, teasing them a little, a cost the Indians bore with patience. One of them took the plastic bags she was handed, turned towards me, spat on the ground and said, 'Garimpeiro, clothes.' She looked around the ring of men for approval. 'Eh?' at good?'

'That's good, that's good.'

Then she put out her hand and asked me, as I understood it, for a present.

'Go on,' they said, 'give her something.'

I went to my rucksack and took out a spool of fishing line, which I brought over to her. She held it up and shook her head.

'There aren't any fish left,' the garimpeiros said. 'Never mind,' they told her, 'you can use it to mend your new clothes.'

The two women walked off to join the man, and they returned to the forest, towards their village two hours away.

Barbara arrived in Jeremias a little later in the morning and suggested I return with her to the next airstrip, as she felt it was perhaps more representative of the mines. With her was a short, bearded, friendly man, with a certain dignity and quiet, called Balão, or Balão Mágico – Magic Balloon – on account of his sizable belly. He led us twenty minutes upstream towards the airstrip of Chimarão.

I marvelled as we walked at how transient every aspect of life seemed to be. The paths were without bridges, though hundreds of people followed them every day. It was necessary in places to wade across streams or to wander some distance to find a tree which had fallen across the main river. These tracks backed and doubled on themselves, looping around craters and fallen trees. The camps, though men might live for months in them, were without walls, and the poles broke in places through the tarpaulins of the roof. Nothing was immune to being overturned, in the interests of what might lie beneath it. I was always aware that the scene reminded me of something, but it was not for some days that I recognized – in the smoke and noise of the miners' engines; in the mineral whiteness of the bones of the earth; in the contrast between the sunburnt ground the mining had stripped bare and the sombre greens of the forest around it – the volcano fields of Central Java.

There was diesel at Chimarão and the men worked like ants. Water sprayed in careless arcs from the bottoms of their pits or churned over graders. The noise of their machines was constant, like a waterfall, or the beat of blood in one's ears. As we crossed the river, just three or four metres wide, I thought of how it must once have been, the trees intertwined above, the cool green space in which butterflies danced, a jaguar drinking in silence at a pool of coloured fish. The Mucujaí had once been clear; now it was a trench of moving mud.

Balão took us up to his camp. His reassurance, his unassertiveness made me watch him. He was as solid as a pig, intelligent, authoritative. He said little. The camp was pitched at the forest edge, shaded by trees, perched above the wasteland the men had made. The people there looked as if they had been chipped from stone. They were all low, solid, of squares and triangles, and grey with dried clay. They sat at a table under a tarpaulin drinking coffee, and watched us with friendly eyes. The owner of the camp, and of the claims which the men in this camp were mining, was clean and delicate beside them, fine-boned, large-eyed, with a slim intelligent face. He was, I later heard, of all the bosses the least trusted.

Chimarãozinho was working for his father, the man who owned the airstrip, after whom it was named. He had acquired his own name from the herbal tea he drank, and his son, by extrapolation, became 'Little Chimarão'. Big Chimarão had walked with Balão through the forest for twenty-one days, to stake a claim and found the airstrip which later made him rich. They had lived on the manioc meal they carried and the roots and stems of palm trees. At one stage Chimarão fell ill, was found by the Yanomami and nursed slowly back to health before continuing, to find the gold which was in time to become the undoing of the Indians. Having established his business and hired miners, Chimarão retired to Boa Vista, and Chimarãozinho took over. He was ill suited to the forest, suffered from cold and found the mud and privations tiresome, and, I felt, had secured little respect among the miners. But his team was composed of mature, self-assured men who managed themselves, and was among the stablest on the airstrip.

Chimarãozinho had three claims, each being worked by four or five men. In the four days we stayed in his camp we followed the mining process, and began to understand a little of how the men from Maranhão survived in their disorderly world.

They would start excavating with the help of a high-pressure hose, pumping water from the stream and spraying it at the gravel banks, then hoisting the debris up a suction pipe and into a grader, where any gold in the sediments would settle. Water had already done the job of hardrock miners, levelling mountains, crushing stone, sifting out the ores and depositing them in concentrated bands, gold, tin ore and many others. Over the two billion years in which rain had attacked the Guiana Shield, the water had sought out and laid aside deposits of minerals as grand as any mined by men in the roots of mountains. The streams, weaving through their valleys on changing courses, stocked their own treasuries, classified by weight. So the men were looking for deposits of pebbles, walnut- to fist-sized, particles laid down by fast water, where the gold would fall. The mud and fine gravel interleaved with these beds contained lighter minerals, grains deposited on the insides of meanders, in eddies or in backswamps.

In the hole Balão worked in, the men had sprayed and pumped for fifteen days, searching for a gold-bearing bed. They had now cleared the deposits to a depth of four metres, and their excavation was perhaps fifty metres in width. The sediments they had removed were piled around the pit or had slid into the stream. In the two days before we arrived they had struck gold. In the pit the four men stood in water to their knees, hosing and digging at the lodebed, and tending the pump which propelled the mud and rocks from the bottom of the hole up into the grader. The men were washed, all day, in spray and mud.

The grader was a series of three boxes, arranged in a standing Z on a firm section of the riverbank close to the hole. A hose entered the topmost of the three, and water and rocks chugged down from one to another over a series of baffles. On the floor of each box was a fine net, with a carpet underneath. The rocks would bounce off the floor and the smaller, denser particles of gold would sink into the mat. Mud churned from the bottom of the trap back into the stream.

Every few days after gold was first found the trap would be broken down and emptied. We watched the men rinse the sediments in the grader into a barrel, which was carried to a clear stream flowing from the forest. One man stood in the stream with a goldpan, a shallow Chinese hat of iron, in which he spun the mud and rocks poured into it from the tub. As the pan was gyrated the particles lined up in order of density, and the panner discarded the lighter stones with a sweep of the hand. The heavier fragments were repeatedly washed back into the barrel, and I saw that its inner wall began to glitter.

'Gold *sharami*,' said Chimarãozinho.

After many separations only gold was left in the tub, mixed with an equal quantity of cassiterite, an ore of tin. Tin, being almost as dense as gold, is hard to separate.

One of the men took out a bottle of mercury, and squeezed a

silver spray into the pan, which was stirred into the other metals with a stick. The gold and mercury combined, to form an amalgam, of bigger, denser particles, which could then be panned out from under the tin. It looked and felt like heavy silver sand. It was washed into another pan, which was carried to where a fire had been made of sticks and oil. The amalgam was heated, and mercury, the god of traders and thieves, left as a white smoke.

Mercury is a poison which builds up through the foodchain, accumulating in greatest concentration in animals which feed on other animals. The drops of metal which may fall from the pan into the river do little lasting harm, as metallic mercury passes out of living tissues. But the vapour, when it leaves the goldminers' fire, floats into the atmosphere above the forest, to be brought down by a fall of rain. In the acid streams and backswamps it washes into, bacteria transform it, and it develops the deadly capacity to be absorbed[2]. Moving from plankton, through insects and small fish, into the bodies of the larger fish in the main rivers, it accumulates to cause tissue damage and sterility[3]. As bigger animals, like humans, catch and eat the fish, mercury seeps into the liver and the nervous system.

The effects of mercury poisoning take many years to manifest themselves. As I write, only one certain case has been recorded in the Amazon. But the results of subsisting on contaminated fish have been well researched among the fishing families of a Japanese bay contaminated with the mercurous effluent of a photographic factory. Minamata disease involves the degeneration of the nervous system. The fishermen lose the feeling in their extremities, then their coordination begins to collapse. Over the years, if they have absorbed high doses, their vision deteriorates, they convulse, and paralysis, then death, creeps upon them. Were all the miners to be removed from Roraima, were the natural systems to recover and the Yanomami to restore the foundations of their subsistence, mercury, inconstant, everlasting, would still be creeping from the mud into their tissues for decades.

As the alchemy in the pan progressed, gold emerged; and in two handfuls of yellow dust I saw the meaning of the pits, the river of mud, the fallen forest, the invading army. The men began to smile and joke. It was a good haul.

When the gold had cooled Chimarãozinho took out a delicate set of scales, and weighed it with care at 211 grams. While the seam lasted the four men could expect to find a similar quantity every week. Chimarãozinho took 70 per cent, and the remainder was divided equally between the four. The sixteen grams of gold they each received was worth three months of manual labour elsewhere in Brazil.

Not all the men in Chimarãozinho's three teams came from Maranhão; but those who did differed from the people they had left behind. They were alert and eager to learn, some of them asking us to teach them English. I felt that Maranhão had been doubly impoverished: not only had the peasants there lost their inheritance; they had also lost their bravest spirits and their best brains. Among these people was Antônio, Big Moreno, a man who could learn at extraordinary speed, and spoke with candour.

'If you steal a chicken,' he said, 'you spend much of your life in prison. If you commit a huge crime, the sort of crime the government commits, you become a hero, a pioneer. It is the garimpeiro who is blamed for what is happening here in Roraima, not the establishment that sent him here. It is the victim who is blamed for the assault.'

My admiration for Balão grew with the days I spent at Chimarão. He was as imperturbable as tar. A vocational goldminer, he seemed to have little interest in the money he made, and neither wasted it nor had plans for its use. He had worked in mines for the ten years of his adult life, as a diver, an explorer and now a digger. His expeditions, though he spoke little of them, had been prodigious. He had trekked for months in the north-west Brazilian Amazon, in Venezuela, Guyana, Colombia and Peru, with nothing but a gun, a pick, a pan, a knife and fifty kilograms of manioc meal, staking claims for other people. He knew the forest better than any other man I met there, and had a physical robustness and a capacity for emotional detachment which seemed to render him immune to what most of the others suffered. When Chimarãozinho left the camp for two days he took control without a word being uttered.

Among the other garimpeiros was Rosinaldo, from Manaus, who, before he had travelled to Roraima, had worked as a diver. Divers were the men who mined gold from rafts, downstream on the deeper rivers. It was lucrative and the most dangerous job in the world. Air was supplied by a compressor sold for spraying paint onto cars. The men would dive as deep as forty metres with the nozzle of the airhose in the mouth, a lead belt around the waist and a suction pipe which was connected to a pump on the raft. The divers would stay on the riverbed for three hours, sweeping the suction pipe over the bottom. The sediments were so churned that they could not see their hands in front of their faces. Eleven of Rosinaldo's friends had died of nitrogen narcosis. Crawling along the bed of the Rio Madeira, bare-skinned, they had developed hypothermia, and had been faced with the choice of dying underwater, paralysed with cold, or releasing their belts and corking to the surface.

Others had been killed by their partners. If the diver found a rich bed, and had not worked for long with the two men on the raft, they might stop the compressor, and divide the extra share between them. Rosinaldo had nearly been killed when the men on the surface were disputing the rights to their claim with another raft. When he heard the engines of the other team closing with those of his own, he dropped his equipment and surfaced immediately, before the enemies cut his airpipe. The three men of the diving team shared 40 per cent of the find between them, and the takings were said to compensate the risk.

But in my estimation the toughest member of the camp, and the one who seemed to hold the men together, was Graça, the cook. She was a stout, hard-eyed, humorous woman, the only person from whom the men seemed willing to take direct instructions. I would watch her standing at the griddle, shaking her wooden spoon at the men as she lectured them on politics, farming or mining, while they sat obediently at the table in the kitchen shelter, not daring to disagree. She was married to one of the miners, and was paid four grams of gold a month for every man she fed. This, she said, was ten times the amount she had earned before, working sixteen hours a day to support her family, in a night restaurant and a day restaurant in Boa Vista. Her children had farmed a small patch of land outside the town which, she told me, 'produced nothing, almost nothing, in eight years. All we grew was cheap, all we bought was expensive. But this' – she swept her wooden spoon around the mines – 'now this is living.'

There were a number of women at Chimarão. Every camp had a cook and several of the men had brought their wives, who helped with small chores. But most were prostitutes, who had moved in from the brothels of Boa Vista in search of gold or husbands. Many found both. They told me that the miners were on the whole less assertive, more trustworthy, than the men they met in the towns.

Barbara reported this too: she said that they were careful to avoid even the commonplace physical contact of Brazilian greetings.

Though there was violence in the mines – murder is the commonest cause of death amongst men in Roraima – gentleness was the dominant quality. Away from their families the men had tried to recreate the consideration they missed. In the most trying conditions, in which they worked, ate, washed and slept in the same camp, in which conceit, ambition and frustration could be expected to define their relationships, where there was no law but the law of the gun, men had chosen to live not in conflict but in communality. There is a myth of Latin American machismo invented by the developed nations, where the Latino is reputed to be even cruder, less sensitive and more arrogant than such exemplars as the young Briton. It is rarely realized, and is nowhere less true than in the mines of Roraima, in which men could be expected to be men together, and women to be brutalized.

Most miners never escape their poverty. They live on hopes, the stories of other men's success, the possibility that the next bed of pebbles will be the one which puts an end to their troubles. Though the men at Chimarãozinho's camp were doing well when we met them, their luck had been lean before, and their expenses were enormous. Chimarãozinho, from his 70 per cent, paid for their food and equipment; but they handled their own transport costs and their medical bills. Each flight to or from Boa Vista cost eight grams of gold, and getting home was still more expensive. They could expect to pay regularly for medicines or spells in hospital: half of the 40,000 miners had malaria[4], and many others suffered from the diseases they had brought to the Yanomami, or new ones they had in turn contracted from the forest. One miner told me there was no point in returning home with less than $5000; or by the time the transport and hospital bills had been paid there would be little to give the family. Some people on the Mucujaí had worked for six months and had still to find a gram of gold.

Those who did succeed had a tendency to waste the wealth which came too suddenly to seem true. Papillon, the Frenchman, had told me, 'Garimpeiros love being in debt,' and there were some famous examples. One man, having flown to Boa Vista, arrived at a brothel and announced, when asked who he wanted, 'I'll have them all.' When he failed to fulfil his fantasy, he asked all the girls to remove their clothes, and he covered their naked bodies with banknotes.

There was, however, no need to behave spectacularly to waste money. At the canteen on the airstrip one gram of gold bought four cans of beer, and many drank their more modest hoards in a single night with their friends.

Boons encouraged other excesses. When hoards of gold began to glint in men's eyes their gentleness dispersed, and it was commonplace for confederates to kill each other to increase their share of the bounty. Two stories I heard are illustrative. Two men who worked their own claim in Roraima had been digging for some weeks, when they decided the task was too great for them, and hired two others to help, promising to divide equally any finds they made. Soon afterwards they struck a concentrated seam, and found four kilograms of gold. They returned to Boa Vista to celebrate, where the four hired a house and drank for several days.

The two owners of the hole, in their cups, began to feel they had been cheated of some of their rightful wealth, as most of the work had been theirs. They decided to kill the other two. They suggested a celebratory feast that night and sent the two men to the shops to buy food, plotting to kill them as they returned to the house and take their share of the gold. While the other two were in the shops, one of them had the idea of killing the two owners of the hole, to increase their own share. So they bought a bottle of poison, and mixed it into the food. They duly returned to the house and were shot dead as they crossed the threshold. The two owners went ahead with their feast. A neighbour passing some days later noticed a bad smell, and entered the house to find four dead men and four kilograms of gold. Back in Britain, on recounting this story to a friend, I was amazed to discover that it had been precisely presaged by Chaucer, in his *Pardoner's Tale*.

The other story concerned what was reputed to be Roraima's record strike. The four men of a hired team had each been paid six kilograms and, again, two of them decided to kill the other two. They attacked them in the forest, shot them both in the head and returned to the camp to take the gold. But one of the men, with a bullet in his brain, regained consciousness some minutes later, got up and ran away. He got to Boa Vista, where, from his hospital bed, he successfully sued for the return of his gold. The two killers arrived at the hospital and sprayed his chest with submachine-gun fire. Two days later he recovered consciousness again, and when last I heard was living with six policemen he had hired to protect him.

For those who found no gold, life was scarcely less hazardous. Some men, unable to afford the flight, walked the several weeks back to Boa Vista, though on the whole friends or bosses would take pity on them and lend or give them the money they needed. In Boa Vista they could beg or work to earn a passage home. Others joined the bandits in the woods, the fugitives from the law in other parts of Brazil, who made a living waylaying miners on forest paths and killing them for their gold.

The miners kept the modest quantities of gold they earned in plastic bottles suspended on strings in their underpants; one man described it as 'keeping all your precious possessions together'. The camp owners moved their money out as quickly as they could. It is said that only 15 per cent of the gold found in Roraima is registered and sold officially[5]. The rest is smuggled, most of it crossing the Venezuelan border in some of the small planes always travelling to and from the airstrips. As the authorities have allowed the pilots of Roraima to forge their flight plans to travel to the illegal goldmines, there is nothing they can do to stop them forging their flight plans to travel to Venezuela.

The gold travels on to the Caribbean or elsewhere in Latin America. The big owners use the smuggling routes to bring cocaine and mercury into the mines, and some of them are said to work with the Colombian drugs cartels, replacing traceable bank deposits or dollar hoards with mutable gold. Several are known to have marijuana plantations of their own on the north Roraiman border. The smuggling makes a nonsense of some politicians' claims that the mining in Roraima is an economic necessity. For the nation the revenues are small; for most of the miners the work does nothing but postpone, or accelerate, their destitution.

Just as the mines, their improvised paths, the lack of bridges, suggested transience, so the men appeared to invest little in making their lives more comfortable in the camps. It was as if they lived, with their hopes, elsewhere. So, though at night the temperature could fall to ten degrees, and rain swept through the shelters on horizontal winds, the camps had neither walls nor beds. Many slept in their hammocks without blankets, a feat I found unintelligible; and the miners' clothes seemed never quite to dry. Every moment of life, sleep included, was a trial of strength. The men started work before dawn and finished at nightfall. Some were required to carry diesel from the airstrip. It arrived in sixty-kilogram drums, approximately their own weight, and they lifted it in cane backpacks, without waistbands, up mountain paths, over log crossings, through swamps, across streams. In the basin of mud in which they lived, the temptations to abandon the routines of cleanliness must have been great. I did, but they were scrupulous. As it was difficult ever to be dry, most of the men had footrot, which they treated with diesel oil.

As well as malaria the garimpeiros suffered yellow fever, typhus and leishmaniasis, the disease of the mucous membranes which, if untreated, eats away the mouth and nose. Many had minor wounds: gashes in their hands and feet, or missing fingers. They rotted quickly. One man showed me a swelling on his leg which was worrying him; when I scrutinized it I saw it was a tumult of worms. There were no doctors in the mines, and the men there treated themselves by conjecture.

Murder was the first cause of death, followed by plane crashes. The men said that Roraima was markedly more peaceful than some of the other mines they had worked in; in the town of Itaituba, outside the famous Serra Pelada mine in southern Amazonia, there had been as many as forty separate murders of a Saturday night. In parts of Rondônia, in the west, mineowners defending their new claims posted guards in the forest instead of warning notices, and they shot anyone venturing in. Nevertheless, at least one man was killed each night on the strips along the Rio Mucujaí.

The men worked even after dark, if they had been interrupted in the day by a broken pump or a flooded hole. Flaming torches lit up the pits in which they waded, in oilskins and hoods, amongst sprays of red earth. It looked like a mediaeval view of hell. From the woods there was gunfire: bandits, I was told; duelling drunks; or the execution of a thief. In the bar young men with pistols in their pockets drank their gold quickly and shouted and collapsed among tables. The bar manager was a delicate, middle-class man, with gold-rimmed spectacles and a degree in journalism. This, he told me, had been a mistake: he had wanted to study symbolism in the theatre.

The miners stayed in their camps for two or three months at a time before flying to Boa Vista to drink, whore and relax. Some, who had not found gold, would stay for up to a year. Whilst in the mines they rarely rested, working through Carnival and Christmas. Except for the rare vocational miners like Balão, mining was just a temporary elusion of poverty. Most intended to dig for two or three years. If they found gold they would use it to buy a house in their home state, or cows if the family still had land, or land. Most found only disappointment, and bought nothing but a passage home.

The miners' attitudes to the Indians were mixed. Many of them were concerned for their welfare, but even these men tended to believe that the troubles of the Yanomami were in some way the result of their backwardness. They were ill because they had no western medicine, they were hungry because they did not grow proper food and they had overexploited their fish and game. It was for their own good that the Indians should be introduced to the benefits of civilization. They wanted to help them in this respect, to teach them to be proper people. They gave the children Portuguese names and bounced them on their knees. The Indians, they said, wanted them to stay, as they needed their food and medicines, and wanted to progress.

It was hard to tell how much of the expressed concern was genuine. They seemed to be aware that the more desperate the Indians became the greater would be the pressure on the government to remove the garimpeiros. They also knew that as the Indians became dependent on them, the harder their recuperation would become. Like people craving a drug destroying them, some would try to keep the miners in their territory. This reliance had already been exploited by the governor of Roraima, who had helped two, possibly bribed, Indian chiefs to come to the federal capital, demanding that the miners be allowed to stay.

But whether their compassion was genuine or not, the goldminers were undoubtedly the worst of all outsiders to be looking after the Indians. They had little understanding of their needs, and regarded them as children, who had yet to grow up into adults of the modern world. Much of what they gave the Yanomami hurt them: the refined food they were unused to; clothes they knew nothing of and shared, without washing, spreading skin diseases; medicines administered for the wrong diseases; alcohol; pornographic magazines; and shotguns which frightened the game and exacerbated violence between the Indian villages. And, as well as their disease and misunderstanding, the miners brought sex and murder.

Most of the garimpeiros denied that anyone had sex with the Indians. It seemed to be true that the majority abstained, not least through fear of how the Yanomami men might avenge their women. But there were some men bold or frustrated enough to try.

Yanomami women were said to be unwilling, though there were reported cases of a despairing resort to prostitution for food. There were also reported cases of coercion, and I heard that miners might force the Indian men to drink alcohol at gunpoint, so that they should not be disturbed or attacked while assaulting their women. We saw one child, possibly two, who seemed to be of mixed blood.

The miners and the Indians lived in a state of mutual fear. When the mines were first opened there were several conflicts with Indian villages. The Yanomami, armed only with arrows, warning people before they attacked them, were easily overcome by the less scrupulous garimpeiros, and were sometimes ambushed and murdered on their way to negotiate. Rogue garimpeiros continued to attack Indians without contrition. At the beginning of 1989 a miner shot an Indian boy out of a tree above a path, saying in his defence he thought he was a monkey[6]. In July of that year two Yanomami women and the children they were carrying on their backs were shot dead from behind when they had taken some food without permission.

The Indians had been known to seek spectacular revenge. Two months before we arrived, a bartender at the nearby airstrip of Junior Blefe, nicknamed, on account of his debauchery, Já Morreu – meaning Already Died – accused an Indian of stealing a box of his cartridges, and shot him in the chest at point blank. For three days the forest was still. No Indians came to the airstrips, and the miners began to feel uneasy. On the fourth day 400 Yanomami warriors sprang from the woods at Junior Blefe, armed with bows and shotguns. All the miners left their pits and fled. They arrived at Jeremias, pursued by the Indians, and all fled from there. Four airstrips evacuated downstream, before the warriors found someone who looked like Já Morreu, killed him and returned to their villages. Já was never seen in the mines again.

A few miners sided with the Yanomami. One man we met, Paulo, a mechanic, was fascinated by their society and the way they used the forest, and defended their lifestyle in arguments with the others. I heard of another garimpeiro who had left the mines and gone to live with the Indians three days' walk from Chimarão. He was reputed to have hair to his waist, to wear no clothes, and to fight beside them in battles against the miners.

Throughout our third day at Chimarão rain swept down the valley and swelled the turbid river. As I lay in my hammock writing, Balão, Antônio and two other men came to me and told me to put out my hand. They placed in it a nugget of gold, of about one gram. I tried to refuse, but Antônio said, 'No, you must have something to remember us by.' I was touched, and could think of no way to thank them. The simplicity of their gift had no equivalent in my world.

Watching the rain when they had gone, I realized that life in the mines was fundamental. There was no ritualization of its dreams and its conflicts. The men were digging for gold, they resolved their quarrels physically, they lived without the constraints of a stylized society. It was like a folktale. It seemed to me that they dealt with the commodities of life, while we work with the symbols for those commodities. Gold is ritualized into currency, and the search for it into employment, investment, paperwork. Mortal fights have been stylized into boardroom manoeuvres, political arguments or verbal disputes in the pub; banditry into fraud or sharp practice. We seem to crave these fundamentals. Our mythology – the Wild West, the Knights of the Round Table, life after the global holocaust – seeks a period in which the currency of life is traded back for reality, in which people respond to their needs directly. I felt that having made ourselves rich we have insulated ourselves from surprises. Only the poor wake up to find their houses gone, their crops destroyed, their children massacred. Yet we still have the fear, the hope, the courage, the aggression designed to help us through these moments, and we still need to exercise them. We invent quests and conflicts to take the place of the fundamentals we have lost.

The life of the miners was perhaps more honest than, but in no sense morally superior to, that of other peoples in the world. Yet I have to admit I found it attractive. The rawness of the mines gave life a thrilling simplicity. Their social system was as close as any state has come to sustained anarchy. It was, as if any were needed, the definitive refutation of the wishful motto 'Order and Progress' on the Brazilian flag. It was this chaos and dissolution, I felt, just as much as the lust for gold, which had attracted the true Klondikers: the few lawyers, doctors, executives and foreigners who had joined the exodus as volunteers. It was life which had drawn them from their air-conditioned offices.

When the rain stopped I walked up a clearwater stream into the forest. Water sparkled over the sand, and its reflections played

Right: A treefrog of the closed canopy forest.

Below: The forest canopy at dawn.

Left: Milton Monteiro, where the police shot his father.

Right: Dona Maria José, cracking babaçu nuts.

The men of São Sebastião show what the police did to them two nights before.

Houses burnt down by the Barbosas' gunmen.

Manoel Barbosa, who hires the gunmen, with his granddaughter. The villagers accuse him of torture, murder and arson.

The third of Barbosa's gunmen raised his hand to stop me. Then he raised his gun.

Above: Beside the airstrip at Jeremias: murder and flying accidents are the commonest causes of death.

Right: Miners working in the valley at Chimarão.

Above: Edilson, one of the men of Chimarãozinho's camp.

Right: Burning the amalgam. The white smoke is mercury, the yellow residue is gold.

Below: A Yanomami family waiting for food at Jeremias.

Right: An Indian woman bargaining for food, with nothing to trade.

Below: Barbara Mann and a Yanomami woman, sheltering from the rain near Macarão.

Left: Miners in Boa Vista, waging war against the church.

Right: Forest land cleared and burnt by settlers.

through the leaves of arums and wild bananas. Hummingbirds buzzed between flowers. The forest was tall and slender, broken in places by the steepness of the slope, and lilies, orchids and passion flowers crowded the lightspots on the ground. Damselflies paused on leaves like tensed springs.

Thirty minutes from the mines, out of the sound of the pumps, I stopped and sat on a rock overhanging the stream. I watched a butterfly, shaped and painted as if it were reversed, a design of eyes and mouthparts on the back of its wings, even the antennae of elongated wingtips twitching with deceit. Fish fluttered through a pool. On the rock I reflected that it was the riches of the Indians' world which had led to their impoverishment.

We decided to walk down the Rio Mucujaí, to find an Indian settlement we had been told of. For much of the time we had stayed at Chimarão there had been rain, and now the paths were sapped with liquid mud. Many pumps had been flooded, and the men were hauling them from their holes on rafts.

At Jeremias we were told that the trail was impassable downstream, and Estamarta, one of the helicopter pilots, offered us a lift. He and his partner had bought a helicopter for $100,000, and paid for it with one month's work. They charged the miners twenty-eight grams of gold to carry a pump from the airstrip to a mine two hundred yards away, and several hundred grams to bring supplies from Boa Vista. Estamarta would take us for nothing. I had never been in a helicopter before and he dropped and tilted over the trees to thrill us. He landed by the owner's complex at the airstrip of Macarão, and took off with a wave as soon as we were out.

'*Buruburu sharami,*' said Barbara, Yanomami for 'helicopter good'.

Macarão was a desolate place. Among the shacks overlooking the mines, chickens foraged through rubbish and piles of unwashed plates. Outside the owner's hut three men sat at a table. Two played cards, another read from an exercise book. We asked if we could stay.

A man turned and stared at us. He had the highboned face of an Andean Indian, scars on his nose and cheeks, and a revolver in the pocket of his waistcoat.

'Stay? Sure.'

We sat down at the table. The man with the gun, Zé, stroked his ragged moustache as he watched us, then returned to his cards. I asked the man with the exercise book what he was reading.

'I'm learning Yanomami.'

I looked at his list of words. There were just thirty translations, but they included the names for vagina, penis and anus.

'Why are you learning these?'

'*Rapaz*, you know.'

'You have sex with them?'

He shrugged and grinned.

A small alert man named Marcinho arrived at the huts. He said he knew the Indians well, and agreed to take us to their village. We left our packs in Zé's cabin and passed through the mud into the forest beyond.

A few minutes through the trees we came to some shabby tents, built from sticks, tarpaulins and banana leaves. Two women sat in their shade wearing *tangas* – traditional tasselled loincloths – and holding babies. This, said Marcinho, was a temporary camp, erected by the Yanomami to be closer to the miners they depended on. The women smiled without interest and let us pass.

We stepped from the forest through a garden of bananas, emerging into a field of fallen trees which surrounded an Indian roundhouse, a *maloca*. It was a building of thatch and wooden walls, perhaps thirty metres in width, with a high conical roof open to the sky at the top. Inside we saw that the Indians lived in a deep corridor between the courtyard and the outer wall. It was a simple and sociable arrangement. Hammocks were strung between the wall and an inner ring of stakes; the thirty people living there could see each other at all times, and meet in the central yard. Yanomami communities are extended families; before the miners arrived the biggest malocas housed several hundred.

We stood in the courtyard and the man Marcinho said was chief tottered out with several others to meet us. Most of them were sick. The old man laid a hand on my shoulder and another on my hip and grinned. I did similarly. We stood there for perhaps a minute, grinning and nodding, then Marcinho said, 'Have you got anything to give him?'

A priest we had met in Boa Vista had told us that the relationship between miners and Indians had come to depend so much upon begging and giving that it was now difficult to make friends without donations. He had suggested, however, that it was better for the Yanomami if we traded presents, rather than merely handing them over. I brought out a mirror and a pair of barber's scissors, and, with signs and the few Yanomami words we had learnt, asked what he could give us in return. The chief disappeared into the living space for a while, then emerged with a bow and two arrows. He took the scissors, screwed up his eyes, lifted a strand of hair and cut it with a jagged motion. He held it up for all to see, laughing. He tried it several more times, until we suggested he stop, before the Mohicans returned to the native Americas. The weapons were a little short of two metres long. The bow was of palmwood, strung with a cord of woven bark. The arrows were shafted with the stems of a pampas grass, flighted with the black feathers of the currasow, and tipped with heavy wood, onto which a sharpened monkey bone had been bound. They were designed for ground-living game; the arrows used to kill monkeys were poisoned with the extract of a vine.

Barbara gave balloons to the children who came into the courtyard. She was probably the first blonde woman they had seen, and was scrutinized accordingly. The women wore tangas of cotton the Yanomami grew, dyed red with the seeds of the *urucūm* bush. The men wore shorts given by the miners. I took out my camera and asked if I could take a photograph.

'*Brokay*, die!' The old chief waved his hands in the air to stop me.

'Go on,' said Marcinho, 'take it.'

'He said he didn't want it.'

'Well, it's up to you,' he said, then turned to the Indians. 'They're fine, they're from FUNAI.'

'Marcinho,' said Barbara, 'we don't want you to do this.'

'It doesn't matter, they don't mind.'

He strolled into the living space and took a banana. He was showing off to us, the king of the Yanomami.

Across another stream, also disembowelled by mining, a path led to a larger maloca. In the courtyard we met young Indian men, fully dressed, who spoke a little Portuguese. They seemed to find the presence of the goldminers exciting, and asked for presents. Barbara gave them balloons. We stepped into the living space. Several women and their children were there, cooking, talking, resting in hammocks. In a glance I could see that the impact of whites and their culture had been insignificant before the miners had arrived: the body of their old life, though paralysed, was whole. Most of the utensils of the maloca were indigenous, and were carefully hung from the walls and the roofbeams. No place had yet evolved for the gifts of the miners, and these lay scattered on the floor, deteriorating.

The new culture had been laid upon the old with the congruity of make-up on a statue.

The hammocks of the Indians were spun from cottonheads, white, cross-hatched with blue. Baskets of several sizes, woven from bark and vines, were hung from the walls: for collecting forest fruits or grubs, for winnowing grains and for carrying firewood. Gourds, fire-blacked to preserve them, had been split to make bowls or cups, or were slung in reed baskets from the rafters, holding water and plugged with leaves. Beside the hammocks of hunters were suspended the bones of the animals they had killed, and the neck-capes of currasow birds. A green parakeet sat in the thatch of the roof. In three thousand years life had changed slowly. In three the world had been upended.

A woman the miners called Claudia took my arm and guided me to her fire. The garimpeiros had rechristened all the Indians they knew, as the Yanomami refuse to reveal their names to outsiders, either because they fear they might be used in witchcraft, or because etiquette demands secrecy. Claudia showed me her daughter, of perhaps ten years old, lying in a hammock, watching us with frightened eyes. With her hands Claudia explained that she had shooting pains in her head and stomach, and had been unable to eat for three days. I indicated that there was nothing I could do, I knew nothing of medicine. Claudia grasped my arm again and looked into my face, searching me for an answer. I thought for a while, then took a gourd and some of the sugar and salt the miners had given, and made up a strong solution. I tried to indicate that this could not cure the child, but might help to sustain her. Claudia held my eyes with hers and smiled her gratitude, as if I had summoned a miracle. The whites had caused the problems. The whites could solve them.

She took up the gourd and was raising the girl's head so that she could drink, when rain began to patter on the roof. She lowered the gourd abruptly and stood up. She waited until the rain had ceased before she tried again. When the girl had drunk, Claudia took my hands and said with her face and eyes, 'Do as I do.' She ran her hands down the girl's body from head to waist, repeatedly, blowing on the skin and chanting in her breathy voice, '*o' kai, o'kai, o'kai na, haray, haray, haray, temeni, temeni.*' She then massaged the girl's arms and legs. She stood back and beckoned me to do the same. I rubbed and blew for thirty minutes, the chant a dizzy conjuration in my head, Claudia urging me on whenever I made to stop. When the girl became tired, Claudia told me to sit down beside her at the fire. She began to tell me something, which seemed to be a story, in her soft voice. Her speech was rich with glottal stops and the harmonics of breath.

As Claudia narrated, I took notes about the maloca. At length she broke off and asked for the notepad and pen. She looked at my handwriting then, grasping the pen in her fist, she tried to copy the shapes I had made. I took the pen from her and drew some simpler patterns, which she represented with some success. She began to laugh, and several other women came to the fire and watched. I drew Claudia and some of the animals of the forest, and either the subjects themselves or my renditions of them were hilarious to the Yanomami, and the drawings were passed from hammock to hammock around the maloca with snorts of laughter. After perhaps an hour of this, Claudia stood up sharply and said, ''Way! 'way!' and gently bustled us out of the house. The honesty of the valediction charmed me. As we returned through the banana garden we met a procession of men and women holding the pinions of the plants above their heads like parasols. In the green luminosity of these leaves they seemed not to be of any world I knew.

As we sat at the table outside Zé's hut with several hard, lethargic men, listening to the gunfire in the woods, two strange figures stepped up from the mud of the mines. The first man was slim and dark, with a long face, a spare beard and calm, Egyptian eyes. He carried a rifle. The second, following at a distance, looked thin and misshapen. He wore a wide straw hat, hiding most of his face, and an oversized shirt and trousers, rolled up to reveal ankles and wrists of a strange slenderness. His chin, feet and hands were discoloured by mud. He came to the table and took off his hat. The man disappeared, and in his place stood a beautiful woman.

Beneath the mud her face had the bloom of an apricot. There was a tremor in her lips. From her hair, crushed by the straw hat, emerged ears which looked naked and shy, as if they wanted to bolt back into hiding. She shuddered as she sat.

'Get me some cigarettes,' she said in a hoarse, humorous voice.

One of the rough men at the table started to his feet.

'Go on, get them.' He almost ran to his cabin. She looked around. 'These people are useless.'

She fumbled a cigarette from the packet, her hands trembling a little, and lit it. She paused, drew deeply, and blew into the air. She seemed to shiver with nervous energy.

'So gringo, what are you doing here?'

I stammered an explanation; it sounded more like an excuse. She watched me for a second then seemed to lose interest. She stood up.

'Wait there,' she told the man with Egyptian eyes. She pounced into one of the cabins and slammed the door.

Her escort sat on the bench quietly, cradling his gun.

'Who, I mean, where from ... who is that girl?'

He watched me with his calm, beautiful eyes.

'*Puta.*'

He kept watching me, no shadow of emotion on his face, neither communicating nor receiving. He was guarding the girl? He nodded. I tried again. He had lived here long? I began to draw from him, slowly, his remarkable story.

João's father was a West African, who had settled in the northeast of Brazil and married a caboclo woman. He was brought up on a smallholding with twelve brothers and sisters, and at the age of fourteen walked away from home, with nothing but the clothes he wore. He walked until he reached the Amazon, having stopped to work on farms, road projects and mines; then travelled, on foot and by boat, to the far west of Brazil. With a gun and pan he had strayed far into Peru and Bolivia, and his discoveries had prompted some of the invasions of those lands by Brazilian miners. He had killed 'only three men in my life, *senhor*, and all the deaths were necessary. But' – he looked around for a second – 'I would kill that many again, were I to spend a month on this strip.' He told me that Macarão was the most violent place he had ever visited. Every night there were men killed, and even the hired guns were frightened. He was working for the prostitute as her protector for a week or two, as this paid well; but he would soon move out and find a place which had yet to be explored, and begin his travels on foot again.

We had been talking for half an hour when the doors of the cabin burst open, and in the frame flickered the incandescent vision of an angel. The girl glowed in a long flamenco skirt, a white blouse, with her hair up, gold on her ears and fingers. She paused for a moment, her hands in the air, then strode into the sunshine and the stupefied stares of all the men. She cast her eyes on João, her lips trembling with energy, her hands on her hips.

'What are you waiting for, little boy? You want me to *fazer um programa* on the airstrip?' João stumbled up, his calm dispersed. She swung off up the airstrip towards the bar at the far end, the explorer stalking humbly behind her.

A few minutes later there were shots from the far end of the airstrip, and soon after that the two of them came running back into Zé's compound. Her face was aflame, eyes glinting, lips alive with sullen fire. She flung her handbag down on the table, swore and strode into her cabin, slamming the door. João sat down, angrily kneading the stock of his gun. Someone had fired on them from the forest. He had sent two shots back but missed.

Zé, the man with the scarred face of an Andean Indian, the owner of the airstrip, arrived from the mines and sat at the table. He and João discussed the shooting. The man who had fired on João was lying close to the airstrip in the forest.

'He's just after a fight,' said Zé. 'He's probably too drunk to hit anyone. I might kill him later.'

Zé admitted to having murdered five men. The first, I learnt later, was his business partner, Macarão, the original owner of the airstrip. Thereafter he had killed two men who had interfered with his financial interests, then two men in drunken fights. I was told he had degenerated since procuring the airstrip, had sunk into drunkenness and an ostensible desire to risk his life. He had hired several gunmen, for no reason we could divine but to liven the place up. The airstrip under his leadership was said to have become the most dangerous, and the dirtiest, in Roraima. He was generous and solicitous, concerned for our welfare. He told us, 'My house is your house. Sleep wherever you will, eat what you like. It is all yours.' We slung our hammocks in his back room, helped by Ananias, a grey-haired carpenter who had built the cabins. He was a drunken, gentle man, who kept out of trouble, and told the most unlikely stories.

João, Zé and the girl were to return to the bar, and asked Barbara and me if we would join them. Night had now fallen, and we walked slowly up the airstrip, all of us tense, João and Zé peering into the darkness with their guns raised. The shooting from the forest had died down for a while; it recommenced soon after we reached the bar. On the crude dancefloor Ananias had built there were as many prostitutes as miners. All the men carried guns, even as they danced. Rifles and shotguns were laid on the tables with drinks, and fingers tapped a nervous few centimetres from the stocks. The girl pulled me to my feet and made me dance with her.

An argument started at the bar. João became nervous. He said it was about to get bad, we should get out before the shooting started. Zé was trying to get into the argument. João took him by the arm.

'Come on Zé, let's go.'

'Sure, catch you up.'

João corralled Barbara and me onto the airstrip. We started back towards the cabins, but then João turned and saw that Zé had managed to join the dispute. Several men were shouting, and Zé's gunmen and some others were picking up their weapons.

'Wait here,' said João. He ran back to the bar and started trying to reason with Zé. Zé was shaking him off. We had been left at the point on the strip where several people had been shot at, and missed, by the drunkard in the forest.

'Let's get back,' said Barbara.

We half raised our hands in the air and called out into the darkness, 'Look, no guns,' and began to walk, slowly, down to Zé's huts. As we turned into the compound a barrage of gunfire came from the direction of the bar, then there was silence. As I crossed the back room towards my hammock, Ananias asked sleepily from the darkness, 'Anybody killed?'

'I don't know.'

'Oh.' He turned over and went back to sleep.

In the morning I learnt that one man had been shot. He was being flown to hospital with a hole the size of an apple in his chest. Ananias shook his grey head when he heard this. 'They like shooting too much. They think they're in the *bangi bangi*: in the westerns.'

We spent the next two days visiting Claudia's maloca. On the first we were stopped at the tented camp closest to the mines by a young Yanomami man who spoke some Portuguese.

'What you give?'

'Nothing.'

'Not come.'

We bargained for a while, until I yielded and gave him a mirror, whereupon he pronounced us friends and let us through.

Claudia had been administering the salt and sugar, and her daughter was a little better. We made her a mash of beans, sugar, and vitamins and minerals I had brought from my medicine kit, which she swallowed with discomfort. After the healing ritual Claudia asked me to start drawing again, and for an hour or two the maloca was overwhelmed with laughter.

Barbara helped the women with some of their tasks, teasing cotton from the seedheads they had gathered. I wandered over the maloca, trying to work out what the many utensils were used for. I found amid the garimpeiros' rubbish on the floor a pornographic magazine. I carried it towards the fire.

'You don't want this, do you?'

They indicated that they did and told me to put it back on the floor; it seemed to be an object of curiosity.

By the final visit I felt we had made friends, that Barbara and I were welcome for our company, not for anything we could bring them. It was then that we met a garimpeiro who told us that he visited the Indians three times a day. He loved them, he said, and wanted to help. But every way in which he had tried could only have made their lives worse. He had attempted to treat a boy with tuberculosis, buying the medicine from his earnings. Though he had administered it for a fortnight, the boy had remained ill, and the miner had given up, pronouncing the medicine useless. Tuberculosis requires several months of medication, and anything less is likely to enable the disease to become resistant to treatment, and to spread through the community unimpeded.

I was impressed by the Yanomami, by the way that they retained their warmth, their outer tranquillity, their sense of humour, while the plagues of men and microbes destroyed all they valued. Their destruction was cultural and spiritual as well as physical: their bodily and spiritual lives, like those of many indigenous people, could be considered inextricable. All they believed in had gone, and all they now had was unbelievable. It had no place, either in their houses or in their pantheon.

The best-known spokesman for the Yanomami Indians, Davi Kopenawa, said, 'The hills are sacred places, where the first Yanomami were born, where their ashes are buried. Our old ones leave their spirits in these places.'[7] When their lands are destroyed they are also desecrated, and with this sacrilege is vitiated the Indians' self-respect and self-sufficiency. Having been the masters of their world they become the slaves of someone else's.

It is true, as the garimpeiros claim, that only a small proportion of the Yanomami's forest has been destroyed, perhaps 1 or 2 per cent.

But the fraction they have transformed, the rivers and their valleys, is the sacrum without which the body of the forest collapses. It is in the river that the small animals develop, the big animals hunt, and the Yanomami find the fish on which they depend. A forest with rivers of mud is like a house without a roof: it is structurally unchanged, but uninhabitable.

Many of the gardens the Indians had planted had been destroyed by miners, often starving when supplies failed to arrive, or craving vegetables and fruit. The trees the Yanomami grew were cut down for their fruit, the miners mistaking the possessions of the Indians for the natural bounty of the jungle. The birds and mammals they hunted had been driven away by the noise of the mines, and by the shotguns both the miners and the Yanomami now used. They had no remaining means of keeping themselves alive, and had moved their malocas to the airstrips, where the miners could supply them with both food and new diseases.

It was clear that while the garimpeiros remained in the Yanomami territory the Indians would decline until the tribe became extinct. Claudia's village, I was later told, had lost around 40 per cent of its people. There were mountain ranges in Roraima where 90 per cent of the Indians had died, and villages in which not a soul still lived[7]. Overall, 15 per cent of the Yanomami were believed to have lost their lives, and the plagues had just begun to spread. The Indians, whose natural resistance defended them against epidemics of their own diseases, succumbed rapidly to the African and European sicknesses the miners introduced. They suffered above all from malaria and tuberculosis, diseases which also killed the miners; but many too died of influenza, chickenpox, mumps and common colds, or were incapacitated by river blindness, malnutrition and the deep anaemia associated with malaria[5]. Only the action of voluntary groups, working in Roraima before the miners arrived, vaccinating the Indians against measles, had prevented the disease which might rapidly have killed them all. By the time we arrived in the mines the government, though its own laws demanded it, had done nothing to save the Yanomami.

The defence of the Yanomami is the responsibility of FUNAI, the government's Indian protection agency. But it was FUNAI, charged with preserving the Indians' lands – legally inviolate since 1934 – which had worked hardest to give them to the miners. In August

1987 FUNAI had already helped other government bodies to expel the voluntary medical teams trying to protect the Yanomami against disease. In September 1988, as the miners' invasion became a serious threat to the survival of the tribe, it was FUNAI that deregulated 76 per cent of the Indian lands, opening them to economic exploitation.

This meant that the Indians became the legal owners of only two of their original nine million hectares. They kept the patches of land in which they happened to be living at the time of the invasion, and lost their rights to the rest, which they had used for hunting, fishing and farming. As FUNAI had expelled, along with the medical teams, the only anthropologists working with the Yanomami, there was no one to tell the government that the Indians could not survive on the isolated patches of land to which they were now entitled.

From then on FUNAI campaigned to keep the garimpeiros in the Yanomami lands, even though the miners had now taken not only the territories they had been given, but also the patches left to the Indians. When a federal judge ruled that the miners should be removed from all the Indian lands, FUNAI threatened to challenge his injunction in court. Eventually it persuaded the government to strike an unconstitutional deal with the miners' unions, permitting them to remain inside three 'garimpeiro reserves', two of which were within the Yanomami lands. As Davi Kopenawa and the voluntary organization working to defend the Indians pointed out, not only would the miners in these reserves continue to infect the Indians near by, but they were well placed to reinvade the remainder of the territory.

As the health workers, priests, anthropologists and even the one FUNAI official who spoke Yanomami and sympathized with the Indians had been expelled, FUNAI itself took responsibility for the Indians' welfare. To report that it failed to look after them would be to suggest that it had tried. It is fair to say that not a single Indian living in western Roraima at the time of our visit owed his life to the recent work of FUNAI.

As the situation of the Yanomami became worse, the FUNAI officers working in their lands were withdrawn. A human rights team visited the airstrip at Paapiú, in the centre of the Yanomami lands[5]. There the FUNAI post had been not only abandoned, but left unlocked. The departing official had told the Indians that from then onwards they should treat themselves. He left his medicine cupboards open.

97

FUNAI ran what it called a hospital in Boa Vista for receiving sick Indians brought in by miners. It was, to judge from the descriptions I had read, more like a graveyard[5,8]. For several days at a time the Indians dying there would receive no food. There was no attempt to isolate those with infectious diseases, and several died of illnesses they caught since arriving at the hospital. Sanitation appeared non-existent. Had the health programme been designed to eliminate, not to save the Yanomami, it could scarcely have been more effective.

Since its inception FUNAI has been notorious as an instrument not of the Indians but of the people exploiting them. But with the appointment in 1985 of Romero Jucá as its president, this role became overt. Jucá, a friend of President Sarney's, introduced enterprise to the agency's agenda. He began selling the timber and minerals in the Indian reserves of the western Amazon to businessmen. He opened the territories of several of the largest tribes to developers, and publicly supported the presence of garimpeiros in the Yanomami lands.

President Sarney rewarded him for his diligence by appointing him, in September 1988, unelected governor of the new state of Roraima. He had anticipated the promotion, and his last significant act as president of FUNAI was to implement the 76 per cent reduction of the Yanomami territory. As governor of Roraima he became the principal beneficiary.

Governor Jucá knew that his political rise thereafter depended upon elections. For five years he had enjoyed high authority without having been tested by plebiscite; but when Roraima was to achieve full statehood, at the beginning of 1991, its representatives would be elected. He needed votes, as his higher ambitions began, according to the national press, with a seat in the federal senate.

The established population of Roraima was ill-disposed towards Jucá. In Boa Vista he was known as 'Nestlé's Milk', as he was said to have received milktins filled with gold dust for certain commercial favours. But while the residents of Roraima were unlikely to elect him to the senate, the visiting garimpeiros were more amenable. They and the people supplying them could stay in Roraima only with the tolerance of the authorities, as their presence in the Yanomami territories was illegal. Jucá could show them that their destiny was dependent on his. The miners and their suppliers were registered as Roraimans, and became the electoral majority.

Romero Jucá worked to secure the presence of the miners in Roraima. He lobbied to legalize their presence, and to spend state money on modernizing the mining process. He laid plans for the building of a city in the heart of the Yanomami territory, to supply the miners and process certain ores[9]. For the tribespeople of the Amazon these projects simply put a nature to his name. In the Tupi-Guaraní group of Indian languages the word *jucá* means death.

But Romero Jucá, like Captain Xâvier, was not ordinarily corrupt. The authorities' tolerance of mining activities which were unlawful in almost every respect suggested a commitment to mining in Roraima at the highest levels of government. All the miners' airstrips were illegal, as they were unsurfaced and therefore unsafe; pilots every day falsified their flight plans, as none of their journeys into the territory were legitimate; no attempts were made to collect tax from the miners or to prevent smuggling by the owners; and all the environmental legislation governing both Indian reserves and national forests was being ignored. Like colonists, the miners in Roraima seemed to be welcome. They brought to the state what the government appeared to believe was progress.

Next to Jucá the Minister of Justice, Saulo Ramos, became the miners' stoutest patron. He contested the judge's ruling that the garimpeiros must be removed from Indian lands. He called the civil servant in the Attorney General's office who was trying to enforce it 'a youth who has only read one book of law.'[10] As the judge's ruling was drawn directly from the new Brazilian Constitution, this regrettably would appear to have been one more than Mr Ramos himself had mastered.

The Minister claimed that there were insufficient soldiers and policemen to expel the miners, and the chiefs of the armed forces claimed that there were no resources to supply them. But as the garimpeiros themselves were aware, it was not force that was required to remove them, but a curtailing of their diesel supplies. Without fuel the owners could not run the pumps, and could not afford to support their teams while they were finding no gold; and the miners would be forced to leave. The police, as the Indian support groups pointed out, would merely need to stay in the airports and ensure that no diesel was loaded[4], as they were pretending but failing to do when we left for the mines.

The armed forces had refused to act. The army claimed it would not fight its own nationals: something strikers on a picket line in Rio de Janeiro would have disputed, had they lived to do so. The airforce claimed it had no role in preventing civil violations of the airspace. While it thus ignored the 300 aeroplanes daily traversing Roraima, probably the worst place in the world for flying accidents, I had read in the newspapers that it had immediately apprehended and prosecuted the owners of a hot-air balloon, flying a few metres above the forest thirty kilometres from the airport at Manaus, as it constituted a hazard to air traffic. Instead, the armed forces' only significant contribution to the situation had been a negative one, as they had built or extended three of the airstrips the miners were using.

The interests of the Brazilian business community in the continued occupation of the Indian territory were no less evident than those of the government. While the likes of José Altino – the air-taxi operator – and the owners of the principal Roraiman newspaper were the garimpeiros' most visible advocates, it was the private mining companies which were said to have invested most in the invasion. Several people, in and out of the mines, suggested to me that the invasion of the garimpeiros was being used as a lever, to prise the area open for the use of the big companies. Though they apparently competed with the garimpeiros for Amazonia's mineral resources, mining corporations were said to have funded some of the initial invasions of Roraima.

It was claimed that the mining firms were using the garimpeiros to destroy the Roraiman forests. They knew that if they moved in directly the national and international scandal this would cause would leave the government with little choice but to close their operations down. But the government could, as it did, claim that it was incapable of expelling 40,000 garimpeiros. When the Yanomami lands ceased to support either Indians or valuable wildlife, they would lose their worth as anything other than a goldmine. The big firms could then, as they had done elsewhere, apply to the government to take over the mining operation, exploiting the resources more thoroughly, without the smuggling and tax losses of the miners. As the garimpeiro operations were inefficient and partial, the majority of the gold, as well as the substantial tin deposits, would be left to the big businesses. Twenty-one big mining companies had applied for exploration rights in the Yanomami area.

*

As I write, in summer 1990, the Indians' prospects are little better. The new government has succeeded in reducing the numbers of miners in Roraima from 40,000 to 5,000; but despite President Collor's pledge to defend the remainder of the Yanomami, there are several reasons to suppose that his administration has no greater commitment to their protection than President Sarney's.

When Fernando Collor took office he promptly sacked Romero Jucá as governor of Roraima, and the people campaigning to protect the Indians celebrated. But when the new governor, Rubens Villar, who had been the coordinator of Mr Collor's election campaign in the northern region, opened his mouth, it was as if the ghost of Jucá had somehow got into his skin. 'We cannot stay with our arms crossed, watching a mountain of gold,' he declared. The Yanomami territory 'is enormous: we will have to review this.'

Collor appointed as the president of FUNAI a friend of Romero Jucá's. Cantidio Guerreiro was said to have supervised Jucá's sales of timber from Indian reserves in the state of Mato Grosso, and it was believed to have been Jucá's lasting influence in government which secured his appointment.

President Collor's most televised commitment to the Yanomami's preservation was his demand that holes should be blown in the airstrips of the garimpeiros. Unfortunately this seems to have been little more than performance politics. Of the 270 airstrips in the Yanomami territory, only fourteen were dynamited, and within a month nine of them were again in use[11]. Having built the airstrips themselves it was not beyond the wit of the garimpeiros to repair them.

The voluntary health teams FUNAI had expelled from Roraima were allowed to return, but against the will of the Indian protection agency, which has now succeeded in sabotaging most of their operations. FUNAI's own health programme, resumed in March, seems to have brought the Yanomami nothing but extra miners: José Altino has been providing its transport, in return for being allowed to resume his carriage of miners and supplies back into the territory[11].

None of this, chaotic and dishonest as it may be, is to suggest that President Collor and his government are deliberately exterminating the Yanomami. Indeed the attitudes of some members of the new administration contrast markedly with those of President Sarney's ministers. But anything other than the surest commitment to the protection of the Yanomami is to preside over their destruction. The power of those who see the Yanomami as nothing but an obstacle to progress is mounting. As I write, Jucá is attempting to reclaim the governorship of Roraima, and José Altino is campaigning to become a federal senator. In his televised manifesto he has denied that the Indians are dying, and informed the garimpeiros that they are free to return to their lands.

The campaigners trying to defend the Yanomami fear that the way the two governments have treated them might become a model for the handling of other tribes in Amazonia. Garimpeiros are taking root in the Indian lands of the western state of Rondônia. In the far north-west of the Brazilian Amazon the more integrated tribal people have already expelled the first garimpeiros from their lands, and are waiting for the subsequent invasions. Mining is already long-established in tribal territories in the south. In October 1988 President Sarney cited his plans to protect the Yanomami as an example of the government's commitment to conservation in the Amazon. It is.

6

WE STAYED AT MACARÃO for four days, trying to learn more about the lives of both the miners and the Indians they were displacing. In the afternoons we saw the Yanomami processing onto the airstrip, wearing the clothes the garimpeiros had given them. One woman, bunches of leaves on her arms and dried grass in her earlobes, hobbled past in a padded bra and sheer pink trousers she must have been given by one of the prostitutes. The men carried shotguns. Several of them came to the compound and demanded shirts, hammocks – which they used for mending their malocas – and food. At the shabby pharmacy beside the airstrip Yanomami women begged drugs for their children. Thinking myself unobserved, I tried to take a photograph of one woman and her sick baby being given medicine. I heard a whistle, lowered the camera and saw the woman's escort aiming his shotgun at me, about to fire. The Yanomami, as the miners had told me, always warn before they shoot.

As Claudia's daughter recovered, word spread that a medicine man had arrived, and several children were brought to me with tuberculosis or violent fevers. I tried to explain I knew nothing; but there was no one I could pass them to. I made a solution of sugar, salt, vitamins and minerals, which I administered in cupfuls. The father of one Yanomami child tasted it himself, pronounced it weak medicine, and poured it on the ground. I did not argue.

Every evening there was gunfire. On our last night three or four men were murdered. Bandits had caught three miners in the woods, shot two of them dead and left a possible survivor, hit in the chest at point blank. A Yanomami man, having learnt the lessons of the superior civilization, had come to the airstrip to borrow a revolver, returned to his maloca, and shot dead the Indian who had taken his wife.

Before leaving Macarão we asked the miners what they felt about the three garimpeiros' reserves. They were dismissive. Settlement offended the life of the garimpeiro, by nature nomadic and irresponsible. 'Garimpeiros don't like reserves,' one man said, 'they like gold. You might as well stay at home and sit on your rump.' If the police came to move them out of Macarão they would either leave for another state, or move to the reserves then wait, creeping back into the rest of the forest when the guards left.

As the river had dropped we could walk the buckled route back to Jeremias. Lauro, the owner, had left to manage his affairs in Boa Vista, and the airstrip was being run by the Professor, the genius behind his enterprise. The Professor had once been the director of the University of Rondônia; but had left for the mines when his salary was cut and a politician was appointed rector. He had a pointed black beard and gold-rimmed spectacles, and an intense, ascetic manner. He had designed the airstrip; and now he supervised the construction of Lauro's mines and the rebuilding of the broken planes. He told me he wanted to work with garimpeiros for the rest of his life; it was more challenging than academia.

The police had now done as they had promised, and supply planes had, for a few days, stopped arriving from Boa Vista. The Professor and the other businessmen of Jeremias seemed to accept that they would have to leave, and extra mechanics had been brought in to help repair one of the crashed DC3s, so that their machines could be lifted out and moved to one of the three reserves.

At Chimarão the garimpeiros of Chimarãozinho's camp were resigned to their reported fate. Chimarãozinho had closed down one of his three pits to save fuel and was dismissing some of his men. The remainder would work for a fortnight until, he calculated, the diesel oil ran out. The miners were composed. Most of them had moved several times before, when seams had been exhausted, the owners had disinvested, or the police of various states had closed them down. They would, they told me, miss the friends they had made in the camp; but that was a commonplace in the life of the garimpeiro. While they each had different plans, no one was uncertain about what he would do.

Rosinaldo had heard on liana radio, the miners' communication network, that his wife had given birth to a daughter. He would return to Manaus to see his new child, then join a diving team. Tatuzinho – Little Armadillo – would go back to Maranhão to visit his new wife. He had left her to travel to the mines twenty days after the wedding, and they had been apart for several months. He would spend almost all the gold he had earned in getting home; but there would be no work to keep him there. He would return to the Amazon, to find another mine.

Antônio – Big Moreno – would work for two more months as a miner, here and in one of the three reserves, hoping to lay aside some capital. Then he would return to Maranhão and train as a teacher, as it was teachers that were needed most. He would learn English and travel. Others would move directly to the mines in Pará, or those said to be opening in the north-west of the Amazon. Graça the cook would follow Chimarãozinho.

'I love the mines because they are made for us. Not for them,' she said, pointing in the direction of Boa Vista.

Chimarãozinho said he would travel to one of the reserves, take samples and see whether he could find a lucrative claim. He said that he was not dissatisfied, as he had made a profit; but it was the Indians who would suffer.

'They won't stay here. With absolute certainty I tell you they will leave this place and follow us. They'll come to the reserves and build their malocas around the airstrips and beg for what we can give them.'

I had the discomforting feeling that he was right.

The departing men measured out their final yield of gold, then ate. Balão gave each a nod and a grunt and returned to his pit. They set off for Jeremias to wait for a plane.

We walked upstream an hour or two to Malaria, a quiet, windblown litter of huts where men slept on their arms in the blue shade of the bar. A tall thin man appeared from the dust and sunlight. He looked like an Old Testament prophet. He was covered in hair and mud, with a straight beard, torn trousers and gold teeth. He laid his body down flat along the bar.

'We'll blow the place apart before they take it from us,' he announced.

Eight of the richest mine owners, he claimed, Lauro among them, were assisting the expulsions of the miners. They had formed a cartel, led by José Altino, called the Grupo Sahara or Zé-Arara. When the police had pulled the garimpeiros out, these owners would move back in with their own men, and monopolize the mining.

'*Filhos de puta*. We're ready for them. We'll put our equipment on the airstrip and set light to it when they come in to land. Then we'll shoot them down. There are two thousand men round here, all armed. They haven't a hope.' He swung his body upright. 'If the bandits are killing garimpeiros for a wristwatch and a couple of grams of gold, why not offer them a kilo for every head of a policeman they take? They'll have to line them up on the airstrip to get paid though.' He lay back on the bar. '*Porra!*'

I asked him what he thought of the three reserves.

'There's no gold there; but they'll be good places for growing cocaine.'

We returned to spend the night at Jeremias. The planes had been liberated again, and were bringing in supplies once more. In the morning I was told that the federal police were due to arrive that day, to confiscate weapons in advance of the expulsions. Since dawn miners had been moving in and out of the forest, burying their guns in plastic sheeting. I wanted to stay and see the police operation. Barbara had heard about another Indian settlement, further from the mines, and set off for the day to find it.

The garimpeiros were tense, stopping work to watch whenever a plane banked over the mountains, sitting on diesel cans outside the control shed to listen to the two-way radio. After lunch in Lauro's house, two Yanomami warriors came to the door with shotguns, clutching their bellies and saying, 'Stomach die.' They finished off the food we had left in the serving bowls, eating enormously with a delicate, uncertain way of holding the spoons. When they had ingested a significant fraction of their bodyweights, the two warleaders stole into the kitchen to see if they could find any more. There was a crash and a shout, the men fell backwards through the door, and the fat black cook came out behind them like a mother hen, brandishing a ladle. She slammed the kitchen door and stood in front of it with her arms crossed. The two warriors slunk away unhappily with their guns.

At four o'clock a plane soared in towards Jeremias unannounced. Someone shouted 'police!', and the men ran round unstrapping their remaining guns and loading them into the Professor's arms. He ran with them towards his room, to lock them in a cupboard. He dropped the guns in the corridor, and rifles, revolvers and ammunition bounced across the floor. The plane landed and the pilot began to unload the food he had brought from Boa Vista. His radio had broken.

By night Barbara had not returned, and I was worried. In the morning Paulo, the mechanic who defended the Indians in arguments with the miners, had come to Jeremias to meet us, and we set off through the forest to find her.

At Chimarão we had been told that she had passed by on the previous morning and had not returned, and we were directed towards the airstrip of Junior Blefe, where Already Died had provoked the Yanomami uprising. We walked swiftly, and when we arrived there we were told she had left that strip the previous afternoon, to return there by the same evening: she had not appeared. A man with a drinker's face and a black eye knew how to find the Indian village, and we set off, running, into the mountains.

We soon began to find the narrow prints of Barbara's plimsolls, moving away from us, a day old, overlain by the naked tracks of the Yanomami. I tried to imagine what had happened to her. I felt she had most likely been killed by bandits, or might have succumbed to sickness or snakebite. I kept my eyes to the ground, absorbed in anxiety. But every few minutes Paulo would stop ahead of me and shout, 'Look at that water, look at those trees; so beautiful, isn't that beautiful?' and I would stop and gaze for a moment, and see flowers flaring in a spot of light; damselflies like a faint glaze on the air; and trees weighed down above clear water by moss and epiphytes. It was impossible not to be enchanted.

We ran for an hour and a half, following Barbara's footprints, slipping on the clay path. Sweat blinded me to the forest. I was aware only that we were climbing, and we were far from the mines. Breath came as if drawn through a sheet; we began to stumble. There was light ahead of us, and I saw that we were reaching the top of a mountain. We stopped.

We had broken through the trees on the edge of the valley. Covering the far flank were groves of banana plants. Women moved gently among them, dressed only in loincloths, carrying baskets of fruit. Hills stepped away into silence, forested, undisturbed. We remained hidden by the forest for some minutes, watching. We had reached the Yanomami's own land, the world behind the mountains.

We walked carefully down to the lap of the valley and up into the gardens, calling out in Portuguese, 'Friend, garimpeiro Yanomami friend.' They stood still and watched us come close. I put out my hands and they shook them with shy grins.

'White woman,' I said. 'Have you seen the white woman?' I mimed Barbara's height and long hair.

They laughed and pointed up the slope behind them, into the forest. We began to run again. Beyond the trees was a cluster of malocas, larger than those at Macarão. People rambled in and out of them, carrying bows and arrows, mattocks and baskets of food. They pointed us on, down through the forest on the other side of the mountain. The three sweating men blundered through their world, tripping on roots, falling onto trees. We turned a corner of the path and stopped.

In the glade beside a stream were three small huts. Outside them a crowd of people sat or knelt, adults and children, the warm honey of their skins cooled by the stained-glass shades of the forest. The women wore feathers in their ears; the painted spots and stripes of wild cats; and 'jaguar's whiskers': stems of dried grass piercing the septum of the nose and the cheeks close to the mouth. The Indians were quiet, watching and listening. In the middle of the circle, radiant as a flower in the green dark of the forest, was Barbara.

She turned and smiled. 'Glad you could make it.'

I sat down on the bank beside her and took off my shirt. The young man next to me put his arm around my shoulder and held my hand in his. The people smiled and watched us calmly. Two women came out of the huts and gave me fragments of manioc bread with beetle grubs, blunt grey maggots with hard heads, which tasted like nuts. The youth held onto my hand, and said nothing.

I was beckoned into the huts, where three old men lay dying in their hammocks. They were naked, as Yanomami men used to be, with a cord about the waist, tied around the top of the foreskin. One old man waved me over. He looped his arms around my neck and smiled weakly. He looked up and down my body, fascinated, and rubbed his hands over my stomach, marvelling at its flatness: he, like all Yanomami, was bellied. He lay back with a smile, like an old Chinese professor who had just upheld his hypothesis.

The two garimpeiros left us, and the young Indians led Barbara and me up towards the malocas, in a quiet procession of golden skin. Some of the women had tied rivershells to the cords of their tangas, which jingled like a windchime as they walked. Others had added the feathers of parrots and grey owls, and some people wore flowers as northern women would wear earrings. It felt wrong to be carrying a shirt amidst brown skin, so I gave it to the youth whom I had sat beside. In the maloca I took off my shoes, and I felt liberated of possessions, with nothing but the shorts I wore, a notepad and a pen.

I sat down and little children clustered around me, grinning and giggling, hiding their faces if I looked up at them. At first they tugged gleefully at the hairs in my armpits – the Yanomami do not possess them – then they discovered the hairs on my feet, which they considered, to my pain and their consequent delight, legitimate souvenirs.

A teenager was rolling a plug of tobacco and ash to push into his lip, and when I asked if I could try some he gave it to me. The leaf was of a species stronger than the one we import, and as I sucked it my hunger abated and I felt careless. To distract the children from my depilation I took out my pen and drew, on every arm presented to me, a different forest animal: lizard, beetle, currasow, tapir, peccary, jaguar, butterfly, fish.

A young man came through the crowd and told me with his hands that I was to help build an extension to the maloca. A group of youths had raised a frame of slim poles; now they wanted me to climb to the top and pull over it a tarpaulin they had been given by the garimpeiros. I tried to indicate that they were smaller and lighter than I, but they stood with grim faces and crossed arms until I mounted the frame. I climbed five metres, and the slight sticks swayed in the mountain wind. The tobacco had made me feel dizzy. I pulled the tarpaulin over, tied it as swiftly as possible, then slid down to the ground.

'Now you can mend the rest of the maloca,' the young man told me with his arms and face.

He enjoyed his authority. The tasks he ordered seemed to me to be impossible, I had to swing from the purling of the maloca to tie a cover to the tips of poles several metres above the courtyard. The children, seeing that I was malleable, called out instructions too, '*Tuxaua* – Chief – do this, *Tuxaua* come here,' until I could no longer tell what needed to be done and what was being invented to test me.

When at length I came down from the roof I asked Barbara why the young man was so bossy.

'Oh, he's the chief,' she said.

'But he's only eighteen or so.'

She looked around, at the bright faces of the children and the teenagers who now sat watching us. 'All the older men are dying or dead.'

*

In the living space of the roundhouse most people seemed to be ill. An old woman looked as though the fluids had been sucked from her body, leaving just a skeleton in a loose skin. One boy lay in his hammock with such a fever that I could feel his temperature before my hand had reached his forehead. Barbara said the people had indicated to her that the sick had been blown at through a tube: she assumed this meant they had been hit by darts from a blowpipe, but she could find no mark on their bodies. We later learnt that the Yanomami believe they can be cursed by an enemy blowing through a magic pipe, and this was their explanation for the plague.

As I sat by the hammock of a fevered boy, two old women broke through the screen of banana leaves, walking on their haunches, roaring and sweeping sticks across the ground. They seemed to see nothing, and I was hit on the shins and ankles before I could get out of the way. The women stamped around the hammock, screaming, beating the air with their sticks, their eyelids, I saw, pressed shut.

In the courtyard I was stopped by the chief. With gestures and a few words of Portuguese he asked me how long it would be before all the garimpeiros went away. He put one hand to his cheek, by which he meant sleep and, I assumed, night, then put out both hands with his fingers splayed: will it be this many nights? I shook my head, gathered up the hands of some of the children close by and put them all together: this many. He nodded, disappointed.

The roaring continued for most of the day. One of the two old women, the faith healer, was visiting the hammocks of all the dying; shouting, screaming, stamping her feet, sweeping the bad spirits away into the forest with her hands. I was later told that female faith healers were almost unknown; only the absence of old men could account for it. Barbara, the day before, had been asked to take over. Today it was my turn, and I was led to the hammock of a teenaged girl, shivering hot and cold, her teeth grinding, eyelids fluttering. I started as I had done at Claudia's, running my hands gently over the skin and breathing the words I had learnt; but the old woman stopped me. The spirits were robust, and would respond only to violence.

I stamped and shouted, sweeping my arms through the air as she showed me, scooping something from the surface of the body and pushing it away from the maloca. The old woman watched me, her approval mounting with my vehemence. As I roared her incantations I tumbled the words, and as she did not correct me I reverted first to Portuguese then to English.

'Disease go away, bad spirit go away, go away, go away, go to Captain Xâvier, go to Jucá ...'

I danced harder, bursting into athletic springs, leaping over the hammock, shouting. I began to feel dizzy, as if I had been blowing too hard, and, as my chant lifted me, I lost full consciousness, and felt I was soaring a little above the ground, sustained by my shouts. I stopped suddenly and fell against the women behind me, my head swooning, sweat starting from my skin. The old woman put her arm around my shoulder.

'*Amigo sharami.*'

I learnt later that faith healing has been known to dispel diseases Northern medicine could not address. As the Yanomami were convinced that many of their afflictions were caused by magic, they were also able to believe that magic could cure them. I believe that this transference of a physical trouble for which there was no known physical redress to a psychological realm, where treatment was available, might have evolved as a strategy for survival.

But we, of course, blundered through their mysteries. I knew nothing of their faith, only that they nominated blood as the metronome of life: too much of it made time run fast, too little of it, slow; that to mature naturally humans need to keep the world in order by following the rituals which surround the shedding of blood in puberty and death. These things would take years of study for us to begin to understand. While we stumbled in their world, the miners marauded through the layers of their faith, seizing and tearing what appeared to be simple only because they had not the understanding to know its complexity. The flames of other knowledge flicker, as the faith healers die, and the outer world usurps their truths.

The young 'chief' came to me and held up a cake of soap.

'Wash,' he said.

Barbara had already warned me about the ceremony to come. Fascinated by Northern bodies, the Yanomami would baulk at no impropriety to see more. She had, as instructed, spent much of the previous day removing and replacing her clothes, while the village stared, amazed, at her pointed breasts and blonde pubic hair. I took the soap and trod reluctantly down to the water's edge, followed by all the young men, women and children of the village. I stood beside the stream in hesitation.

'Wash,' said the chief.

I took off my shorts, stepped into the water and soaped. The young men stood on the bank with grave expressions, their arms folded, like farmers assessing stock. The women looked on with consternation, discussing the spectacle in worried tones. The children giggled wildly. I rinsed quickly and left the water, pulling on my shorts before I had dried. They seemed satisfied and let me return to the maloca. I joined the old women, who fed me with toadstools, baked plantains and beetle grubs.

Insects are an important source of protein for the Yanomami[1], supplementing the fish and game they catch. They also make ponds in the forest to attract frogs, and harvest them and their tadpoles. They eat fine-grained clays, which supply some of the minerals they need. These customs revolt the garimpeiros, who try to teach them to consume the food of proper people: rice, beans and beef. These are less nutritious and cannot be produced by the Indians themselves. Some of the younger men are persuaded to change, however: it is hard for them to see that so many people, with such material advantages, could be so wrong.

But most of the Indians still take their protein from fishing and hunting and their carbohydrates from their gardens. They fish with bows and arrows or a poisonous bark mashed in the water. They hunt tapirs, wild pigs, agoutis and monkeys; but above all the currasow bird, which is like a slim black turkey. The men when they walk carry a pouch of spare arrow points, agouti teeth for sharpening them, and magic potatoes for bringing luck to their hunt[2].

They garden without breaking the soil, much as the Kayapó do, planting their different crops in the parts of the field which suit them best. The bananas, manioc, sweet potatoes, peppers, pineapples, sugarcane and cocoyams they grow are mixed with medicinal or magical plants, psychotherapeutic drugs, dye and fibre crops. The gardens continue to produce long after the Yanomami cease cultivating them, as many of their crops are designed to sustain people foraging in the forest, all around the village's land.

My brief aerial view of the Yanomami's territory might have suggested that their lands are uninhabited, as almost all the ground is covered by forest. It was on the basis of a similarly superficial survey that FUNAI concluded the Indians were not using their lands, and they could therefore be confined to the plots on which their malocas happened to be. But researchers with a knowledge of botany have shown that there is scarcely a corner of a village's territory which has not at one stage been cultivated; and hardly a tree in the forest will come to the end of its life without having once been used for its fruit, its wood, its medicinal leaves or bark, the bees' nests or the game it harbours. The survival of the forest in their territory is a mark not of a place unused but of a place used sustainably. It is because they have treated their land with such subtlety that the Indians are considered unworthy of its tenure.

Every few years the village moves between 10 and 30 kilometres, through a country landscaped by legends. Each valley, every streamside, mountaintop or boulder has its own mythology. There is no dissociation between the landscape of the mountains and the landscape of the mind. The tribe defines itself by its land, and the land is peopled with spirits by the tribe. Removing an Indian from his forests is not as simple as taking a farmer from his fields: he becomes detached from the physical foundations of his belief, from the landmarks by which he navigates the spiritual highways of his world. No relocation by outsiders, however sensitive, can rechart the geography of sentience.

In the sunstriped shade of the maloca girls carried banana leaves piled with manioc roots or fruit. The people talked quietly, poking at their fires, cooking. Before the whites arrived the life of the Yanomami had been leisurely. Their gardens, well planned, using the natural features of the sites they chose, producing long-lasting rather than annual crops, needed little attention; just as banks of shrubs in Europe require less maintenance than herbaceous borders. Without defined periods of planting and harvesting, and the storage and trading that a single large harvest would demand, the Yanomami avoid the stresses of an accumulative society. They devote most of their attention to the social arts – talking, resting together, nursing babies, feasting, fulfilling the rituals of marriage, puberty and death – in other words, entwining the threads which hold a society together. They would be amazed at people who need to seek a lifestyle.

The Yanomami still suffer from a reputation for arbitrary violence, which now seems to have been undeserved[3]. The anthropologist who propagated this impression in the 1960s has subsequently reassessed his work, and he and others have found that his initial accounts were exaggerated. There is infanticide, whose function is the subject of some debate, and there is violence between villages, but it is now known that most of this aggression is ritualized into duels or formal wars. There are strict rules of combat, and rigorous purification rituals for anyone who kills another.

But it is the first impressions which have remained in Northern minds. They corroborate our mystification of other people, allow us to continue to horrify ourselves with the strangeness of others, and congratulate ourselves on our own decency. It is such conceptions which help governments to claim that their tribal people are in need of correction, of integration into a respectable society. The more they are represented as fierce and immoral, the easier it is to justify their subjugation, for their own sake as well as that of the nation. They cannot have lived a happy life, the authorities can argue, when ruled by such fearful gods.

But it is not the Indians who consider their habits repulsive or their spirits terrifying. It is we who are frightened by their lives, and we are frightened because we do not understand them. Yet civilized people claim to wish to rid the Indians of the things they find fearful, for the good of the Indians.

It is impossible to appreciate the impact of the changes developed societies have imposed on the lives of tribal people, without imagining how our own lives might be, were they to be forcibly changed by aliens such as, for instance, the Indians. This, if we are to understand what has happened to the Indians, is worthy of our speculation. Were the Indians, through some inconceivable circumstance, to evolve a power, physical and psychological, to subjugate us as we have done them, and were they, also inconceivably, to become, as we have been, aggressive evangelists of their own ways of life, we could expect them to destroy all they considered frightening, unnecessary and distasteful about our lives.

Finding in our technology a system which they could not penetrate or understand, they would destroy it in all its manifestations: transport, heating, electricity, communications, sewerage, manufactured goods. Our houses, being incomprehensible to a communal society, would be burnt, and replaced with shelters of sticks and leaves, in which fifty or one hundred people would be forced to live. Our religious institutions, austerely frightening to the uninitiated, would also go; our clothes, considered unnecessary by people who come from a place where they are not required, would be taken from us, and in the winter many millions would freeze to death. We would be denied access to conventional medicines, and encouraged instead to use bark, leaves and roots to cure ourselves, though we know nothing of such things. There would be no food we did not hunt or cultivate ourselves. We would be forbidden privacy, the music we know, reading and writing, and even, if the examples of the world's proselytes are to be followed, our own language. We would be forced to abandon our own morality, our ambitions, our understanding, and aspire to those of a culture we could not understand. We would be denied ourselves.

The results, of course, would be devastating. In terms of their physical impact they would be comparable only to a nuclear holocaust; in terms of our disorientation, to pandemic mental illness. It would not be an invasion to which we could adapt, as post-Roman Britain adapted to the arrival of the Angles and Saxons, as there would be no points of contact between our own culture and that of the invaders.

All this may seem improbable, ridiculous; it might appear unlikely that any invading society, however ignorant, however lacking in compassion, could fail to see that such changes could only destroy the people it claimed to be developing. Yet I have chosen my examples with care. They are the exact converse of the changes still being forced upon tribal people by cultures which claim to be educated and civilized. And the impact, both physical and psychological, has been exactly as we might imagine the effects on ourselves to be. When tribes are developed by people who do not understand them, they are simply destroyed.

Brazil and the other Amazon nations are not the worst of the world's offenders. The governments of Indonesia, China, Bangladesh and Guatemala, for instance, have refined the extermination of their ethnic people to a delicate art. Yet still in Brazil, a nation which is in some respects as civilized as any, communal houses are burnt down and replaced with homes for nuclear families; Christian evangelists are allowed to convert unwilling populations; tribespeople are encouraged, cajoled or forced to wear clothes; Indians are denied access to their traditional medicines and foods, and forced to use those they do not understand and might be unable to endure; traditional social relationships, communality, rituals and languages are widely discouraged. Tribal people are taught that all they believed in and knew was wrong, and all that the new society can replace this with is right. Their humanity becomes somebody else's.

It might seem that the introduction of things, such as clothes and technology, to a people who have no place for them is less destructive than the removal of things, such as clothes and technology, from people who need them. But one of the features of the imposed development of tribal people is that the civilized society does not know what it is removing. Nakedness, for instance, is a commodity when climate and lifestyle make the wearing of clothes impractical. By encouraging, or forcing, people to wear clothes, we are not just giving them something they do not need, but taking away something they do. When communal houses are burnt, and replaced with rows of huts, it is not only a frame of sticks and leaves that is being demolished, but also a community whose complexity no honest anthropologist could claim to understand. When the land is taken away, so is the people's sense of self.

Most of these things are not, as I write, yet happening to the Yanomami. Their contact is too recent, the penetration of government is insufficient. But other Amazonian tribes, living where the alien culture has had more access to their lives, have suffered, and are suffering, all of these impositions. The Yanomami wait their turn.

In the evening, though by now stumbling with tiredness, I cut wood as I was instructed, while Barbara was painted by the women of the maloca. Her face was patterned with gold spots and laughter lines; she looked leonine. Then the women called me, and I sat and was painted in black: straight strokes on my face in a startled cat pattern, wavy lines down my chest to my shorts. The dyes were resinous and fragrant. I was glad to sit down, glad that the day's labour was over. They rubbed our arms and legs with red urucûm seeds, and then they began to laugh. They sprang up, pulled us to our feet and propelled us into the centre of the maloca. We had been painted for dancing.

We stood together sheepishly. I tried to hide behind Barbara, hoping I might be forgotten. The chief jumped up and down in front of us, his arms in the air, stamping his feet.

'Ha! ha! ha! ha!'

He backed away around the courtyard, and we had no choice but to follow him, jumping and stamping our feet, our arms raised. He then left us and joined the crowd of spectators, sweeping his hand around the maloca to show that we were to carry on. We plodded round and round the courtyard, in opposite directions. If we slowed down the chief jumped into the ring and admonished us.

'I think we're getting married,' said Barbara as we passed each other.

The sun sank, night fell and the stars appeared, and still we were obliged to dance. I felt my legs turn to wood. At length I stopped, suddenly, and even the chief's exhortations could do no more for me. We leant against the walls of the maloca, sweating and panting. The Yanomami were delighted.

The people soon moved to their hammocks. The chief sat beside us and spoke in Yanomami, with sign language and a little Portuguese. He said he wished the miners, FUNAI and the police would all go away and leave them alone. But later he told us that the maloca was bad and Boa Vista was good. Boa Vista had no diseases, lots of presents, and priests who would look after the Yanomami. They should go to Boa Vista to live. He lived in a world of mirrors, where every image had its counterpart, and nothing once taken to be solid could now be trusted as a certainty. He wore shorts, a shirt and football boots the garimpeiros had given him, and a string led into his underpants. When he pulled it a plastic bottle materialized, which he shook to show us there were grains of gold inside: his certificate of citizenship of another world.

I was given a cotton hammock, which a boy helped me to string over a fire. We hung it too high, and within a few minutes I was shivering. I curled up and said nothing, but a young man left his hammock in the darkness, came to me and slipped his hand under the sheet to feel my chest.

'*Tuxaua* cold?'

'Cold.'

He returned to the darkness and appeared again, to give me a tracksuit jacket he had found.

On the other side of the maloca the chief turned on a radio the miners had given him, and found liana radio.

'... from Pará José Ferreira says to tell Chico and Paulinho he's found gold on the Rio Preto and to come and join him. A message here for Marcos Andrade Lima from his brother in Santa Teresinha. Your wife has died. Now here's a hit the whole nation's playing, "I Want To Be Your Only Girl", by Maria Santos ...'

From the riverbank frogs called like chinking glass.

We returned to Jeremias against the pleas of the Indian children.

There we found that the police had visited the previous day, and they were due to return for a meeting with the bosses of the camps. We were told they had found few arms, but had caught one man with cocaine, beaten him and taken it. Lauro said he would not be charged; the cocaine would inexplicably be found in the pocket of somebody richer, who could pay more for their silence.

A Superpullman helicopter arrived the following day, carrying fifteen policemen and two FUNAI officers. The police were a rough, indisciplined bunch, unshaven, some long-haired, swinging automatic weapons with the safety catches off. One of the two FUNAI officers was the man who spoke Yanomami, whom Jucá had expelled with the priests and voluntary health teams in 1987. FUNAI had begun its health programme for the Indians and, watched by the world, had agreed to send someone who spoke their language to assist. Francisco Bezerra, a lean, grey, modest man, who had lived for twenty-five years with the Yanomami, had been sent to assess the Indians' needs. He did not know if there would be funds to do as he would recommend.

He told me that if the Yanomami are asked in Portuguese what they think of the garimpeiros, they will say they are friends. They know the penalties for not concurring. But if they are asked in their own language they say they wish they would go away. They know that the miners, though they depend on them, will destroy them. He said that the Indians understand and respond if the trouble is taken to explain how some of the miners' merchandise might be bad for them. He was telling people, for instance, that if they ate sweets they would need dental care, while if they kept to their own foods it would not be necessary. Those he had spoken to took his advice. If FUNAI let him stay, his would be one voice against 40,000. But it would be a Yanomami voice.

Francisco felt that if the miners were removed immediately from the whole Indian area it would still be possible for the Yanomami to recover; but that if they remained much longer the tribe would be lost. The Yanomami had been saved before. When smaller groups of garimpeiros were expelled in the mid 1980s, the Indians who had become dependent on them almost died of famine. Within a year, however, they were working in their gardens again and supporting themselves once more. Now they needed the most sensitive patronage: enough food and assistance to allow them to survive the return to self-sufficiency, but not so much that they became dependent on FUNAI.

There would certainly be problems. Some of the younger men had developed a taste for the life the garimpeiros had introduced them to, and took pride in the clothes, the shotguns and the alcohol they had been given. If they wanted, Francisco said, to take up the life of outsiders and move to Boa Vista – even when people such as he had explained all that would involve – then they should; but if they stayed at home without reverting to their traditions they would disrupt the vulnerable social systems of the majority. He wanted FUNAI not to take away the Indians' clothes, but first to make their use safer – by showing them when to remove them and how to wash them – then, away from the culture which had encouraged their use, let them rediscover the advantages of nakedness.

From what I had seen of the damage to the environment, I felt that, were the garimpeiros suddenly to leave, the natural systems would become reasonably productive again after twenty or thirty years. The rivers would clear and become habitable to fish, which would spread from the small streams the miners had not excavated. Trees could not return to the raw gravel of their banks until smaller plants had first colonized, and some topsoil had gathered around them. But the holes the miners had dug could become ponds sustaining fish and frogs. Many of the animal species the garimpeiros had driven away would not return, and mercury, of course, would lurk as a perennial threat. But such a recovery cannot begin until all the miners are expelled, and the government ensures that they cannot return.

The police had confiscated all the two-way radios on the strips along the Rio Mucujaí. This seemed at first to be sensible, as the bosses could no longer order fuel and supplies; but then I realized that all transport had by this means been halted. Without details of local weather conditions and air traffic, the pilots from Boa Vista would not fly to the strips. As the armed forces had failed to provide alternative transport for the garimpeiros, no one could leave, even though there were people now queueing at the airstrips to get to Boa Vista or the three reserves. The DC3 at Jeremias had been repaired and had left the previous day; and the miners appeared to have been abandoned.

In the morning hundreds of garimpeiros whose diesel had come to an end assembled at Jeremias, waiting for a flight out. There were others queueing beside airstrips all along the river, and beyond

Macarão they were said to be starving. Some bosses at Jeremias had stored diesel, and claimed they could stay until the police deadline, sixty days thence.

No plane marked the sky. I was ready to leave and, like the miners, I now began to feel trapped. I spent the day writing and reading. Barbara played cards with the helicopter pilots.

On the next day, 24 January, the police arrived again, now unannounced and on foot. Their helicopter had broken down and they were hungry and cross. Four policemen pushed open the doors of Lauro's house, where they found me writing at the dining table. One of them told me to stand up.

'Where's your cocaine?'

'I haven't got any.'

'It'll be easier if you give it up before we find it.'

They pushed me against a wall, frisked me, and tipped my pack onto the table. I was frightened that they would plant drugs or confiscate my notebooks. They questioned my authorization. I had none. A man arrived with a video camera and filmed several pages of my hieroglyphs, and they took away some printed papers for translation.

They lost interest in me when they found the Professor's locked door. They shouted for a key. No one answered, so they kicked it down. They tipped out his drawers, found nothing, and moved to the kitchen. There, though the cook protested, they emptied the fridge and loaded their arms with all the tins they could carry, and strode out into the sunshine to eat. Later I was told that they had visited one of the camps, and confiscated the gold chains.

At night I heard the bosses fending off their boredom by speculating about Barbara and me – who were we, why had we stayed so long? I thought only of escape, and could not sleep. There were no planes in the morning, and people suggested we might be trapped for weeks. But in the afternoon I heard the noise of engines, and miners ran from their huts and shelters to watch the sky. The old DC3 the mechanics had mended was banking ponderously over Jeremias. It fell and thudded over the clay. Lauro climbed out of the cockpit and the miners milled beneath him. The Professor gave us tickets. The plane turned and prepared for take-off. I picked up my rucksack and found Barbara.

'Got all your stuff?'

'George.' She hesitated. 'I've decided to stay. This place—'

The last of the miners with tickets were climbing into the plane. The propellers were racing.

'The pilots say they'll give me work. It'll be great. I—'

The steps were being drawn into the plane. Barbara gabbled a message for her friends in Manaus and I ran across the strip without her, feeling the wind of the propellers on my face. I was pulled through the hatch and the DC3 taxied immediately. Lauro hauled back and we lifted sharply from the end of the runway, to avoid the mountains. I looked down and saw Jeremias, the men, the tarpaulins, the pits, and Barbara, waving from the airstrip.

We landed at Alto Alegre – Happy Halt – a windy frontier town of red roads and shut stores, where people waited morosely for buses or for accidents. There were no police on this strip to stop the loading of supplies, and Lauro could move in and out unimpeded. We hired a truck to Boa Vista, and drove for several hours across the ranchlands.

On 26 January I visited the garimpeiro syndicate in Boa Vista, where the union members were preparing for a demonstration. I interviewed their leader Baixinho – the Little One – who stood and shouted answers to my questions while thirty or forty men around him cheered. They would be marching against the church that day, as the Bishop of Roraima and the other *comunistas* had been lobbying President Sarney to close the mines down. This march would be a warning to them; next time they would set light to the churches.

The procession of 150 men – reported as over 1000 by certain regional newspapers – marched around the town's perimeter, heralded by firecrackers and trucks playing music and speeches through loudspeakers. The banners they carried read 'The bishop wants to snatch the bread from the mouths of our children' and 'We garimpeiros want work.' They arrived in the central square, and gathered about the statue of the garimpeiro with his pan.

Baixinho spoke, excitedly. 'It is the americano gringos who are trying to close us down, as they want the Indian land for themselves. We all have faith in Christ. It's only the Bishop of Roraima who's not on the side of God but on the other side. What sort of Christian is it who says he supports the Indians, when we all know he is keeping them as slaves to mine his own gold? We're with Jucá. We'll fight with him.'

I had tried throughout the day to secure an interview with

Romero Jucá – who was still at the time state governor – and I was finally led through the Governor's Palace to meet his Press Secretary. He was a neat, polite man, who emphasized repeatedly the governor's commitment to order and control. In his panelled office he told me that Romero Jucá wanted to control the mining process, so that the garimpeiros became more efficient, generating money for the state and all its people. The order he was bringing to Roraima would be of benefit to the Indians too, as he would give them the right to some of the gold the miners found. Then they too could become rich, and Roraima would progress into the twentieth century. Order, control and progress: the Brazilian flag fluttered outside his office. From within the Governor's Palace there came only the sedate noise of air conditioners and conversation, but from the middle of the plaza the muffled shouts of the miners declaring war against the church could still be heard. Beyond the flag a smokebomb had been ignited in the grass, and I watched the garimpeiros fade from view.

7

It is not the miners but the farmers who are the colonists destroying Amazonia. In terms of their effects upon the Indians the garimpeiros are enormously important; but they do not, as I saw, lay waste to more than a small proportion of the forests in which they work. There are, on the other hand, few practical limits to the damage the farmers cause.

While most of the miners I saw in Roraima came from Maranhão, the peasants now cutting and burning around the south and along the flanks of the Basin have come from all over Brazil. Many have left their home states, as I have shown, through the agencies of expulsion or technological change. Others are escaping from their financial troubles. Brazil's economic crisis, exacerbated by a concentration of capital as intense as the concentration of land, has overburdened farmers already struggling with small plots and low prices for their crops. Many who worked for larger landowners are losing their jobs, as agricultural employment is declining throughout the nation. At the same time one and a half million people are entering the labour market each year. As the size of peasant families has tended to grow, farmers find that their smallholdings can no longer support them.

Peasant farmers are likely to cause the Amazon's least eradicable problems. While at present they account for only a little over 20 per cent of the destruction taking place there[1], they are harder to control than the other destructive agents. Were the government, as it now promises to do, to make a serious attempt to curtail deforestation in the Amazon, it would quickly discover that it was dealing with a problem far deeper than environmental destruction. There is no profit in attempting to stop the slash-and-burn farming there if the farmers have no other means of survival. However rigorous is the government's satellite monitoring of the fires and application of fines, the peasants, through necessity, will find a means to continue.

Though the big landowners cutting cattle ranches from the Amazon have supporters throughout the government, they do not have the force of numbers which the colonists now command, and are in theory easier to restrain. As settlers become the majority of the electorate in all Amazonian states, there are increasing political difficulties in trying to control their cutting, or to forbid their access to new land.

The destruction the colonists cause is far out of proportion to their numbers. It is true that the Amazon's population is rising faster than that elsewhere in Brazil, and indeed one researcher suggests that even were the Brazilian Amazon's borders to be sealed in 1990, the 16 million people now living there could multiply to as many as 50 million by 2030[1]. As the borders are not to be sealed, the eventual numbers are likely to be much greater than that. But in an area the size of the Amazon even 200 million need not be an overwhelming population, were the farms there small and sustainable. But while most of the immigrant families the government sponsored first acquired 100 hectares, and those financing themselves tend to purchase smaller plots, it is not these first farms which define the limits to the devastation they cause.

For settlement in the Amazon is seldom final. Even before arriving there, most of the migrants settling in the west of the Basin had moved through other parts of Brazil at least three times, and some, remarkably, had tried to recommence their lives on as many as twenty-five occasions[2]. In the Amazon they are even less sedentary. Within a few years most move from their initial settlement sites, many travelling to fresh frontiers, where they open new plots, burning more forest. There are several reasons for this perpetual restlessness[3].

The fortunate settlers are generally those who arrive first on a new frontier, with sufficient capital to secure their residence for long enough to obtain titles to their land. They can then sell these first plots, whose value rises as the frontier develops, and move on to buy larger, cheaper landholdings on another virgin frontier. They may be the ones who break the cycle of their poverty, and establish a foothold on the glass cliff of prosperity. Others move because they fail, either because they get the worst land, or insufficient of it, or because of their lack of capital. Inadequate investment increases the chance of crop failure, and those without money to fall back on are particularly vulnerable to the market distortions and poor transport of the frontiers; which mean, in some places, that crops cost more to grow than they do to buy.

Many go because, perhaps not for the first time in their lives, they are expelled. Ranchers move in behind the settlers, buy up the land that those who were already leaving have to sell, and consolidate their properties by seizing the remainder. Already, in the state of Rondônia, 3 per cent of the landowners possess 60 per cent of the land, and throughout the Amazon the concentration of property holding is approaching that of the home states. Like rust developing under paintwork the settlers, sealed against the floor of poverty by violence and deprivation, can only move sideways.

The peasants' insecurity exacerbates the damage they cause. As they cannot ensure that either their finances or the ranchers will allow them to remain to reap the benefits, they do not invest in the land improvements and perennial crops necessary for a sustainable livelihood. Instead they farm as if at any minute they could be forced to leave, using crops which produce rapidly, but at the expense of the exhaustion of the soil. This in turn increases their chances of failure and remigration.

Among the safest places for peasants to move to are nature reserves. This is because, by contrast to the private landholdings which quickly monopolize the rest of the regions made accessible by roads, there are no gunmen in the reserves. For many Amazonian politicians the destruction of a nature reserve is a political boon, as it enables them to grant free land in exchange for votes. So when the federal government declares an area to be totally protected, the announcement is often accompanied by a rush to occupy it.

Life in the colonization sites of the Amazon is difficult for everybody there; but many of those who have substantial landholdings are glad to have moved. The land they possess means that in some respects their lives have improved since leaving their home states; though in other senses there is a deterioration. Many are blighted by the Amazon's fecund diseases: just in the state of Rondônia 200,000 settlers suffer from malaria. Healthcare, transport and education are generally even worse than in Maranhão. The peasants can make a profit on their holdings only by cutting and burning a significant proportion of their land each year, and this requires the labour of a large family.

An extensive survey of peasants settled in Rondônia in the

western Amazon revealed that 28 per cent considered their lives had improved since arrival in the Amazon, while 45 per cent claimed they had become poorer[2]. Those most disadvantaged may either lose their land and join the miserable troops of the migrant workers, making fencing posts for ranchers or charcoal in the sawmills; or pawn their tools when they have planted their crops and use the money to travel to the mines. If they find no gold they cannot return for the harvest.

All the evident troubles of the settlement sites – the disease, the poor infrastructure, the presence of the ranchers – are overshadowed by the nature of the soils the peasants are attempting to farm. Only 7 per cent of the Amazon's soils are considered to be suitable for conventional peasant agriculture, and most of the places in which these soils are accessible have already been heavily colonized.

The biggest agricultural problem is a lack of available phosphate. There is a reasonable quantity in the soil, but when the neutralizing minerals released by the burning of the trees have been washed away, it becomes inaccessible to crops, and they begin to fail. On most of the farms in the Amazon this takes place after two to four years. The same patch of land can then be farmed again once it has been left fallow for at least fifteen years, and the deep-rooted trees returning to it draw more neutralizing minerals from the earth. But most of the farmers who stay on their plots have neither the land nor the patience to wait that long before they return to where they first cut into the forest. When the soil is reopened too early it cannot recover for decades.

There is little that can be done with an infertile Amazonian soil. The peasants cannot afford the required fertilizer, and nor can the nation. If the government's recommendations for fertilizer use in the Amazon were to be followed, Brazil's deposits of phosphate would be exhausted within four years. Without such applications, farming in the Amazon is, for most, as painful and as futile as raiding a wasps' nest for honey.

The farmers have the additional problems of having been set against nature, and of living in an extensive land. As they try to combat the plants and animals of the Amazon, rather than, as the Kayapó do, work alongside them, they are commonly defeated by weeds and pests. And as they do not have a tradition of turning and facing their problems, but tend to flee, as they are encouraged to do, to seek their solutions elsewhere, they can never establish themselves sufficiently to raise their standard of living. It is instructive to see that many of the peasants possessing one hectare of fertile ground in Java, where the land is crowded and the people have no option but to concentrate on the little they have, are more prosperous than those farming one hundred hectares in Brazil.

The people and the forests of the Amazon also suffer from bad advice. Scientists and development consultants have tended to work with a single model of farm economics, developed and found to be profitable in the temperate lowlands of the northern hemisphere. Peasants have been encouraged to abandon their subsistence farming, and concentrate instead on growing a single crop each year, using technology and chemicals to supply what the land lacks. While this might, for a few years at least, generate income for the nation, for the small farmer it is disastrous. Only the big landlords can invest sufficiently, and be assured that they will not die of starvation if the strategy fails. The small farmers are soon ruined, and forced to sell their land to the big owners.

It is not only this inverse distribution of wealth across the population which has accompanied these agricultural changes; but also an inverse distribution of wealth over time. From the United States to Bangladesh the Green Revolution, as these developments were optimistically dubbed, has proven itself unsustainable, as farming which is insensitive to the characteristics of the land has led to soil erosion or nutrient loss, salination and resistance to pesticides, and increasing costs for all farmers. The resources of the future are used to pay for profits in the present.

Some of the worst advice has come from the most respectable sources. An entirely misguided study by the United Nations' Food and Agriculture Organization, which failed to take account of mineral loss, climate, pests, drought or finance, suggested that the Brazilian Amazon could support up to ten people per hectare, allowing the astonishing total of five billion people to survive there by farming[4]. With such advice the Brazilian establishment should take only part of the blame for the troubles it has helped to precipitate in Amazonia. Just as Northern governments opt to listen to the scientists who tell them that there is no evidence for the greenhouse effect, the Brazilian government could be expected to heed the studies of the Amazon which best suit its own political purposes.

*

For all of these reasons, many people are moving from the land to the towns, where the majority of Amazonians now live. Some towns are now doubling in size each decade[5], attracting not only failed colonists, but people from other parts of Brazil. Manaus, which now supports 1.2 million people, receives a further 80,000 each year, more than its total population in 1920. These immigrants alone require fifty new houses each day, and were the authorities in Manaus to keep pace with the needs of the population, a new school would need to be built in the city every three days. Hospitals, transport, sewerage and electricity supplies are overloaded. But in the Amazon cities, by contrast to the megalopoli of the south, nearly everyone has a house.

The city dwellers too are a serious threat to the environment. Much of the food Amazonians now consume is imported; but this situation is changing, as successive governments have attempted to make the Basin productive. The inhabitants of most Amazon towns are reliant upon fish, and to this end the rivers are being exploited to the point of likely ecological collapse. In a misconceived attempt to boost meat production, the authorities have been encouraging settlers and ranchers to cut the flooded forest. The result is that the protein production falls dramatically, as the fish of the forest are replaced by unproductive cattle pastures.

While most of the settlers entering Amazonia now pay for themselves, the infrastructure of colonization was laid down not by the peasants but by the government. Since 1970 Brazilian governments have been investing heavily in the movement of settlers to the Amazon, for several reasons. Of these it is probably fair to say that the least important was the welfare of the people being moved. Colonization has long been used as a means of avoiding land reform, and of generating substantial profits for construction companies, many of which have uncomfortably close relationships with members of the government. Like goldmining it increases the numbers of loyal voters in a state, and to this end certain state governments have invested in advertising campaigns in the rest of Brazil.

But above all settlement has been used to boost national prestige. In the 1970s Brazil's military leaders chose to portray their nation as a pioneer state, whose advance into the Amazon would be the first step towards becoming a superpower. Such propaganda helped to boost the popularity of the government during the time of the most ferocious state repression. Allied to this purpose was the aim of national integration, taking control of the Brazilian Amazon before it was annexed by other – unidentified – nations. To this end the people living in the Amazon were encouraged to be representative Brazilians, and much of the failure of the first farmers there can be ascribed to the fact that they were advised to farm like those in the temperate south, despite the great differences in climate, soils, infrastructure and markets.

The first big project was the construction of the notorious TransAmazon Highway. With the help of the World Bank and the InterAmerican Development Bank, settlers were encouraged to move from the North East of Brazil along a road built to cut across the southern Amazon. The project took no account of the fact that only 3 per cent of the soils in the region are fertile. Even though the project spent $39,000 on each person settled[6], it failed to provide them with essential supplies. Few elected to travel there, and of those who did, most soon left, but not before the road had cleft a previously inviolate part of the Basin.

The other great government-funded colonization scheme was in the west, and it was this that led to one of the world's greatest environmental tragedies. The project involved the extension of a road from the south of Brazil into the state of Rondônia. By contrast to the TransAmazon Highway project, the Rondonian scheme attracted vast numbers, partly by means of government advertising, partly as the result of inaccurate rumours that the soil there was good: regrettably only 10 per cent of the state's land is suitable for farming. Between 1975 and 1988 one and a half million people arrived in the virgin state, and by 1989 26 per cent of its forests had been destroyed. Again, a substantial part of the funding came from the World Bank, whose present attempts to make amends seem destined only to exacerbate the situation. Perhaps the most damaging result of the Rondonian settlement scheme is that the state has become the gateway to the rest of western and northern Amazonia. It is from there that colonists are now flocking towards the states of Acre, Amazonas and Roraima, the last great wildernesses of the Amazon.

8

THE ENCOURAGEMENT OF settlers and the neglect of the Yanomami are just two manifestations of the regional policy introduced with military rule in 1964. The doctrine which has guided it was summarized in one of the slogans of the military leaders: '*Integrar Para Não Entregar.*' This means 'integrate [the remote territories] so as not to deliver [them]', into the hands of foreigners or subversives. To this end a project began under the administration of President Sarney which threatens to be among the most destructive of the government initiatives in the Amazon.

The Brazilian Amazon has been protected so far by the fact that most of the development there has taken place along just one – albeit enormous – front. While the infrastructure of change has already been laid down over much of the south of the Basin, the Brazilians have as yet done little to threaten either the central core or the northernmost forests. With the exception of the mining in Roraima, oil and gas exploitation in the state of Amazonas, several dams, a paper pulping project in the east, and the rudiments of some settlement and cattle-ranching schemes, Brazilian development north of the River Amazon has so far been insignificant. The integrity of the northern forests has served to limit the speed of development throughout the Amazon: because of the roads which link them, two development frontiers can approach each other with considerably greater speed than twice the rate of advance of a single front.

But since 1985 the Brazilian armed forces have been trying to implement a plan to turn the northern border of Brazil into a development zone. If they succeed, this will involve the opening of a region 6700 kilometres long and 150 kilometres deep; or 20 per cent of the Brazilian Amazon. As the northern frontier is to be linked to the south, the two are likely to be drawn together around the Amazon's core.

The project is called Calha Norte, which means Northern Channel, referring to the area north of the River Amazon. The army intends that the military garrisons it is establishing there be accompanied by settlements, ranches, and minerals and timber operations, to be implanted from the Atlantic to the western frontier. Mining companies have already applied to prospect most of the land in the region.

The project has been held up, mainly by bad planning and a lack of finance. So far the armed forces have only succeeded in building short sections of the road designed to follow the entire frontier, and few of the accompanying settlements and ranches have yet been established. But President Collor has renewed the government's commitment to Calha Norte. While he says he would like the scheme to become an instrument of environmental preservation, there has been no corresponding change of vision among the generals administering it.

Calha Norte threatens to take over most of the lands owned by Indians around the northern frontier, where some of the most populous of the remaining tribes in Amazonia live. Among the stated policies of its administrators are the integration and development of the tribal people living there. It is these plans which have given rise to the Indian movement which may prove to be the one means by which the project can be stopped.

For the 18,000 Tukano Indians of the north-west of Brazil are the only people who have in any sense managed to deflect or delay the army's enormous scheme. It is paradoxically because the Tukano have a long history of repression that they are now equipped to defend themselves against this latest threat to their lands. Unlike the Yanomami, they have suffered for decades at the hands of rubber slavers, soldiers and missionaries. The Salesian Catholics working among them were absolutist. It was through their indoctrination of the Indians that they unintentionally armed them with the understanding they needed to confront the white man.

The Tukano, who live in the region known as the Dog's Head, bordered to the east by the upper Rio Negro and the north and west by Colombia, emerged from the horrors of fundamentalism, slavery and military onslaughts significantly changed. They wear clothes, live in individual houses, drink too much alcohol, and are in most cases literate, numerate and fluent in Portuguese. They have lost their traditional music and dancing but, perhaps because the changes were gradual and their forests have not been damaged, they remain in touch with some of their traditions. Like several Indian groups in the Amazon, they are now making efforts to reclaim their tribal identity.

The slavers and the missionaries taught the Indians a certain shrewdness in dealing with the white man. This and their knowledge of Brazilian law have helped them to win several small but significant victories over Calha Norte. The Indians of the central Dog's Head, while they have lost most of their battles, have succeeded in preventing the construction of one of the army's biggest barracks in the north-west, stopping a road and two ranches, and forcing unwilling officers to inform them about Calha Norte's plans. These are but pebbles flung into the path of an advancing tank, but they are perhaps the most important external obstacles the project has yet encountered.

The Calha Norte frontier in general and the Dog's Head especially are closed to outsiders. So, though I had been invited by the Indians who lived there, my journey would have to be clandestine. I was told that were I to be caught by the soldiers garrisoned in the area, my notes and films would be confiscated, and I would be expelled from Brazil. For this reason I could not visit the part of the territory which had already been closed to the Indians by a mining company, as this was well guarded; but I felt I could escape detection travelling through the middle of the Dog's Head, where the most voluble of the Tukano activists lived.

I had intended to travel in February 1990, but had fallen ill, and was forced to wait until I was sure I was no longer infectious. So by the middle of March, when I was certain to be safe, I had lost touch with the Indian leaders I had met at a demonstration elsewhere in the Amazon, and was worried that I would be unable to find them. I took a small plane from the airport in Manaus and flew north, across the unbroken lands of the central Amazon.

The aeroplane followed the Rio Negro, whose waters rolled towards the Amazon with thunderous gravity. As it tilted the river burnt white, a steel plain in a soft sea of trees. Only in the riverside gardens of caboclos was the mat of the forest worn thin; elsewhere it ranged unblemished into the distant lower sky. These were the plains I had read of, the undiminished heart of Amazonia.

We landed for a few minutes at Barcelos, a village halfway across the northern Amazon. A line of girls in Fernando Collor teeshirts sat on a bench in the shade beside the airstrip: a reminder that the new president had taken office that day. They seemed to be waiting for something, perhaps an elemental apocalypse announcing that the political order in Brazil had changed; but the sky remained blue and steady. Oil drums were stacked in hundreds at the head of the strip; only later did it strike me that they might have been supplying the miners in Roraima, since the police were said to be checking the planes in Boa Vista.

After an hour of flying, foam streaked the channel of the Negro. Approaching São Gabriel da Cachoeira, the town on the nape of the Dog, I saw mountains emerging from the plains, as abrupt and smooth as flowerpots upended on a lawn. This was the edge of the old Guiana Shield, and the peaks were the last bollards of resistant rock extant after two billion years of weathering.

The road from the airport passed the barracks of the biggest garrison of the north-west, where men with crewcuts exercised, and notices announced 'Army: National Presence'. São Gabriel is a town of low houses and only two paved streets, tucked into one bank of the Rio Negro, beside the rapids through which boats from the south cannot travel. Before Calha Norte was introduced it was the last point of steady contact with the outer world, beyond which only Indians lived.

Only when the elements of the Amazon Basin are reduced to a scale that a human being can respond to do they become impressive. On the main channel of the River Amazon, where water, forest and sky extend in their different planes beyond the limits of the eye, the view is so partial as to be meaningless. But at São Gabriel the black waters are just one kilometre wide, and the forest is palisaded by mountains. Ink and feathers jostle through rocky passages in the river, surging in places into standing waves. Whirlpools suck the edges of forest islands. In the shallow eddies children played and Indian women washed their clothes. Boys fished from the roofs of riverboats.

The Indians of the Rio Negro had set up an office in São Gabriel, where, I had been told, I might find people who could take me into the Dog's Head. By good fortune the office was crowded. On the day before I arrived, there had been a meeting between the representatives of the Tukano and a government official, and now all the sixty-four chiefs of the central Tukano territories were waiting to return home. They would leave the next morning, to travel up the Negro then along the Rio Uaupés, and they told me that I could join them. In such a crowd the chances of avoiding the soldiers were high.

The chiefs were darker than the Yanomami, taller, with stronger features and a little more beard. They seemed acute and well organized. The president of their association, Pedrinho, told me that the meeting of the day before, like all the Tukano's efforts, was an attempt to put their theoretical entitlements into practice. The Indians had fought for their rights to be defined by the 1988 Constitution; now they had to persuade the authorities to uphold them. He believed that, with determination, they could reclaim some of the lands which Calha Norte had taken from them.

The chiefs told me to return early the next morning to catch the boat. I wandered through São Gabriel. The evening light flattened the coconut trees against the blue mountains, deepening the red-brown skins of the Indians by the river. It was a peaceful town. I had my hair cut by the wife of an army sergeant, who told me that São Gabriel was almost free from theft; since the Indians had expelled the garimpeiros who had once invaded their lands, nobody locked their doors.

I walked down the river beach to join the chiefs in the morning, and to my surprise I saw a white man, sitting on the rocks beside the river. He was thin, muscular, with a long beard, a hooked nose and a broken straw hat. He waved and called out to me, and it took me a second to realize that he was speaking in English.

'Where you going, mate?'

I had seen no other foreigners in São Gabriel; I was intrigued by this man, an Australian in torn clothes, without shoes. He told me he had just come down from Venezuela.

'How did you come?'

'That's me boat.'

In the water beside the rocks was an Indian canoe. He and a Swiss man had travelled from Puerto Ayacucho on the Orinoco, through the Casiquiare, a natural channel in the forest, and into the Rio Negro. It had taken them three and a half months, crossing lands which were almost uninhabited. They had been captured by bandits, escaped and had then capsized in some rapids and lost all but the clothes they were wearing. They had made spears and bows and arrows and hunted fish and raided turtles' nests. Once they had eaten bitter manioc and had nearly died from cyanide poisoning. The Indians taught them to find edible fruits and palmhearts, and they stored dried fish in the baskets they wove. They had arrived in São Gabriel penniless, and were now contemplating their three months' journey to Manaus, where they could arrange for money to be wired to them.

The sixty-four chiefs had already crowded into the boat they had hired and were waiting for the captain. It was one of the two-storey, boot-shaped craft peculiar to the Amazon, with the captain's cabin and wheelhouse on top, and the passengers' quarters in the open hold. It was licensed for thirty-five, and several of the chiefs had brought their wives and children, so that even when moored it sat disturbingly low in the water. People filled every available space, sitting in the gangways, lying on the roof, draped over the rails. Already a few were drinking *cachaça*, sugarcane rum; but they were friendly, careful people, and joked and laughed softly in their common language, one of several spoken in the centre of the Dog's Head.

Captain Siqueira arrived drunk, two hours late. He was half Tukano, half white, fat, friendly and lecherous. He spent an hour tinkering with the engine and lubricating his own inner workings, then he clambered into the wheelhouse, and we set off with a salute of fire-crackers and empty bottles into the mid-morning sunshine.

The water was just beginning to rise after the dry season, and navigation was a delicate art. The river ran smoothly only where it planed over rocks; around them it disintegrated into waves or whirlpools. We zigzagged across it, paddling around the rocks as a duck might, finding the point at which to dart up the channels between them. The engine laboured against the weight it propelled, and water surged across the bows every time we turned into the rapids.

From the forest above São Gabriel the mountains rose without reference to the land around them. From the river they looked like human molars. Only on the crowns was there vegetation; the walls were as smooth as enamel. I guessed that some of them might have been among the few spots in the tropics which had never felt a human foot.

As I sat on the bows, my feet in the river, I spoke to the oldest of the chiefs, asking him how life for the Indians had changed since he was born. I found that he seemed somehow to have confused the time of his childhood with that of both his ancestors and the Biblical deluge.

'Yes, *senhor*, there were no clothes then, only loincloths made of bark. We made fire with sticks, rubbing one into the other, and we lived in houses, yes, so big. So it was in the time of the old ones.

'Before the flood there were only three languages on earth. One the whites spoke, one the blacks spoke and one the Indians spoke. Then all the people of the earth came up this river and licked the Mana rock, a great rock in the shape of a saucepan, and they went away each with their different language, English, Palestinian, Tukano and all the others. So it was in the time of the old ones. I remember we still treated ourselves with plants from the forest and we played pipes. Even in the time of Noah, when the Tukano people came out of the sea, they ate manioc, the bread of the earth which God gave them, not the rice and beans he gave to the whites. That is how God favoured the Tukano.'

I was later to read an account by a German traveller, Theodor Koch-Grunberg, who had visited the Tukano territories between 1903 and 1905[1]. He described longhouses in which one hundred or more lived; parties for all the people of the region, with panpipes and dancing long into the night; and giant signalling drums to summon them. I stopped when I came to one of his photographs, astonished. It was the old man I had sat with on the boat. For an eerie moment I thought he had transported himself across the century, and then I realized that it must have been his grandfather. Even then the Indians had been struggling with the army, which had been burning down their communal houses. Things seem never to change in the Amazon, only to get worse.

After two hours spent lumbering through the rapids the cachaça bottles were falling fast around us. From the top deck there was high-pitched laughter, and I became less certain that our erratic passage was the skilful manoeuvre I had first imagined it to be. We passed wooded islands, smelling the flowers on the trees, scents which mingled with the resin of the boat and the warm subtle smell of the Indian men, like baking bread. Even here political advice was painted on the rocks: 'Francisco is a monkey. Vote for Edilson.'

As we came to the confluence of the Rio Negro and the Rio Uaupés, down which we were to travel, I saw on my map that we were re-entering the northern hemisphere.

The old man pointed north, up the Rio Negro, and told me, 'We don't go that way. Far over there are the Yanomami. They would kill us if we went there, and take all our clothes. Yes, *senhor*, they would take all our clothes.'

Where the rivers met was an island, and above it the last of the rapids, a dangerous passage between high rocks. The boat felt as insubstantial as a bottle. The waves surged and roared around us, snaking into the stern, while the drunken Odysseus in the wheelhouse above steered us through the crisis. Logs were tumbling through the falls; around a settlement on the far bank children paddled the safer water in canoes. I could hear the tones of the water change as the bows of our boat bucked into it.

Above the rocks the river was smooth, and we chugged into a calm yellow evening, the water ringed by fish, the forest on the banksides quiet. In no place had the trees been visibly disturbed; I had read that the Tukano take pains to preserve the bankside forests in order to protect the fish they hunt[2]. They consume more fish than any other tribe in the Amazon, and most of the fish feed in the flooded forest. I had learnt that FUNAI and the administrators of Calha Norte wanted to replace much of the riverine forest with cattle pasture. Calha Norte was also said to have encouraged the Indians, in some cases obliged them, to introduce cattle to the limited tumps of dry land close to the riverbanks, the only places where the manioc they depended on for subsistence would grow.

The day's one meal was passed round as the sun sank, a bucket of rice, spaghetti and manioc meal, which we scooped out with our hands. When the nightjars came out over the river, the shouting from the top deck degenerated into grunts. As an empty bottle splashed into the water I heard, '*Porra*, there's only three left.'

Upstairs I found six or eight men in and around the wheelhouse, who had finished most of a case of cachaça, the sugarcane rum they had bought. The chief of Urubuquara, a big man with a broken-up face, saw me and announced, 'I tell you I will have nothing to do with FUNAI, or with Calha Norte, or with the government. They'd better watch out.'

Captain Siqueira was now lying on the deck like a dead and swollen pig, snoring; his helmsman was slumped against the back wall of the wheelhouse with two fingers on the wheel, his eyes unmoving and his mouth hanging open. The boat was named the *Santa Marta 3*. I could guess what had happened to the other two.

After dark we moored at the foot of an Indian village and slung our hammocks in the eaves of the houses. At dawn, when the *zogi-zogi* monkeys were calling, we were woken by a shout from the boat, and while the land was still blue we stowed our belongings and swung out onto the river. One of the drunks of the previous night sought me out and asked if I had slept well.

'Yes thanks, but not as well as you must have slept.'

'Ah, cachaça. It's an old tradition of ours, very traditional.'

I thought this unlikely, but I later read in Koch-Grunberg's account that the Indians of that time had condensed alcohol in stills behind their houses. They had learnt the process from the missionaries. Nowadays cachaça can be bought in bottles in São Gabriel for a little more than the price of beer.

I had imagined we would have been spared the spectacle that day; but to my regret the small party of drunkards found another case in the hold. By nine o'clock the shouting had resumed, and we swayed across the burnished river as crookedly as we had among the rapids. The forest was dark and trackless. It was now broken every few kilometres by an Indian village: a cluster of palm-thatched huts above a beach, with a small white chapel and a white cross. By noon we had reached the settlement in which the first of the chiefs lived, and all the men disembarked to meet their friends. We were fed in a big hut where the chief and his family lived, with manioc bread, pepper soup and fish, while the men from the boat recounted their news. Then the villagers led us through their gardens, and cut from the trees coconuts, oranges, and the Amazonian fruits *umarí, cupuaçú* and *ingá*. We stowed the bunches in the hold, and the chiefs reorganized the baggage to make more room. They shouted instructions to each other, disordered the luggage which had already been tidied, and so confused Captain Siqueira that he retired to his cabin and took to his bed. There seemed to me to be too many chiefs and not enough Indians.

As we resumed our journey upriver I sat next to a man who began complaining bitterly about Calha Norte and the reduction of Indian lands. He was wearing a teeshirt a soldier had given him, which read 'Calha Norte: Faith, Hope, Determination'. The river glared flat as a sheet of steel, flashing heat under the awnings of the boat, seeking out each corner of shade into which the people had crept. After two hours someone on the top deck shouted, and the boat slowed so that we could see a dolphin rupturing the glassy surface.

The man in the Calha Norte teeshirt said: 'The *boto*, he's great. He's our companion. He follows our boats, and when the fish jump because they are frightened of us, he moves in and snatches them. He never sleeps, day or night, all the time fishing, right up into the small streams and into the forest. He drives the big fish into shallow water, where we can get them with a spear.'

The lunch bucket came round, with what seemed to be sick inside; but the men said it was boiled manioc meal with fish flakes. We used coconut husks as spoons. Later we stopped at another village where we were fed again, and given bundles of smoked fish wrapped in palmleaves. The chiefs seemed to have relatives in every settlement. The Indians of the Dog's Head allow themselves only to take spouses from another language group[3], so families may be spread across several hundred kilometres. This has afforded the Tukano of the Uaupés considerable unity, a key to their partial success in their struggle against Calha Norte.

As we were making to leave the village, one of its elders arrived on the bankside, asking if a man he named was on board. The man came out of the wheelhouse on the top deck: it was the helmsman. The elder started shouting at him from the bank, 'You son of a whore, you dog ...,' breaking into a Tukano language as he became angrier. Someone gave him a glass of cachaça to calm him down; but he drained it in one swig and it seemed to have the opposite effect. He leapt onto the boat, scaled the ladder to the top deck and threw himself on the helmsman. The two men, both in their fifties, set about each other with kicks and blows, until the village elder fell through the hatch onto the bottom deck, and was helped back onto the land.

Towards evening we reached the village of Bela Vista, distinguished by the cavernous ruin of a brick building with arched windows, enmeshed in flowering vines. This was the headquarters of Manduca, the notorious slaver and tyrant of the first decades of the twentieth century. Manduca had been the local chief of FUNAI's antecedent, the Indian Protection Service, and he had taken the valley of the Uaupés as his personal fief. In the brick building was once stored the rubber and fish his Indian slaves had collected for him; if they brought insufficient they were tied to a post and flogged, and several dozen were said to have been flogged to death. He was reputed to have forced his attentions onto 200 Indian women, and any husbands objecting would be shot. One night in the

1930s, when he was drunk, an Indian mixed the extract of a plant into his coffee. For two days he was unaffected, then he collapsed in screaming pain and was taken to São Gabriel by boat. By the time he arrived he was dead, and the doctors there found that his intestines had been shredded into little pieces.

Now that they were used to me, the captain and the other drunks were ceaselessly playing tricks. In the evening they crept along the top deck and dropped a praying mantis onto my stomach. To their disappointment I was not startled but captivated. The mantis stood on its hind legs and raised its splendid green and yellow wings, flaunting red eyespots like Uccello's Quattrocento dragon. It drew back the cage of its arms and swayed and feinted at my finger like a shadow boxer; a ballet dancer sired by a basilisk.

The river had again become cropped with rocks. The helmsman was now rigid with inebriation, and Captain Siqueira, who was scarcely more shipshape, took his place. Because of the late start the day before, and the various delays caused mainly by drunkenness, the chiefs were anxious to get home, so we elected to continue upriver by night. After dark we reached the village of Açaí, where two or three of the men lived. A few of the drunkards followed them into the village. Captain Siqueira wanted to join them but he could not get out of his chair, so he sat drinking by himself.

We waited for an hour and the men did not return. Two of the chiefs were sent to find them, and they too disappeared. Three more men were despatched half an hour later, and no more was seen of them. A storm broke over us and all the people crowded below decks, where they sweltered together until the hold looked like the galley of a slave ship. A third posse left and at length returned with all the men, most of whom were scarcely able to walk. By this time Captain Siqueira had drunk himself into stupefaction. One of the original drunkards fell off the gangplank into the water. They climbed onto the top deck to join the captain.

Someone started the engine, and Siqueira steered the boat out into the river. We reversed a few hundred metres to get clear of the rocks, weaving jaggedly. There was a thud and the boat stopped. The people below decks fell silent. I heard only the rain, which poured like gravel onto the roof. Then a groan shuddered through the hull, and the boat settled into the water, like a bull dropping to its knees. 'We're sinking,' someone shouted.

Suddenly everyone was shouting. The chiefs' wives snatched their children and tried to climb over the men crowded onto the landward side of the boat. People scrambled along the handrails. The boat began to list. We were still close to the shore, and someone lashed two gangplanks together, which reached the shallow water. People surged around the gunwale, shouting, slipping over, trying to pass their baggage to those now on the gangplank, pulling each other out by their clothes. The children screamed. Rain matted people and their possessions together.

I climbed the steps to the top deck to find my rucksack. Siqueira sat senseless in his wheelhouse, while the other drunks lay sleeping in the downpour. In Siqueira's cabin I found a woman nursing her baby, unaware, as the rain had drowned out the noise below, of what was happening. I hustled them down to the galley. Back on the top deck I tried to kick the drunks into life. I pulled Siqueira off his chair and he managed to lower himself through the hatch. All the men but one dragged themselves away and down to the lower deck. The one man lay on his back and stared at me, appearing to see nothing.

'Come on, the boat's sinking.'

'Uur, uh.'

I tried to lift him by one arm. He pulled it away from me. I stopped for a second, frightened, uncertain what to do. A shudder ran through the boat.

'Get up. The boat is sinking. You will drown.' I took his face in my hands. 'Tonight you will die.'

He continued to stare at me. Fear made me angry. I kicked him in the side.

'*Puta que pariu!* Get up, you bastard.'

I grabbed his wrist with both hands, dragged him to the hatch and dropped him through it. The shock woke him up, and he crawled down the gangplank and into the shallow water, where he sat, in the rain, staring at the boat. I found my pack, wrapped my equipment in plastic bags, and joined the last of the people jostling around the gangplank.

In the rain people clawed at the rivercliff like rats I had seen flooded from the houses of a town in Africa. Softened by the deluge the clay and rocks they pulled at came away in their hands. It looked like a terrible nightmare, the people backlit by lightning, their hair and clothes tarred to their bodies, some of the bundles falling from their arms into the river. Someone found a stream which cut the low cliff and we climbed up through that, then walked through the forest towards the village. On the edge of the trees were some broken-down huts, and we slung our hammocks beneath the shreds of roof through which rain was not pouring. Scorpions and spiders, taking refuge from the storm, hid behind each pillar and frond. I lay shivering in my wet hammock, reflecting on the evils of drink.

To their credit the captain and the helmsman had sobered up and supervised the beaching of the boat at night, preventing its capsize. By six in the morning the pump was running, and they and some of the chiefs were trying to mend the hole. The engine was damaged but could run at half speed. Pedrinho, the Tukanos' president, found me and led me into the village, where he had an uncle and an aunt, old gentle people with hard faces. They gave me breakfast: smoked fish, pepper soup and two types of *mingaú*, thick drinks made from manioc. Among the high colours of the morning the bad dream dispersed.

I met Pedrinho's cousin Alberto, who had resigned from the army six months before, having served as one of its only two Tukano officers. He was a quiet man, patient in answering my questions. Many Tukanos, he told me, were recruited into the army, which had an overt policy of training as many Indians of the region as it could. At the time of my visit there were 300 in the 5th Frontier Battalion, the main force in the Dog's Head. Most of them joined for the salary or, Alberto believed, because it afforded them respect as Brazilians. Nearly all left after just one year. He had stayed because he was liked by his commander and had been invited to take an officers' course. He had left because of the government's decree reducing the lands of his people.

Nearly all the Tukano soldiers, like Alberto, returned to their villages at the end of their terms. The human rights groups supporting the Indians had complained that their recruitment was a means of dividing and weakening the villages. But from what I saw in my time in the Tukano territories, the conscription was, whatever its intentions, having the opposite effect. When they returned home the soldiers brought with them an inside knowledge of the organization which the Indians identified as their principal enemy. As a result some of the most capable leaders were among those who had served in the army. Like the missions, the armed forces had inadvertently given the Indians the means to oppose them.

Another advantage of Indian recruitment was that many of the soldiers serving in the Indian lands were Tukanos. Disputes between recruits and the villagers with whom they were stationed might have been intense, but in practice many of them already knew the people they were living with. The white soldiers and officers, by contrast, seemed to treat the Indians with disdain. There were 3000 in the region, and they had taken no precautions to avoid introducing their diseases, repeatedly infecting the Indians with tuberculosis, measles, diphtheria and influenza. Some of the Indians were resistant to these; but in every village there were excessive numbers of sick. On occasions the Indians would be conscripted into performing small tasks for the army, like carrying supplies. Though they asked for cash for these services, they were paid in cachaça.

By mid morning the boat was almost ready. Captain Siqueira sat on the grass above the riverbank, drinking. I tried to suggest, obliquely, that drinking might have had something to do with the shipwreck of the night before.

'Ah, *senhor*, no. The old boat was just trying to get out of the rain. It wanted to be in the houses, like us.'

He winked, then threw back his head and laughed.

In the afternoon the river narrowed between islands of *tucumã* palms. Herons and sandpipers left the banks at our approach, and parrots foraged back and forth across the channels. Heat pounded from the river like the flexions of a strip of metal. I sat in the shade, talking to an Indian girl who leant on the rail. Siqueira lurched along the gangway, his eyes red. He sank his fingers into the flesh of the girl's waist, grinned and flashed his eyebrows at me.

"*Tá bom, eh? Eh, senhor?*' he cackled. The girl pushed him off and stalked away to the other end of the deck.

By four o'clock we were taking in water again, so pulled into the forest, while two men dived to plug the hull with sacking. By late afternoon we reached Pedrinho's village, and he invited us to his house to eat manioc bread and giant catfish, which was, I decided, among the best food in the world. The catfish, one of the migratory species now shoaling in the Uaupés, had the texture and taste of scallops. The bread, or *beijú*, a coarse pancake, expanded, when soaked to the crust in pepper soup, to fill the stomach. With it was a mingaú of *açaí*, a palmfruit whose strange taste I had already acquired.

We were now in the middle of the Dog's Head, and I had decided to stop in Taracuá, the next large settlement we were to come to.

Beyond that there were garrisons, and in the biggest of the communities – Iauareté on the Colombian border – the greater part of a battalion. Two of the senior Tukano leaders, Moura and Sebastião, had invited me to stay with them in Taracuá, from which the campaign of the Uaupés people was coordinated. The boat had been moving slowly since we had damaged the engine, and it was not until ten o'clock that their settlement came into sight. I was disappointed. The village was charted by electric lights. The huts were overhung by the silhouettes of three large buildings of brick, one of which seemed to be a cathedral.

As we approached with a broadside of firecrackers, a crowd of people, perhaps one hundred or more, assembled on the beach. When we landed I was led towards Sebastião's house by a procession of children, over a modern bridge and past a television aerial bound to the top of a wooden pole. I was told that a generator had been installed in the village two years before.

In the morning Sebastião and Moura led me through the village. Many of the houses were still thatched and made of wattle and daub, as were those downstream; but some were now roofed with tin, and a few were built of bricks. A television had been given to the village by the government. On all sides was the forest, and from the top of the hill above the village I saw the confluence of the Rio Uaupés and its tributary the Tiquié, shimmering through the trees. Canoes were on the water, fishing.

I had imagined the church to be one of the monstrous impositions of the last century, as it seemed designed to intimidate rather than enrapture. It loomed in white above the soft darkness of the jungle, the black figure of Christ between the belltowers holding out his arms as if about to swoop upon the village. I was surprised to find it had been built in 1952. The Catholic Salesian missionaries had been invited to Taracuá in 1922 by the Indians themselves, to defend them against the greater evil of the rubber slavers, the notorious Manduca among them, who had been spreading misery and disease along the Rio Uaupés. They took the places of the Franciscans, whom the Indians had expelled after their brief mission of the 1880s, when the monks had exposed the sacred musical instruments of the shamans in church. For the Tukanos music was the medium through which their gods revealed themselves, and the magic of the instruments was so strong that it could destroy the uninitiated.

For most of the century the Salesian missionaries had been the instruments of the establishment, and the Tukanos told me they had been subdued by them just as they had by the government. But now there was a war being fought within the Salesian church, between the traditionalists and the new liberationists, who preached an awakening similar in tone to that which the Indian leaders themselves had been urging.

We met the padre, a cold German man who soon dismissed us. Sebastião took me to the mission school, where he was one of the teachers; it was an airy cloistered building which might have been lifted from Rome and dropped unmodified into the forest. Several nuns in white robes herded the Indian children into classrooms. One of them – I shall call her Sister Primeira as she wished not to be named – joined us, and agreed to show me around the classrooms. I was amazed at how rapidly some features of the church had changed.

In the last two years, at the insistence of the Indians, new classes had been introduced. The children were now being taught, as well as Portuguese, arithmetic, national history and religion, the Indian skills of pottery, basket-making, weaving and woodcarving; the Tukano language, music and dances; and the history and legends of the tribe. All the teachers were Tukanos. Sister Primeira told me that she and the other liberationists now wanted the Indians' education to reflect their own lives, not those of their conquerors. It was not until I learnt that Sebastião's father and all the Tukano of his generation had been taught in Latin that I realized how great the change had been.

The new teaching seemed to be regarded as a threat by the authorities. The Salesians had recently been warned that they might be expelled from the Tukano lands, and the army was trying to replace the Salesian schools with colleges administered by the government, employing teachers from elsewhere in Brazil.

'Now we want to help the people to become autonomous,' Sister Primeira said. 'Calha Norte wants them to remain dependent on the white man, like children. In the old days the mission was working alongside the big economic interests, as a means of imposing the will of the whites. Now that we are no longer prepared to do this the army wants to get rid of us.'

Calha Norte's publicity had claimed that the project was bringing to the Indians the benefits of the developed world. In Taracuá the army had built a health post to serve most of the Rio Uaupés. Though I arrived during visiting hours, and people were at the same time queueing for treatment in the mission surgery, I was surprised to find that nobody but the nurse was there. A Tukano girl from another village, she sat among open crates of medicine. She was pitifully shy. When I asked if I could see what medicines she had, she nodded, biting her lip. I asked if she had medicines for most of the diseases the people there suffered, and she continued to nod. I had contracted a cough on Siqueira's boat, so I wondered what she would prescribe for it. She pointed to a box of a medicine which was unfamiliar to me.

'That's what I would give for coughs, for coughs and all types of chest disease.'

'Would you mind if I looked it up?' I picked up the medical dictionary on her desk. She nodded and twisted a foot around a shin.

'It says it's for diseases of the urinary tract.'

'I don't know what that is.'

'Have you prescribed it to people for coughs?'

'Yes.'

'What made you think it was the right one?'

'It looked right.'

She was untrained and scarcely literate. FUNAI had promised to send a doctor several months before, but it was now clear that no one would come. The army was, however, determined that this post should take over the duties of the mission hospital, and to this end was trying to close the church's medical practice down.

In the evening I went to church with Moura, Sebastião and his sister Regina, who was one of the most influential of the Indian campaigners. It was as impressive inside as out. The German padre stood behind his lectern at the front of the deep hall, and read in a mumbling monotone. I noticed that at the base of the crucifix above the altar were the words, 'Those who love me fulfil my law.' The people took no part in the service, but sat in silence with their heads bowed. They had been told it was an insult to God to speak Tukano in church.

Sister Primeira later told me that she and some of the other nuns refused to participate when the padre led a prayer about the inferno. They disagreed with the approach of the priest and the other traditionalists, who taught as many lessons from the book of hell as from the theophany of heaven. It seemed to me that it was as much the merchandise as the beliefs of the Europeans that the Tukano were being called upon to accept. Wafers were more godly than manioc bread, white robes than loincloths, organs than panpipes, Latin than Tukano. God clearly lived elsewhere.

The Indians had told me that they had worshipped a God who was everything the Christians claimed theirs to be. He, Eno, was the creator, born of the mother of the universe; the saviour of mankind and the owner of the land. He gave rise to the spirits which inhabit the rivers, rocks and trees, and empowered the shamans, who could treat the sick with medicines and magic. The difference was that there had been none of the terror with which they associated the Christian God. The missionaries had, in Moura's words, crucified Eno.

The missionaries now remained in the Indians' lands on sufferance. The Tukano, having come to learn what their rights were, had threatened them with expulsion if they would not help them. Most of the Salesians had now expressed themselves willing to work with the Indians against the depredations of the other whites; but Moura believed that, even so, they were still trying to evangelize them. Christianity, he said, was by nature antipathetic to cultural diversity.

'Even in the Bible,' he remarked, 'Jesus is a cultural invader.'

Both on the boat and in Taracuá many of the complaints I had heard concerned FUNAI, the Indian protection agency. It was described to me as an instrument of Calha Norte, charged with integrating the Indians into the rest of the population, so that they would not be an obstacle to the economic exploitation of their lands. FUNAI was accused of deliberately dividing the Indians, buying some and setting them against the others. All the FUNAI officials on the Rio Uaupés were Indians, said by the people of Taracuá to have been suborned by high salaries and perquisites. The Tukano man appointed as FUNAI's regional administrator was called by the Indians 'the ghost of Manduca'.

'He has become so fat,' someone said, 'that his face is like the full moon.'

Each of the officials had a motorboat, to be used for FUNAI's administrative work and for the emergency transport of sick people to hospital in São Gabriel. I was told that on one occasion, when an Indian had fallen sick, the FUNAI officer said he could not be taken to hospital, as there was no fuel. The next day the officer was seen motoring to São Gabriel to buy cachaça. The sick man died.

Regina, Sebastião's sister, said that FUNAI was generous when it came to development the Indians considered to be destructive to their way of life, and uncooperative when they asked for help with the progress they felt would suit them best. It handed out cattle like patriotic flags, as if their ownership certified true citizenship of Brazil. The Indians said they did not want cattle, as these destroyed the land they needed for growing manioc; but that they did want to manufacture traditional ceramics, basketware and woodwork for sale outside their area. They were presently producing such things in their houses; but felt that they could increase their productivity if they could start a workshop. FUNAI had refused to assist them.

In Taracuá the FUNAI officer, Laurentino, was particularly unpopular. He was an Indian from another part of the Dog's Head. Sister Primeira had reported that he had intimidated her with a club, and Sebastião that he had threatened him with a shotgun. The Indians had already expelled him once, but FUNAI had sent him back to Taracuá.

I visited Laurentino in his house. He was a nervous man, and so angry that when I interviewed him on tape I had to reduce the recording level by two thirds. He attacked me immediately for having arrived in the Dog's Head without permission, then he turned his attention to the people of Taracuá. He said that he was employed by FUNAI, so he was the government's representative amongst the Indians, not the Indians' representative in government. But they did not appreciate that. They asked other people to help them; but it was FUNAI which was there to look after them. It alone had authority. It was like a mother to them, to help them to develop and to teach them to work, according to the plans of the government.

'If the people are rebelling it is on their account. FUNAI is bringing them benefits. The Indian will never be independent of the whites. He will always need them, as he needs clothes, factories, machinery. If he does not need the things of the white man, why use outboard motors? Why drink cachaça?

'Through the Bank of Brazil they were offered an interest-free loan to set up cattle pastures. They rejected it. This is the sort of idiots they are; they could have been ranching cows. The Yanomami, for instance, they can't develop because they are still blind, they don't have mothers. So FUNAI will bring them the food and clothes and teaching they need. Here it won't be done because of this stupid view of theirs.'

'The people here say they were not consulted about the changes. Is that correct?'

'The Indians were never consulted. Since the first arrival of the missionaries they have never been consulted. Anyway they were consulted. The mayor of São Gabriel visited the villages and told them what would happen. People who say they were not consulted are donkeys.'

In the afternoon of my third day in Taracuá Moura and Sebastião called a meeting in the assembly rooms of the village. Most of the villagers attended, and the two men proved themselves good leaders, firm yet democratic. Many people spoke from the floor, raising problems or suggesting strategies. Afterwards the men and women split into separate groups. I attended the women's assembly. It was they who were managing the Indians' economy. They were producing several dozen decorated pots each week to sell in São Gabriel, as well as dresses and baskets. They needed to develop the market and set up a network of traders within their organization, so reducing the share the white middlemen took. But their priority, as Regina explained, remained to combat the effects of Calha Norte.

Calha Norte, I had learnt, began and has largely continued in secrecy. In June 1985, when Brazil was said to have been freed from the grip of the armed forces, General Rubens Bayma Denys, the Secretary General of the National Security Council, proposed the project to President Sarney. The plan was not revealed to the Brazilian public for sixteen months, by which time Calha Norte had already begun. There was no consultation with the Indians, the scientists who had worked with them, or even, in the early stages, with the government's civilian ministries. Commenting on this, Sévero Gomes, a federal senator, complained, 'The fact that such a serious decision has been taken without the participation of either society or Congress surprises all those who imagined that democratic practices are being exercised in the New Republic.'[4]

From the beginning the project was to be administered and effected by the armed forces. The civilian ministers who were, several months after it begun, allowed to attend discussions of the scheme, found that there was little for them to say. The explanation for this, when it came, was that Calha Norte is principally a security programme. The armed forces drew attention to the Colombian M19 guerrillas, at the time working close to the Brazilian border, and the existence of strategic minerals at certain points on the edge of the national territory. What they failed to make clear was why they perceived the entire border to be threatened, and why their response to the perceived threats should involve mining, timber-cutting, colonization and ranching.

From the sparse information since made available to the public[5], it is possible to divine that the army considers there to be several wider potential threats to the northern frontier: the tension between Guyana and Surinam, which could result in either nation threatening Brazil; Venezuela's policy of securing its own frontier, which could be in preparation to expand and then dominate trade with Brazil; and the work of Indian rights campaigners in publicly opposing Brazilian indigenous policy.

All of these concerns are rather curious. I looked into the military threat that Guyana and Surinam might pose to Brazil, and found that these sleeping giants have a combined population smaller than that of the Brazilian armed forces and their reserves. Neither nation could muster a single tank or combat aircraft[6]. Trade with Venezuela is much in Brazil's favour, and any expansion of it would seem to be of benefit to both nations. The campaigns of Indian groups and the organizations trying to help them have been fought in the open, by democratic means, principally by calling upon the Indian rights already recognized by Brazilian law.

Another of Calha Norte's justifications is the fear that non-governmental groups, particularly foreign Indian rights organizations, would start to establish control over parts of the border country[7]. President Sarney repeatedly claimed that these groups were trying to annex the Indian lands, so that they could then be exploited by foreign corporations. This accusation, which is being repeated by members of Collor's administration, also seems odd, in view of the fact that foreign corporations are already working inside Indian lands with the Brazilian government's blessing: indeed foreign companies have been allowed or invited to lay claim to an area of Brazilian sovereign territory three times the size of England[8].

The Indians and their advocates believe that Calha Norte has less to do with security than with control. It has been described as one of the armed forces' many attempts to ward off the resurgence of a truly civilian state. The secrecy and the means by which the installation of Calha Norte began suggest that the implementation of the project was in effect a bloodless military coup of the northern region, with the connivance of the civilian government. It not only affords the army control of 20 per cent of the Brazilian Amazon, but also helps to justify the inordinate military budget and the armed forces' continuing role in government.

This role has been successfully defended by the forces, to the extent that it is possible to claim that they have as much power in Brazil today as they did during the last years of the military dictatorship. Though the 1988 Constitution denied the armed forces a place in government and disbanded the powerful National Security Council, the generals – and the politicians whose interests are allied to theirs – have found means of preserving their power. President Sarney immediately replaced the National Security Council with another body, which in all respects but name was identical to the first. General Bayma Denys, who was as powerful a man in many ways as the president himself, retained control of this, as well as Calha Norte and other crucial agencies[9]. Though Fernando Collor had promised, before he became president, to limit the power of the armed forces, one quarter of the ministers he appointed are military commanders.

The new Army Minister is the general – Tinoco Ribeiro – who, in 1987, had signed a secret document identifying liberation theology as 'a subversive training ground *par excellence*' and urging that the armed forces should consider, 'beyond strictly military fields, actions in other fields of power'[10]. In June 1990 a treatise was published by the Higher War College, where much of the armed forces' policy is determined, suggesting that the Brazilian government might have to resort to 'the extreme expedient of war' to overcome such obstacles to development as groups campaigning for the environment and Indian rights, and the artists, intellectuals and churchmen who support them.

The armed forces have taken over Indian development policy on the northern frontier. This is worrying in the light of the fact that the previous Army Minister, Leónidas Pires, announced in 1989 that the culture of the Indians 'is very low and – I will say it with all courage – not respectable'. It would be best, he said, to integrate them into society, 'turning them into Brazilians'. When Calha Norte's indigenous policy was questioned by a scientist at a lecture given by two airforce officers in Manaus, one of them answered, 'We won't accept imprecations of the armed forces from any citizens.'[11] The army has expelled all anthropologists from the Calha Norte zone, and now controls 85 per cent of FUNAI's budget in the region.

Since Calha Norte's inception, the original proposal has been amplified to cover the lands all the way around the western frontier to Bolivia. Details of the new scheme have been kept secret, but General Bayma Denys was eventually forced, by the threat of court action, to reveal that it would involve the construction of roads and hydroelectric dams, the development of ranching, extractive economies and timber-cutting, and the 'regularization of the questions of landholding, Indians and goldminers'. Nobody who knows is prepared to reveal what this means.

President Collor visited some of Calha Norte's Roraiman installations just one week after coming to power. He said he wanted the project to continue, and to encourage it to take a role in the protection of the environment. At the same time, however, the chief of his military cabinet said that the colonization of the Calha Norte region had been slower than he had hoped. As yet there has been no sign of a change in either Calha Norte's implementation or the attitude of the armed forces towards Amazonia.

In some respects Calha Norte's security concerns are likely to be self-fulfilling prophecies. The only sizable invasion of Brazilian national territory in the last five years has come about as a result of a policy assisted by the National Security Council: the admission of miners into Roraima. In 1988 and 1989 not only did several hundred Venezuelans illegally cross the border to join the Brazilian miners; but 3000 Brazilian miners expanded their activity into Venezuela, one of the few sources of tension between the two nations. Settling peasants moreover on a remote frontier, at medium altitude – as some of the border lands are – with few opportunities to make a reasonable living from conventional agriculture, close to the smuggling routes into countries such as Colombia, seems to me like a formula for bringing cocaine production to northern Brazil.

It is fortunate for the Indians of the northern frontier that many of the army officers supposed to be administering Calha Norte could scarcely run a bath, let alone a construction project. The road they have tried to build around the border has been repeatedly obstructed by bad planning, and only short stretches have so far been completed. Even so it has succeeded in introducing epidemics to some of the remotest tribal communities of the frontier, and of ruining the lives of the few settlers foolish enough to move to the barren wastes it has subjugated.

But the most important of the army's actions so far has been the revocation of the Indians' rights to their traditional lands. President Sarney, General Bayma Denys and Bernardo Cabral, the man who is now President Collor's Minister of Justice, argued that because some of the Indians were in some respects civilized, they had no further need of their traditional territories, and the majority of the land could be taken from them[12]. The Indians found this ruling puzzling. The Tukano pointed out to me that the wearing of clothes and speaking of Portuguese does little to satisfy their hunger.

Sixty-three per cent of the Tukano's lands were taken from their control by presidential decrees, and registered as National Forest, in which approved development could take place. The decrees were unconstitutional. To attempt to legitimize them the government invited representatives of each subdivision of the tribe to sign an agreement stating that they were happy with the reductions. Some were bribed, some were coerced. I was told that Rolandinho, then the senior chief of the Uaupés region, was taken to the federal capital Brasília, six hours by plane from São Gabriel, to discuss the land reductions. He was presented with an agreement to sign. When he refused he was told he would not be going home. He was kept in Brasília until he signed it.

The Indians still do not know what the effects of the land reductions will be, as these depend upon the future use of the National Forest areas. Though now outside their designated territories, the Indians still use these places for farming and hunting. An old man in Taracuá explained to me that the forests they use have been preserved so far by the fact that comparatively small numbers of Indians were exploiting a large area. If, he said, the same numbers were confined to a small area, they would overexploit its resources, and the forests and poor soils would no longer be able to support them.

Some indication of how the National Forest areas might be used by the developers is provided by what has already happened in part of the traditional Tukano area, the far western lands of the Face of the Dog. There the Indian leaders had signed away some of the Tukano lands after General Bayma Denys had personally threatened them with the removal of nearly all their territory[13]. The general himself had stepped into the issue because the powerful mining company ParanaPanema had already taken over a substantial part of their land illegally, and wanted state approval for its annexation. Having secured this, the corporation posted security guards on the rivers to prevent anybody, the Indians included, from entering the area without special permission. As the Indians of the region were thus deprived of some of the lands supporting them, General Bayma Denys decreed that they should, like ParanaPanema, make their money by mining gold. Over 100 of the Indians became garimpeiros, but were later evicted from their own mine by soldiers[14].

The Tukano of the Rio Uaupés are particularly worried by these developments, because their own lands are rich in minerals. Some estimates suggest that in and around the Dog's Head there are 95 per cent of the world's known reserves of niobium, an element used in making high resistance steel. Around Taracuá there is gold, tin, amethyst, tourmaline, aluminium and reputedly diamonds. Where the Rio Uaupés cuts the Colombian border, at Iauareté, is the most critical of all deposits. The Indians had a long-standing legend about an ancestral shaman, a witchdoctor, with evil powers. He could poison people by singing to them, so that they would return to their houses, eat, and then die in their sleep. The ancestors got together, killed the shaman, burnt his body and buried his ashes. But the ashes became a mineral which causes people handling it to fall ill and die. A mineralogical survey rediscovered this radioactive deposit in 1985; to judge by the Indians' story it must be particularly concentrated.

Mining companies have requested prospecting licences for most of the Dog's Head, and some have already been granted. Most of the companies are unlisted in the public directory of Brazilian miners, which suggests they may be operating fronts for larger corporations or for foreign capital.

The authorities refused to discuss the Indians' future with them. Instead an army helicopter simply arrived in each village, hurriedly erected a concrete marker announcing that the village was part of a reduced tribal territory, and left. When the army chiefs had repeatedly refused to meet the Indians to explain what this meant, all but the villagers of Açaí dug up the concrete markers and threw them into the river. In Açaí there are no rocks, so they took their marker down and used it for scrubbing their clothes.

But it appeared to me, in the several days I spent in and around Taracuá, that the antagonism Calha Norte was causing, like many of its plans, was unnecessary. If only the army officers had stopped to look, they would have seen that the Indians welcome development, as long as it is the sort of development which is beneficial to them, rather than destructive. They would have been willing to cooperate on certain economic projects, if these did not involve the long-term degradation of their resources, or the obligation to adopt the values of a different race and culture. They would probably, for instance, have accepted controlled mining in their lands, had its introduction been a matter of consultation and profit-sharing, rather than imposition. They pointed out that they could even have done the job of guarding the national borders, had they been encouraged to love their country rather than to fear it. But as Calha Norte was conceived in secret by people who seemed to have no respect for the Indians or interest in their welfare, it could scarcely have been better designed to antagonize them.

The Indians themselves had extensive plans for their economic self-improvement, many of which were being foiled rather than assisted by the developers. They said they wanted their own people to receive training as professionals – lawyers, doctors, economists, ecologists and anthropologists – so that they became independent of both the whites who hindered them and the whites who helped them. To this end they were encouraging their school leavers to apply for university, and trying to raise funds to send them there. They were trying to set up a workshop to expand their production of pottery, and they wanted to buy a motorboat to help keep the members of their organization in touch with each other and to run the sick down to São Gabriel. They were trying too to raise money to publicize their cause, so that they could dispute the favourable view of Calha Norte which the government's own publicity was presenting to the nation.

For those who have studied the treatment of Indians in other parts of Brazil there are few surprises in the way the Tukano have been handled. Their usage, while rough, has been mild by comparison to that of the Macuxí of Roraima, many of whose longhouses are still being burnt down by the military police[15], or of the Waimiri-Atroari of the central Amazon, whose lives have been dominated by the most insensitive FUNAI administrators, and whose numbers were reduced from 3500 to 374 in the thirteen years to 1986.

But, while there has been little progress from the presidency, several Brazilian congressmen and senators are now openly supporting Indian rights. After intensive lobbying by Indian groups, their entitlements were clarified by the new Constitution, and in theory the people and all their traditional lands are well protected[16]. The fact that both the president and the armed forces have repeatedly been able to trample upon these constitutional rights is one of many indications that democracy in Brazil is not all that it claims to be. The Brazilian administration is also in breach of clear international guidelines. Simply through its treatment of the Yanomami and Tukano Indians, Brazil manages to contravene 19 of the 28 provisions of the United Nations draft declaration of the rights of indigenous people[17].

In Brazil the government and many of the citizens have asked why it should be that certain people, just by virtue of being Indians, should be afforded so much land. The Yanomami territories have been regarded as the extreme example of this profligacy: the 10,000 people there are entitled – by the Constitution, if not the subsequent presidential decrees – to 9.4 million hectares. This, the government has argued, is a disproportionate amount for anybody to own.

Leaving aside, for the moment, the reasons why the Indians might be entitled to more land than other people, it is worth examining this claim in detail. The size of the traditional Yanomami territories corresponds to the amount of land in Amazonia that the government allotted to state-sponsored ranchers between 1966 and 1985. There were 766 of these ranches; and because the land was unproductive and used for speculation more than for cattle rearing, these acquisitions generated almost no permanent employment. So on this 9.5 million hectares there were 766 owners, most of whom were absentees, and several hundred permanent employees.

The biggest landowner in Amazonia, and this is without taking into account the lands in the Calha Norte area, is the army. The army has been given, chiefly through eighteen months of transfers under the Sarney government, 12 million hectares, in which it is accountable to no one. Nobody knows what happens in these lands, some of which are the remotest in Brazil. Nobody outside the army is allowed into this area the size of England, and the army's given explanations – training and the installation of new military organizations – succeed in sounding both unconvincing and sinister.

The second biggest landowner is a timber company, Madeireira

Nacional SA, which owns 4.1 million hectares, close to half the size of the Yanomami lands. The Jarí company, founded by an American, now owned by Brazilians, possesses 1.6 million hectares of Amazon forest, which is being converted, with accompanying environmental and economic disasters, to paperpulp plantations. The biggest individual landowner in Brazil is a man who possesses one million hectares of the Amazon, one ninth of all the land the 10,000 Yanomami were once entitled to. British Petroleum has or had licence requests covering more than twice the area of their traditional territory[8]. There are 335 million hectares of unproductive farms in Brazil.

While the uses and social benefits of these private landholdings are questionable, those of the Indians' are clear. The Yanomami could not survive as a people without their lands; the Tukano could not survive as a culture. They would, as dispossessed Indians have before them, end up at the bottom of Brazil's great social pit, impoverished, marginalized, and considering themselves to be neither proper Indians nor proper white men.

It is not only the Indians who benefit from their control of the traditional territories. Where these people have been left alone they have succeeded, as they have done for thousands of years, in conserving the forests they live in, with all the worldwide climatic and genetic benefits this affords. They have also sustained a way of life from which we have much to learn, in terms not only of the medicines and other products they might lead us to, but also perhaps with regard to the more important lesson: how people can live together without destroying either their surroundings or their communities. The best use of rainforest land is rainforest, and the best guardians of the forest are the people who live there.

Over the days I spent at Taracuá I was able to see a little of what the Tukano had preserved. Regina led me through the kitchen hut behind her house. She showed me the great urn used to brew *caxiri*, a slightly fermented drink prepared for parties. There was a bamboo horn for calling neighbours to the celebration from along the river, and they would arrive bringing gifts of fish, fruit, manioc or game. She showed me her clay oven and the irregular clay pots used for cooking; her manioc grater, made of a wooden board embedded with chips of stone, and her set of *tipiti*, tubes of woven cane taller than a man, which, when pulled taut, would squeeze the poison from the manioc inside. Her father showed me how to weave a basket for soaking the seeds of the umarí palm in the river, before their oil was extracted to make manioc bread.

I watched Regina's mother Anita making pottery. She mixed clay and ash with her hands and feet, then rolled it and built it into coil pots, which were smoothed and shaped with the shell of a gourd. The pottery was heavy and glazed black, with a pale pattern. Regina gave me a pot to take home. One evening Anita sang some traditional songs in her old strained voice. These were now remembered by few of the Brazilian Tukano, as the missionaries had previously proscribed them; but I had heard that in Colombia the people still sang and danced as they had long done. At night I would lie in my hammock coughing – the infection I contracted on the boat was to last for two months – and at first I thought there was a strange echo in the house. Each time I coughed I would hear a feeble but exact repetition of the noise. This disturbed me. One morning I went into the next room, and found, hiding under Sebastião's table, a parrot.

The Tukano were, and to some extent still are, constrained by what they considered to be the natural order of the world. The materials they used and the forests and rivers they worked in provided a physical framework into which their spiritual and emotional lives could fit. Everything, like the pots and fires in Regina's kitchen, had its traditional place, and the Tukano could identify themselves as a people by reference to their surroundings. They believed that certain forms of behaviour were not only socially undesirable, but an offence against nature. The same theme runs through British literature, right up to the Agricultural Revolution. When man still had a physical link to his natural environment – the soil under his feet, the corn in his hands – he could, some of our classical texts suggest, judge the propriety of his life by the order of the natural world. If something were wrong, or unnatural, about mankind, this would be reflected by disorder in nature, like a hawk killed by a mousing owl.

Our surroundings, which included our possessions, were sufficiently constant to define the limits to life; nature was regarded as broadly unalterable, so it set recognized limits to the human actions which could be considered natural, and therefore appropriate. Evil and ignobility, characteristics of which we now have little sense, were a sinister defiance of nature. Shakespeare could describe the state of a man's soul by drawing on the attributes of the material world. Everyone knew the properties of a crab-apple, a cormorant or a horsecart, as the lives and learning of everyone were closely bound to such things. They were a common language of the soul, by which man could communicate his understanding of himself. And, in turn, the material world was animated by mankind: as character was ascribed to physical entities we now consider inanimate.

Nowadays the material environment is too complex and changes too rapidly for such an understanding. There is no common knowledge of the environment, as the world is a different place from one decade to the next. Rather than constraining ourselves to suit the constancy of nature, we have changed nature to serve what we guess are the constant needs and characteristics of mankind. Having lost our constraints we seem to have lost our place in the world. I believe that the identity crisis we appear to suffer is the result of the disintegration of the natural world which shaped us. Without a natural order we do not know what human nature is.

Modern man's problem is not that he is too materialistic, but that he is not materialistic enough. Our 'materialism' is in fact a lack of respect for materials, the fast and careless use of them, the superficial nature of our understanding of or feeling for them. We are, as a result, a society loosed from our surroundings, like seaweed torn from the rocks and pushed around by the fickle tide of each passing trend. The belief that nature can be infinitely altered to suit mankind is the belief that mankind can ascend to any level, usurping the role of nature as the determinant of physical, and spiritual, possibility. But what we have in fact usurped, to our own discomfort, is the role of man.

I had arranged to travel upriver with Geraldo, a *peripona* from the village of Ipanaré. The peripona, as he explained, were the upstream people whose growth, according to legend, was diverted when they were children from the body into the ears. Geraldo's small stature was indeed offset by his enormous aural brolleys, of almost half the length of his head. He was a neat, gentle man, of wide experience and an ability to explain some of the more complex of the Tukano's beliefs to me, as he knew what white men could be expected to understand.

He was, like all the Tukano, a fisherman and cultivator; but he had also taken a number of roles in the other world. He had worked as a mechanic in São Gabriel, and must have been a good one, as his employer had offered him a house, a pension and a pay rise if he would stay; but he had declined and returned to his village. He had become a goldminer in a small working manned by Indians. This was dry-rock mining, breaking the crumbling sandstone of a mountain in the interior with a pick and shovel, and sifting it through water and mercury. In three years he found around 500 grams, with which he bought an engine for his boat.

He was now the unofficial ferryman of Taracuá, carrying people up- and downriver in what I would hesitate to call a motorboat, as this seems too modern a term. It was built up from a dugout, with poles supporting a roof of palmleaves. It was unstable, rolling to the gunwales if someone shifted his weight, but Geraldo assured me it had never capsized. It looked like a thatched house blown into the water.

With Eduarbato, an old man with a soft strained voice, we set off towards the impassable rapids upstream. On the way the two men told me more about the means by which the Tukano supported themselves. In the wet season they fished in the flooded forest with hooks and lines, using as bait the grubs found in the rotten trunks of palmtrees. There were waterpaths through the forest, as well travelled by canoe as the tracks on dry land were by foot, and along them the people knew all the trees under which fish were most likely to gather. In the dry season they used traps and harpoons. Now it was the time of the catfish migrations: they were shoaling in deep water then running up the tributaries to spawn. Most were caught in cane traps in waterfalls and at the entrances to streams. Geraldo said that the people had stopped using poisonous bark to catch fish, as this killed the young ones as well as the adults.

When someone caught fish he did not eat alone. Always he invited other people to share his catch, in the knowledge that when he had caught none and others had succeeded, their fish would be shared with his family. But people too lazy to fish for themselves were not invited. In August the people would take turtle eggs, sometimes emptying the nests, sometimes leaving some to breed in subsequent years. In the wet season frogs appeared and were eaten. Geraldo did not know where they came from, but assumed they fell out of the clouds.

The people made a small income by collecting rubber and *piaçava*, from which cord was made. This they traded with the big boats coming from São Gabriel, mostly for soap and cachaça. They planted fruit trees, but only for their own consumption.

'The government,' Geraldo said, 'says we are lazy, that we ought to plant more so that we can sell some. But the land can't take it. There isn't much land that we can plant, and we need that for our own crops.' He said that the Tukano forbade people to cut timber for anything other than their own use, as the forest was their wealth, and without it there would be no fish.

We talked about the changes that had taken place, and Geraldo agreed with me that alcohol seemed to be a problem. I told him how it had spoilt the lives of the North American Indians and rendered them less capable of securing their rights.

Geraldo said, 'Yes, it's a terrible thing. People drink too much here. It's irresponsible, especially when they're working.'

Eduarbato said that many of the Tukano now hunted with shotguns, but some still used bows and poisoned arrows. There were two sources of poison, one distilled from a vine and one from a herb, both found in the mountains. It was rubbed into a groove in the arrowhead and caused instant death. People once hunted with blowguns as well, but no longer. He seemed obsessed by jaguars, returning to the theme several times, telling me how they prowled through the village hunting for dogs and chickens, and how they moved in the shadow of a man like a ghost.

'He's a fierce one, this painted jaguar. You must get behind a tree, so that he grabs the tree instead of you.'

Half an hour from Taracuá we were passed by a pair of pink dolphins. I asked Geraldo if the Tukano had any legends about them.

'No, none at all.'

'Because down on the Rio Solimões I've heard that the caboclos say that the dolphin – the *boto* – comes out of the water at certain times of the year, disguised as a handsome man in a white suit, and that it's he who is responsible for pregnancies before marriage.'

'Oh yes,' Geraldo replied, 'he does that here as well. Mind you, I don't believe it is the boto all the time. Sometimes I think it is someone pretending to be the boto.'

We came within sight of Ipanaré, marked by an army sentry post and an asphalted road. The road had been built by soldiers in the previous year, to circumvent the falls upriver from Ipanaré. They could not be negotiated by boat, and the people had traditionally walked around them to the village of Urubuquara – Vulture Water – where they could return to the river. But now the army could tow its launches from one side of the falls to the other and take to the water again within a few minutes.

I had told Geraldo that I was worried about meeting the soldiers, as I was in the region illegally; but he told me there was nothing to worry about, as the sentries there were Tukanos. As we landed and passed the guardpost, they waved to Geraldo and paid us no further attention. At the waterfront we met some of the villagers and were led past a broad patch of bare sand and clay. This, they said, had been a manioc garden; but forty soldiers had arrived one day when the men were out fishing and had bulldozed it. They had intended to build part of a barracks on the site, but the Indians, by lobbying and threatening to take the army to court, managed to prevent its construction.

Along most of the four kilometres to Urubuquara the forest had been cleared and was now growing back. The army had intended to build 600 houses here, to accommodate a battalion between the two Tukano villages; and to open two ranches and a road to Iauareté on the Colombian border. But here too the Indians had stopped the army, proving that even by the terms of the unconstitutional decrees reducing their lands, it could not build in these places.

The new road to Urubuquara was already cracking in places, exposing the clay beneath. Geraldo told me that someone in the army had sold most of the asphalt allocated to build it, so it was paved to a depth of just one centimetre. He also pointed out, with satisfaction, that the soldiers had omitted to dig drainage channels alongside it, and the first rains would wash most of it away. The road had dammed the stream the people used for washing and drinking, which had become marshy and noxious. The pump and watertank the army had promised would replace it never arrived.

As we entered Urubuquara, Eduarbato told me that his house there had been flattened when the road was built.

'They just knocked it over with the bulldozer. It was all destroyed, the doors, the windows, my banana and orange trees. If they had warned me I could have saved the doors and windows and the beams and pillars and used them to build another house. But they did it secretly while I was away fishing. Now I will have to go back into the forest and work for days, with all the mosquitoes and the other flies in there, and the jaguars, finding the right wood. It's just a joke to them, but it was my house.'

He said that when the white soldiers came down the road from Iauareté they would stop to steal the fruit from the trees.

We entered the house of a fat, self-important old man with a face like a walrus, who sucked in his stomach to look impressive. He had once been the chief of Urubuquara, but had been demoted by the people. He announced that we would go to the falls to see where the ancestors of the Tukano came from.

So with the three men I set off across the river in the walrus man's canoe. We crossed the wide pool above the cataracts, then walked down the far bank for some way until we came to the first of the torrents. The river roared over the boulders. The walrus man, with Geraldo's help, explained that in the time of the ancestors sea covered much of the area which now was land. Out of the sea came a giant snake, and it swam down the river until it stopped at the bottom of the falls, at Ipanaré. Then the people of Ipanaré, the peripona, were disgorged from the mouth, and the others came out of its body.

I later read that the Tukano people considered to be the most senior were those who lived beside waterfalls[3]. They had, by tradition, emerged from the head of the snake. It was at the waterfalls that fishing was most profitable, as traps could be set between the rocks. One of the marks of seniority was generosity: those living there were expected to share the extra fish they caught with the junior villages.

Eduarbato, who had been born upstream of Urubuquara, said that his sub-tribe had a different origin story. Eno, the creator, had picked up three rocks, one white, one dark red and one the colour of fire, and had struck them together. A beam of lightning hit the earth, and the people came into being. The walrus man pointed out to me a bump on the upstream side of a rock where, he said, the people of Urubuquara had kicked out the periponas. He then instructed me to take photographs of the falls, and we returned to the canoe and back across the water to his village.

The new chief of Urubuquara, who was the big broken-faced drunkard on Captain Siqueira's boat, was to hold a meeting that afternoon, so we were taken around the village while we waited, being fed various mingaús, beijús and fruit. The people met in an open-sided assembly hut in the centre of the village. The chief told me the story, now becoming famous in the Dog's Head, of how the local battalion commander had been forced to discuss the plans for the Indians' lands.

Concrete markers had been posted in all the villages, and the land between Ipanaré and Urubuquara was cleared of trees, but the army had refused repeated requests to tell the people how their lives were to be affected. The officers just flew from village to village in helicopters supervising army projects, refusing to talk to the inhabitants. The fuel for the helicopters – 120 drums each of 200 litres – was stored at Urubuquara, and every day one or two of the craft came down from the other garrisons or the battalion at Iauareté for filling.

'Well, we're all fishermen, so we knew how to set a bait for a big one. We confiscated all the helicopter fuel one night and hid it in the forest.' He smiled and looked around with satisfaction at the other men. 'For three days the helicopters came down to Urubuquara, landed, couldn't find the fuel, then took off again and returned to the garrison at Iauareté. And for the three days we heard nothing. Then on the fourth day this enormous helicopter arrived, with Lieutenant Schreder and the other officers, and some military police with machine guns, and they marched into the village. They took hold of us and demanded to know where the fuel was.

'Well, we were pretty calm, as we knew that if they did anything to us our association would make an enormous fuss, and there would be trouble for the whole project. So we told them they could have the helicopter fuel, once they had told us what they were doing and where it would lead. They were furious! But we made them sit down for five hours and tell us all about Calha Norte and what they wanted to do.'

The officers told them about the barracks, the second road and the ranches which were to be installed. With this knowledge the Indians were able to launch a campaign to stop these developments, producing pamphlets demonstrating their illegality and threatening the battalion commander in São Gabriel with legal action; and all the plans were dropped. It seemed to be for reasons such as this that Calha Norte's operations were so secretive.

We stayed the night at Ipanaré and in the morning ate a vast communal breakfast of catfish and many mingaú drinks and returned to Taracuá. I arranged to go back to São Gabriel with Geraldo the next day.

*

When I arrived at Geraldo's house at dawn he was sitting outside his door. He seemed, strangely, not to recognize me. His eyes drifted independently. I called out to him and he did not reply. I walked up and put a hand on his shoulder. He started, realized who I was, tried to stand up and slumped against the wall of his house. I was mystified. I asked him if the boat was ready.

'The boat. Senhor Jorge ...'

'Geraldo, you haven't by any chance been drinking?'

He kept smiling, showing the gaps in his teeth, trembling slightly. He took a deep breath and steadied himself against the wall.

'Good morning, Senhor Jorge.'

His wife and I began to load the boat, while Geraldo stumbled about, getting in our way.

''Sall right, Senhor Jorge, all ready. São Gabriel.' He pointed downstream. 'Boat.'

When the boat was ready I sat on the shore for two hours, waiting for Geraldo to sober up. When he had regained some awareness of what was happening, we loaded him in and I hired his brother to steer. His old mother came too, and sat in the stern chewing on her drawn-in lips. As I sat down I saw two bottles of cachaça in the bilges, and I slipped them over the side. When we were making way down the middle of the river, Geraldo stumbled along the boat and sat next to me.

'Not to worry, don't worry about a thing. Everything is organized for you, Senhor Jorge. I have got it all ready.' He drew in his chest. 'I would like to say I am a man of the river. I am a man of the forest. I will tell you about it.'

'Go away and sober up and then tell me about it.'

'No no, Senhor Jorge, don't worry. I'll sing to you.'

'No, Geraldo, you will not sing to me.'

'I know all the traditional songs.'

'Well, sing them when you're sober.'

At length he went and sat beside his brother, prodding him to get his attention, then he returned amidships and started looking for something in the bilges. He moved back to where his mother sat in the stern and asked her, in mixed Tukano and Portuguese, 'Have you seen those two little ones here, mother? I'm sure I put them in the boat.'

'I threw them overboard,' I said.

'You threw them ... ? You ... ? But those were my little bottles. I bought them. I only wanted a sip to make the journey go better. You threw them overboard, oh you shouldn't have done that, Senhor Jorge.'

I became quite angry and repeated some of what he had declaimed about drunkenness two days before, and Geraldo curled up in the stern and pouted. As he sobered he brightened a little, and after some time came and sat beside me, and began pointing out the different trees on the banksides.

At midday an army launch sped down the river towards us. I slipped down beneath the seats, lying in the bilgewater. The white soldiers stood as they passed us and, Geraldo later told me, looked into the boat. They failed to see me and moved on.

At night there was a terrible storm. The black waves rolled the boat from beam to beam and spray lashed into our faces. We had no lights, and Geraldo steered from memory. When I saw that both he and his brother were frightened I too became scared, and when lightning showed me for a flash how low we were in the water and how the waves loomed around us, I thought we were going to die. At length we saw a faint light on one of the banks and steered in around the rocks towards it. We unloaded our possessions and ran to the chief's house. Rain beat through the forest like a signalling drum.

9

THE GREATEST CAUSE OF deforestation in the Brazilian Amazon to date has been cattle-ranching. Nearly all the land cleared in the Basin finds its way into the hands of ranchers, though much of it was first opened to support other developments, such as colonization. Though ranching seems likely, as I will show, soon to be overtaken by a new threat to the Amazon, it may never be an insignificant cause of the forest's destruction. This is despite the fact that its lunacies appear to be universally recognized.

It is now well known that clearing the forest to produce grazing land in the Amazon is even less productive than the colonists' planting of food crops. Even before the grasslands fail, the beef they produce can raise only 6.5 per cent of the income the owners could have made each year from manioc production, and can supply no more than 10 per cent of the protein produced by a plantation of Brazilnut trees[1]. Yet despite having yielded so little, the pastures are characteristically exhausted after three or four years, when they need be either abandoned or expensively resuscitated. Those which are left untended quickly revert to rainforest. This is not as diverse as the forest the pastures replaced, but when it matures it recycles water and accumulates carbon much as the original ecosystem did. But those pastures kept open by burning, fertilization and pesticides for a decade or more may never recover. This land is likely to become not, as was once forecast, a red desert, but an enduring scrubby prairie[2].

As its own pastures produce so little, the Amazon is a net importer of beef. Because of this and fears of foot and mouth disease, nothing but an insignificant quantity of cooked meat has ever travelled from these rainforests to the developed world[3], and it is unlikely that a single Amazonian hamburger has ever been consumed in the North. It is in Central America that forests are cut to supply the foreign meat markets.

Ranching in the Amazon has clearly then not been sustained by beef production. Rather it has been supported principally by government subsidies and the rising price of cleared land. Both of these inducements are now considerably less potent than they were before.

The most heavily subsidized ranches in the Amazon are calculated to have cost Brazil, in terms of direct payments and the waste of resources, nearly five billion dollars[3]. This is despite the fact that they have been of no significant benefit to any in the nation but the few very rich people who received this money, each of whose government handouts and tax exemptions cost the nation over five million dollars[4]. Instead, the ranchers tend to drive out most of the other people living in the areas they move into, bringing violence and in some cases slavery to those who remain.

By the time the government could no longer afford to reward the richest Brazilian businessmen and landowners in this manner, land values had taken over as the most persuasive reason to clear the forest for pastures. The prices of land in Brazil often bear little relation to its productivity, but may fluctuate much as those of other investments, such as stocks and shares. As the speculative value of land rises with the clearance of trees and its proximity to roads, ranchers profit by cutting the forest and lobbying the local government to develop the frontier. The price of grazing land in the Amazon, whether or not it has ever felt the hoof of a cow, has risen by around twenty-five times since the 1960s. It has been described as 'one of the most profitable investments on earth.'[5]

Now, however, it appears that the boom in land prices is over. But there remain several financially sound reasons for cutting the rainforest. Among them are taxes which penalize the maintenance of uncut forest and reward the creation of pastures[6]; the higher chances of being awarded title for land which has been cleared; and government practices which allow a rancher to lay claim to six or twelve times the amount of unowned forest that he has demolished. The creation of cattle pastures is the easiest and cheapest means of transforming the jungle.

Ranching will continue in the Amazon for these and other reasons, among which are the Portuguese traditions by which ranchers are accorded a higher status than cultivators; and, for the poorer farmers, the fact that the cow is still regarded as a good investment. Like the English word 'stock', the Portuguese word 'fazenda' has two meanings: ranch and treasury.

But while ranching is likely to become less important, and the Brazilian government is being congratulated on its new efforts to contain it, we in the North have failed to notice the greater threat which has been creeping into its stead. And this, though it now promises to bring destruction to parts of the Amazon which might otherwise have remained inviolate, has been so little reported that it is likely to take many of the defenders of the forest by surprise.

For in 1989, while using satellites and helicopters to show the developed world that it intended to control the cattle-ranchers, the Brazilian administration issued 4000 licences for the cutting of timber in the Amazon[7]. The timber industry, for so long scarcely significant in the Basin, is exploding. During the 1980s the number of sawmills authorized to cut in the Brazilian Amazon doubled, with the new registrations accelerating towards the end of the decade. The number without licences is said to have increased still faster. And not only is the destruction caused by the timber-cutting itself the greatest threat to the forests in some parts of the Amazon; but it is now this industry which is subsidizing both ranching and colonization. By selling the trees on their land, both the settlers and the landlords can support clearance and farming which would otherwise be economically unsustainable. In some regions it is principally because of the burgeoning timber trade that these destructive activities continue.

Though 28 per cent of the world's tropical timber grows in the Amazon, the Basin has until recently been of little importance either to the world timber market or even to Brazil's own consumers, partly because the forests there are so diverse. In South East Asia, by contrast, the majority of the rainforest trees are closely related, and as the wood they produce is of a similar colour, texture and use, it is easy to exploit commercially. In the Amazon the trees belong to many different families, and the variability of the timber is confounding. Exporters have searched only for a few well-known luxury woods, such as mahogany, while Brazil's own timber market has been supplied by the forests of the south.

But now such impediments are being overcome, and the changes taking place are conspiring to make the Amazon the world's great new timber frontier. The exploitable forests of South East Asia are coming close to the end of their commercial use, and those of West

Africa will follow soon. Researchers experimenting with Amazonian timbers have found ways in which many of them can now be used, and the foreign markets have expanded to allow new species to enter. The forests of southern Brazil have been exhausted, just as domestic demand has intensified, due to the need to house the growing population.

The result is an explosion of an ill-controlled and ruthless industry. The timber-cutters have been scrambling to exploit not only the areas owned by the sawmills or other businesses, but also the forest refuges of Indian and nature reserves. In their haste they are carelessly destroying far more than they use, and opening a rambling web of roads through the rainforest, down which colonists can flood. While only 12 per cent of the timber felled in the Brazilian Amazon is sold abroad[8], and the rest is consumed internally, the export industry is proportionately far more destructive than the cutting of wood for the Brazilian market. The high value of the tree species selected for sale abroad means that the sawmills are prepared to travel further to find them, with correspondingly greater destruction of the forest they move through.

In 1989 and 1990 I visited two of the Amazon's timber-cutting frontiers. The first of these was in the east of the Basin, along the oldest of the development fronts, on the highway from Belém to Brasília. Around the town of Paragominas in the state of Pará the logging industry is now well established. Most of the sawmills are cutting on lands owned by ranchers or in their own timber reserves, but a few have invaded the Indian territories on the border of Pará and Maranhão. I went to see how the logging industry there had developed, and how it was affecting the forest.

I travelled to Paragominas in October 1989, in the middle of the cutting season. Along the road leading south from Belém the bus was passed by lorries laden with logs, sawn timber and charcoal. Through the windows I could see the grazing lands, the ragged fringe of the forest the ranchers had yet to cut, and the sawmills now feeding from it, lining the road for many kilometres. As we crested a hill five hours' drive from Belém, I could see little of Paragominas for the smoke which shrouded it.

Like murky water, the air of the town held in suspension the black and red dust of charcoal and sawn wood. Through it swam the quickening smell of machine oil, the scream of saws, the grunts of unloading trucks. Lorries moved in and out along the service roads, carrying logs to the sawmills then returning to the forest. The men and women around the machines worked like ants, and sawdust stuck to the sweat on their bodies. As trees could be pulled from the forest only in the dry season, and the storage space in the timberyards was limited, they had to cut and sell the trunks almost as they were brought in. Forklift trucks carried logs to the sawing sheds, where they were run onto the blur of a ribbon blade. There were fields of torn bark in the yards, and smoking hills of scraps and sawdust.

In 1970 there was just one sawmill in the county of Paragominas. Now 400 were registered. I found them surprisingly accessible. I wandered around the yards, apparently unnoticed by the frantic people around the saws. When I was able briefly to stop the owners or the managers, my questions were answered frankly.

The mills had already used up the most valuable timbers near by, and those cutters who could were now travelling 100 or 200 kilometres to find the best trees. Some owned substantial reserves of their own forest land, and hoped to be able to stay in the region for many more years; but others, who relied chiefly upon sales by ranchers, had exhausted most of the land available to them, and were being forced to move to fresh frontiers. Some of the businesses I visited had already relocated several times, travelling progressively northwards as they had consumed the forests in the south of the country. None of the cutters I met were managing the land they owned for continuous production; rather, as one sawmill owner told me, they would disinvest when the wood ran out and find a new trade, much in the way of the whalers of the nineteenth and early twentieth centuries.

Others were diversifying. I visited a plywood mill, where I watched the treetrunks being locked into a rotating vice – a sort of lathe – and a blade, like that of a giant razor, lowered onto the surface of the wood. The logs were spun and wood unravelled from them as if paper were being pulled from a roll, then the sheets were pulled taut and cut to length. The foreman told me that even these timbers – commoner and cheaper than the heavy woods the other mills were taking – would be exhausted in the areas his company had secured within ten years.

But while the plywood industry seems to be adding to the destruction caused by the mills producing sawn timber, other developments are more positive, as some of the sawmills are looking for new means of exploiting the forests whose most expensive woods have already been extracted. As the market expands to accept new timber species, some of the mills are moving back into areas which five years before were considered exhausted. Many of them have just begun to explore the blossoming market for veneer, the attractive skin used to cover cheap wood. This and the demand for construction timbers enable them to exploit as many as 150 or 200 species, so that when they return to the ruined forests they can take almost any tree with a straight trunk. Others are raising the value of their wood by manufacturing finished products, such as furniture or tool handles. These developments mean that the sawmills need to cut less forest to make the same money.

Several of the mill owners and managers I met blamed other people for the destruction of the forest. One man asked, 'What about your own country?' He was sitting at his desk and he drew on a piece of paper a large circle and two small rectangles. 'That's Brazil, and that's Britain and that's Japan. Look how small they are; yet it's they who are sucking in the whole world's resources. They chew them up, belch out a cloud of pollution, then spit out some crumbs to sell back to Brazil at inflated prices. And yet you people believe it is Brazil that's responsible for destroying the environment.'

In almost every sawmill I visited I heard about the corruption of government officials. 'If the forest goes,' I was told, 'it is the government's fault. There are companies given money to replant. They never do, and IBAMA [the Environment Institute] never checks. They are thieves all the way up, and Sarney is Ali Baba.'

Some researchers have estimated that as little as 10 per cent of the timber taken in the Amazon is cut with full legal authority. Though most of the mills of Paragominas are taking wood only from land in which they are authorized to work, they succeed in breaking the majority of the laws intended to restrain them. For each area to be cut the mills have to draft a management plan, showing that they intend to harvest timber in such a way that the forest will continue to produce in the future. The government's environment or forestry departments then give them a permit, the equivalent of a ship's manifest, to be carried by their lorries, showing that the timber being transported is legally registered. Not only are the efforts to fulfil the proposed management plans a little pale; but the plans tend to refer to areas far smaller than those actually cut.

In front of many of the mills in Paragominas were notices announcing that they had been granted eight years of tax exemption by the government, as an encouragement to the industry. But I was told by one man that even those required to pay managed to escape most of their dues. This enabled the mills to make a substantial profit, much of which could be channelled into securing new areas in which to cut.

While most of the mills exported a small proportion of the wood they cut, some said that sawing for the foreign markets was often too wasteful to be lucrative. Not only did the importers' demand for wood of the highest quality mean that all but the perfect parts of the trunk had to be discarded; they also required planks of such a precise length that one or two millimetres of shrinkage while they waited for shipping would mean that the consignment would be dropped into the harbour and the mill would not be paid.

Logging for the domestic market was less wasteful, though still profligate. In the forest only the parts of the treetrunks without imperfections would be loaded onto the lorries, the rest would left to rot. At the mill the shape and size of the planks to be taken meant that around 50 per cent of a log cut for the domestic market was wasted, while all but 30 per cent of the export timber was scrapped. Unlike those of other nations, Brazilian sawmills characteristically make no use of the waste wood for panels, such as chipboard. The sawdust is incinerated, and the scraps are usually given to the charcoal burners who work on most of the mill sites.

I followed some of the timber cut for export to the town of Belém at the mouth of the Amazon. Much of it was bought by the Danish company Nordisk, to be sold above all to Britain, the United States, France and southern Europe. One of the firm's managers told me that one half of the volume it handled was mahogany, of which Britain was the biggest consumer, followed by the United States. Mahogany would soon become commercially extinct in the state of Pará, and importers were already paying 45 per cent more for it than they had in 1987.

When I asked about environmental damage, the manager told me, 'Logging has no effect on the forests at all. It is the ranchers who are causing the destruction.'

It was to assess claims such as this that I visited the ranch just outside Paragominas where the American scientist Chris Uhl and his research team were working, looking at the development of the timber industry and its influence on the forest. I was taken by one of the researchers into a part of the forest which had been logged for the first time two months before. Though only eight or nine of the 600 trees in each hectare had been cut, around one half of the canopy had been torn open. Both the falling timber and the bulldozers whose tracks now trellised the forest had pulled down many more trees than had been harvested, and these were now scattered on the forest floor.

One of the research team's surveys had found that when just over nine trees in each hectare were removed, 56 per cent of the canopy was destroyed. In an area of fifty-two hectares they had found nine kilometres of bulldozer tracks[9]. As the loggers had little interest in the future commercial use of the forest, they made no attempt to protect the trees they did not want.

The forest was likely, were it to be left alone, to recover; but the new growth would differ markedly from that of primary jungle. Many of the taller trees would be blown down, and the remaining forest was unlikely to reach the same height. Vines, taking advantage of the sudden openings, would run into the canopy and inhibit the growth of the trees. But in reality the first team of loggers was likely to be followed by another, a few years later, or by ranchers or settlers, and the rest of the forest would be cut and burnt.

I mentioned at the beginning of this book the possible effects of a drought in the Amazon long enough to cause the canopy to lose its leaves. The breaking of the canopy by loggers could have similar consequences. When the lid of the forest is removed, the saturated atmosphere escapes, and the forest floor is exposed to sunlight. After only six days without rain, the leaf litter may be dry enough to burn. Many of the selectively logged forests around Paragominas examined by Chris Uhl and his team had been damaged by fires. As the ranchers near by used fire to clear their pasturelands in the dry season, the flames would run on into the broken forests and catch among the piles of leaves and branches the loggers had left behind, sometimes cutting into the jungle for several kilometres.

The fires which destroyed the forests of eastern Borneo in 1983, costing the Indonesian government $5.5 billion in lost timber revenues alone, had started under circumstances similar to those now prevailing in the eastern Amazonian state of Pará. The forests there had, just like the rainforests of the eastern Amazon, been selectively logged. The cutters had left piles of branches on the ground. The normal rainfall was identical to that of eastern

Amazonia. All that was required to ignite the bonfire of Borneo was a dry season which lasted longer than usual. The Amazon Basin, without the geographical limits which helped restrain the Indonesian conflagration, may be moving towards a far greater tragedy.

While in Paragominas timber-cutting is an economic motor driving the continued clearance of ranchlands, on the newer frontiers of Pará the logging industry is subsidizing small farmers. Chris Uhl and his team have also been working in Tailândia[10], a colonization frontier 200 kilometres to the west of Paragominas, where the landholdings have yet to be monopolized by big investors. By selling the timber on their land or working for the sawmills, colonists can establish themselves – and their destructive activities – on land which they might otherwise have been unable to settle.

In the flooded forests along the big rivers of Pará, by contrast, logging is displacing some of the people – the caboclos – who live and farm there. Timber has been cut from the flooded forest for many decades; but until recently this was a gentle and apparently sustainable activity. The few trees to be taken were felled with axes in the dry season and floated out into the rivers as the forest was inundated in the wet. Now, however, small sawmills are being built in parts of the flooded forest, and in places the ground is being cleared of all its trees. The trees cut from the floodplains may never be replaced, as the land is invaded by vines, palms and aquatic plants[10]. The loggers – many of whom are the caboclos themselves – enjoy a few years of high profits, after which the land may become worthless to them.

There are now around 3000 sawmills – most of them unlicensed – just in the state of Pará. Chris Uhl's calculations suggest that if no more sawmills were installed and timber-cutting were the only means of deforestation there, the whole territory – of 120 million hectares – would be logged in eighty years. If, as seems likely, the number of sawmills doubles in the next decade, there will be nothing left to cut in fifty[9]. Taking account of ranching, settlement and government initiatives in the region, it seems that the forests there could be gone within a generation.

The timber industry in Pará is markedly different to that in the western Amazon, in the state of Rondônia. There timber production increased by nine times between 1980 and 1986[8], and part of the expansion was accounted for by an invasion of the special areas set aside for Indians and wildlife. This is partly because the timber industry in Rondônia, by contrast to that in Pará, receives much of its income from export. As it is the most valuable woods that are sold abroad, and as these are quickly depleted, the timber companies have been prepared to travel far to find them. Of the woods exported in quantity from Brazil, the most expensive is mahogany, nearly all of which is sold to Great Britain and the United States. Much that Brazil produces comes from the state of Rondônia. And much that is sawn in Rondônia is taken, illegally, from Indian reserves.

I set myself the task of following some of this illegal timber all the way from the Indian reserves to the retailers in the importing countries. Though it was widely suspected, no one had been able to prove that timber being sold in Britain or the United States had been taken from reserves in Brazil, and the people campaigning for a restriction of the trade had been deprived of what could have been their most powerful weapon. The timber merchants in Britain and the United States were able to claim, as they had yet to be directly challenged, that the wood they imported came from sustainable sources.

I flew into the Rondônian capital Porto Velho on a drunken Sunday at the beginning of February 1990. Along the city's main roads cars were crawling, festooned with drunkards. They sat on the roofs and the bonnets, legs dangling over the sides, training their livers for Carnival at the end of the month. Other men, also drinking beer from plastic bags, walked beside them, their hair full of streamers, bellies wobbling like wineskins. They pulled down their trousers at the ladies and toasted everybody's health.

Pôrto Velho, like all large towns in the Amazon, is ugly and brazen. Life there is unrestrained, and the vices of drink, sex, amplified music and dangerous driving are surrendered to without shame. But there is a style to the debauchery which sometimes affords it a certain charm. The hopes vested in recent settlement, the excitement of a new life, are evident in the city's excesses. Its carelessness, born of fresh wealth in the city centre, is mirrored in poverty in its suburbs. There the huts of the migrants ramble loosely across miles of broken land, children are barefooted and undisciplined, and cats are skeletons in fur.

On Monday morning, as the town groaned back to work, I visited the office of an organization trying to protect the Indians of the state. The campaigners there had been harassed by the government and businessmen. The organization ran a network of informers around Rondônia, providing, often at risk to themselves, news of incursions into Indian reserves, abuses of human rights and illegal environmental destruction. The network had on occasions been infiltrated, so before I was allowed to follow any of its strands, I was questioned about my contacts and my sources of information, and had to leave for a time while these were checked.

I had decided to concentrate on the reserve of the Uru Eu Wau Wau Indians, close to the centre of Rondônia. It was the biggest of the protected areas in Rondônia, of 1.8 million hectares, and it encompassed some of the most biologically diverse of all forests. Many of the 1200 Indians there had only the slightest contact with the outside world. Most spoke no Portuguese and, unlike some of the tribes in Rondônia, had not encountered the loggers other than through violent confrontation.

Two men had monopolized the cutting of trees in the Uru Eu Wau Wau reserve. They or their associates had started working there when Romero Jucá was president of FUNAI, and he had signed agreements with them and others, allowing the loggers to take wood from Indian reserves in the states of Rondônia and Mato Grosso. The contracts were in every sense illegal. Not only were they for cutting in places reserved exclusively for the Indians, but they required no forest management plans and, like some British privatizations, no competitive bidding. Those tribes in regular contact with whites were offered, in return for the timber taken, roads and tractors. Besides being of questionable social value, these cost the loggers far less than they would have paid other landowners for the wood. Indians with little contact, like the Uru Eu Wau Wau, got nothing.

The contracts had been declared invalid by the courts in January 1989, and the loggers were ordered to cease their activities immediately. But without enforcement and with the acquiescence of the local officers of FUNAI, perverted by Jucá or suborned by the loggers, the cutting had continued unimpeded. Both of the timber millers working in the Uru Eu Wau Wau territory were taking mahogany, and at least one had cut roads into the centre of the reserve to find it. Several of the Indians were reported to have been killed by the private armies the logging companies ran, and many more were believed to have died of disease. The logging operations inside the reserve now covered many tens of thousands of hectares. Yet the cutters were able to work unchallenged, as no one dared to close them down.

I took a bus to the town of Jarú, on the road through the centre of Rondônia along which most of the colonists now deforesting the state had come, and which the World Bank had helped the government to build. Two thousand kilometres from Paragominas, the same scenes spooled past like a repeated film. On both sides of the road were ranches, unproductive, some now weeded over, with small herds of zebu cattle flicking the flies from their ears in the shade of the remaining trees. Beyond them were the distant tatters of the forest. On the outskirts of Jarú were sawmills, but fewer and larger than those of Paragominas. Here big business, aided by gunmen and government subsidies, had tightened its grip, and the smaller operations had been obliterated. Tied to the top of a telegraph pole at the entrance to the town was a dead vulture, its wings spread, dressed in a red shirt. On the shirt had been painted the letters PT: the initials of the Workers' Party, the main opposition to the authorized excesses of the businessmen.

Jarú is a road town, built around the highway and the bus terminal. It is a place in which people wait and watch. What goes past is life and what stays – the men in cowboy hats sitting smoking on the steps of bars, the women leaning in silence in the doorways of shops – seems to be a longing for life. It is a migrant town, where no one can be sure he has ceased to move. The shops bear the names of the states their owners came from, and chart the whole great nation from which the migrants have been wrung.

Outside the slow half-built hotel I stayed in I met two of the original settlers, who had moved to Jarú seventeen years before, when the road had still to be built. When they had arrived, there were only eight houses; now there were several thousand. A father and son, they came up by river and traded their produce that way.

'Yes, *senhor*, just where you see the road, a jaguar was killed there once. In the forest we hunted tapirs, and in the stream running between those houses you could hunt caimans at night, by the lights in their eyes.'

Since then the prices of rubber and cocoa had collapsed, the road had been built from the south-east of Brazil to Porto Velho, and people had arrived in their hundreds every month, stepping out of the buses in the terminal with their baggage and a dazed look, not knowing which way to walk first. The town had spilt along the road, bars and shops had opened, the forest had been divided into farms and burnt, and the ranchers had moved in to replace the colonists.

'In the old days, when there were only rubber-tappers here, before there was a road, they would carry each other twenty kilometres out of the forest on their backs when they were sick. It was different then, *senhor*, it was certainly different.'

The researchers in Porto Velho had directed me to a woman I shall call Gabriela. She was alert and intelligent and, like most of the people of the town, had worked for a while in a sawmill. Now she and several others strove to restrain some of what the millers did.

Gabriela told me about one of the two men cutting into the Uru Eu Wau Wau reserve. José Aparecido da Silva, a rancher who had expanded into timber-cutting, was working in the part of the reserve administered by the county of Jarú. He owned the company Cometa Madeiras Ltda – Comet Timber – one of the biggest sawmills in the state. It had been with Jucá in person that he had exchanged contracts to cut in the Uru Eu Wau Wau.

José Aparecido owned a ranch which touched the northern border of the reserve, and controlled the colonists whose farms continued along the edge of the protected forest. Throughout this farmland he and the state government had built branch roads, two of which ran straight into the reserve. Fifty kilometres from the main highway, the roads were blocked by guardposts, manned by José Aparecido's gunmen. Any vehicle other than one of Cometa's fleet was turned back, including those of government officials. Watchmen were positioned at all corners of his territory: if anyone tried to enter on foot he would be shot.

Within the Indian reserve, Cometa Madeiras had been felling several tree species in an area of 30 kilometres by 20; and the 60,000 hectares were largely destroyed. One of the roads travelled a further 100 kilometres into the mountains in the heart of the reserve, where it branched out to find mahogany. I was later to see this in a satellite photograph: a white smear like a slug's trail leaves the pale pastures around José Aparecido's ranch and slides into the forest.

Aparecido had, of course, no legal right to cut in the reserve; but he was said to have powerful friends in both the federal and state governments. At least one local FUNAI officer was taking regular wages from his operation, and others had been either bribed or intimidated. One conscientious FUNAI official had tried to stop Aparecido's operation. He took a team of men through the back of the reserve and succeeded in confiscating some of Aparecido's machinery. But when the expedition returned the official was arrested by the other FUNAI officers and transferred to another post. The equipment was returned to Cometa. When, in a new post in a different Indian territory, he again reported the activities of illegal loggers, his own superiors threatened him with death.

Gabriela had entered the reserve, disguised, and reached Aparecido's logging operations. There she had photographed his woodpiles and lorries. The operation was even more wasteful than those of the cutters in Pará. Mahogany trees of 300 years old, whose trunks were hollow and useless, had been cut only for their branches, and the rest abandoned. In the forest belonging to the Indians it looked as if a tank battle had been fought.

José Aparecido's assault on the forest of the Uru Eu Wau Wau was just one of the many threats to their existence. In both the north and south of the reserve there were groups of garimpeiros. Elsewhere two state senators and a federal deputy had laid claim to parts of the Indian territory, and had been paying peasants to move in, clear the land and establish title for them by proxy. The state authorities had for five years been lobbying the federal government to reduce the size of the reserve, and, to the dismay of Indian rights campaigners, they had eventually succeeded. At the end of his term President Sarney accepted the petition by a Rondonian federal deputy to reduce the reserve in his favour, granting the deputy the land he laid claim to. At the same time José Sarney decided to cut from the reserve the land the two sawmills and 600 invading colonists had taken, which served, effectively, to reward their theft. President Collor promised to reverse Sarney's decree, but as I write this has not yet been done.

As a result of the many invasions of their territory, 160 of the 1200 Uru Eu Wau Wau Indians are believed to have died in the last three years. Most died of diseases they caught from the invaders; but some have been killed deliberately. There are rumours of posses sent into the reserve by the loggers to pacify the Indians.

The sawmills could only cut during the dry season, which began in May or June, so I would not be able to watch the trees being felled. But I told Gabriela that I wanted to enter the reserve to see the damage they had inflicted, and suggested that I would take a truck and start walking that day. Gabriela told me I would be mad to try: at every point there were guards. She had taken a secret route into the forest which had since been discovered and closed. Even so she had nearly been caught, and was forced to flee.

I told her that I felt the forest was big enough to get lost in; as I was prepared to enter on foot I believed they would have trouble finding and catching me. But she explained that I would be risking not only my own life, but those of herself and the others I knew in the network. If the loggers caught and tortured me, which was not improbable, and I succumbed, which again was not unlikely, they could all be in danger of their lives. I yielded, and as she and the others had already accumulated a dossier of unequivocal evidence – testimonial and photographic – documenting Aparecido's destruction of the forest inside the reserve, I decided to concentrate on tracing the wood to the buyers in either Britain or the United States.

After a day of research and deliberation I arrived at the gates of Cometa Madeiras Ltda. The enterprise was orderly and enormous. There were several warehouses the size of aircraft hangars, and I could hear both saws and plywood lathes in operation. It was many times bigger than the largest mills I saw in Paragominas.

I was stopped at the gates by sentries, and directed to the mill's offices. Inside I told the receptionist that I would like to meet José Aparecido. He was away, but she told me I could speak to the manager if I would wait. I sat rehearsing my role. Gabriela and her confederates had told me that some of the mahogany – they did not know how much – had travelled from Cometa to a timber merchant up the road: Aparecido's laden lorries had been seen entering its compound. But they also believed that Aparecido was exporting some of his wood himself, though they did not know the channels he used.

The manager was a quick, shrewd man, with a neat beard and bright eyes. He ushered me into his office, shut the door and then asked what I wanted. I told him that I was working for a British trade magazine run by timber merchants. They wanted to know whether there was enough mahogany in Brazil to last them another ten years. I had been sent to survey several of the sawmills of the region, to see what their stocks of the wood were, whether they had enough to cut and who they were selling to at present. I suggested that if Cometa could assure my readers of supplies my report should guarantee demand for its wood. He watched me closely while I spoke, then stayed silent for a few seconds.

'We have no mahogany.'

'None?'

'We hardly saw wood at all now. Nearly all we produce is veneer.'

He told me that the mill supplied only the Brazilian market, and that Cometa's affairs would be of no interest to me. He made to dismiss me. I tried to delay, asking some questions about demand for veneer.

He told me that the wood came 'from small farmers who sell it to us'. As he opened the door for me he said, 'It's the garimpeiros who are destroying Amazonia, my friend, not us.'

I felt transparent. I asked hurriedly if I could look around the sawmill.

'No. Anyway, there is nothing for you to see.'

The sentries watched me go, and I walked a kilometre or two back down the road to the centre of Jarú. There I waited for an hour, then I returned in a lorry. I disembarked a few hundred metres from the mill and slipped into the swordgrass and sorb-apple bushes beside the road. I crept to the fence of Cometa and slid along on my belly until I found a gap in the logs which had been piled around it, which afforded me a view. There was indeed a considerable veneer mill in operation; but also, nearer to me, were men in an opensided shed sawing a dark red log. Beside it was another such shed, into which I could not see. From the sound I could tell – as Gabriela had said – that at least two saws were working. Of greatest significance was the wood. Even in the port at Belém, where I had watched the most valuable timber of much of Pará being loaded onto oceangoing ships, I had scarcely seen such stocks. The piles of sawn wood were neatly stacked, most uncovered, some tarpaulined, many of them as big as houses. Gabriela had not exaggerated the scale of Aparecido's operation.

I had failed to find out whether Cometa was exporting any wood directly, so I decided to visit the merchant who was said to buy some of what José Aparecido produced. I had been somewhat abashed by the perspicacity of his manager, so I resolved to approach more circuitously, and apply with more diligence the rule of making the thing I most wanted to know appear the least important of my concerns. I needed to lure the loggers themselves into giving me the information, as such evidence would be unequivocal.

Above: Before the shipwreck: the sixty-four chiefs on the Santa Marta 3.

Right: A Tukano woman bathing, at Taracuá on the Rio Uaupés.

Above: The church in the forest.

Centre right: Cooking manioc meal in a Tukano kitchen.

Below right: A meeting of the Tukano women, discussing the reduction of their lands.

Above: The road the soldiers built at Ipanaré.

Right: Abandoned ranchland. In the distance more forest is burnt.

A logging yard in Paragominas.

Unrolling a log in a plywood mill.

Above: Loading a charcoal lorry, behind the sawmills.

Centre right: A bulldozer track through the forest at Paragominas. Only 2 per cent of the trees here were removed for timber.

Below right: Wood bound for Britain in the port of Belém.

Right: Harvesting the fruit of the açaí palm.

Below: Taking açaí fruit to market. The city can be seen in the distance.

Right: Oscar with the cocoa harvest: cheap enough to feed to the pigs.

Below: One of the medicine markets in Belém: cures for everything from dysentery to bad luck.

Right: Chris Uhl, with a mahogany seedling planted in degraded pastureland.

Below: The peasant syndicate's experimental garden.

Imaribo, the timber company said to be buying some of Aparecido's mahogany, was part of a much larger firm – Gabriela had said a transnational – with affiliates and offices throughout Brazil. In the manager's office were two men sitting behind desks: one – who seemed to be the senior – pale, soft-looking and smiling; the other lean and brown, missing some teeth and carelessly shaven. I surmised that the first had been brought from elsewhere to manage the branch, and the other had worked his way up through the local industry.

The senior man smiled me into a chair. His name was Romero. He listened to my explanation with friendly interest. The other scowled, and merely watched me. My questions were naive: I asked first about the logging seasons and the difficulties of extracting timber, then about timber quality and regional differences, and we slowly moved round to questions of supply. Romero said there was enough mahogany in Rondônia to last for ever. His company only bought and sold, it cut none of its own, and it handled astonishing quantities. His affiliate Madebras, through which the wood was eventually sold, handled 10,000 cubic metres of mahogany each month. It was trucked down to the southern port of Paranaguá along the newly paved Rondonian road – the route that much of the region's export wood took – and the company retained possession of it until it arrived, by ship, in foreign ports.

The biggest mahogany market was Great Britain, followed by the United States. I asked, as an aside, who he sold to in those countries, perhaps I knew of them? He told me and I claimed I could not follow, so I asked him to write down the names. He listed five companies, four of which were operating in Britain and two in the United States. Among them were two of the biggest timber importers in the northern hemisphere, which, as I later found, had produced extensive publicity material claiming that their operations were harmless and sustainable. The companies bringing wood into the United States bought from Madebras every ninety days. Those buying only for Britain purchased less regularly. I asked where the wood came from.

'From the sawmills closest to here, such as—'

'No it doesn't,' the other man interjected. He had been watching us, unsmiling, throughout the interview. 'Not mahogany. We buy none from here. All the mahogany we buy comes from' – he paused and looked down for an instant – 'from the Cáceres Sawmill in Mato Grosso.'

'All 10,000 cubic metres?'

He nodded slightly and the skin around his eyes and mouth hardened. I asked a few more questions, then left.

So Cometa was producing and selling a lot of sawn wood, of which, to judge by the colour of the timber I had seen and the testimonial and photographic evidence Gabriela had collected, much seemed to be mahogany. Yet Cometa denied selling mahogany, or large quantities of sawn wood of any kind. Cometa's lorries had been seen entering the yard of Imaribo, which claimed to be handling, through its associate Madebras, 10,000 cubic metres of mahogany each month. Yet it had provided no convincing explanation of where this wood came from, as it was scarcely conceivable that a single sawmill should regularly be turning out as much as this. Testimonies Gabriela had collected had shown unequivocally, as the manager had started to tell me, that Imaribo was buying mahogany from around Jarū.

So there was evidence to suggest that the five companies in Britain and the United States were unwittingly importing mahogany which had been illegally cut by Cometa Madeiras inside the Uru Eu Wau Wau reserve, in disregard for the welfare of the Indians and the forests in which they lived. When I returned to Britain I endeavoured to follow the wood the companies were buying.

Posing as a builder and decorator trying to buy fittings made from sustainably produced Brazilian mahogany, with the help of headed notepaper and various regional accents, I persuaded two of the five importers to tell me about their wood, and which retailers handled it. One of them, James Latham PLC, is among Britain's largest timber merchants. James Latham's hardwood manager told me that his company was buying 95 per cent of its mahogany from a single supplier, which operated in the east of the Amazon, and claimed to replant the trees it cut. The remaining 5 per cent was bought when insufficient could be provided by the main supplier, and came from sawmills in other parts of the Brazilian Amazon. To test the manager of Imaribo's claim that he, through Madebras, was supplying some of this mahogany, I later made a witnessed phonecall to James Latham in the guise of a commercial agent. I told one of the tropical hardwood buyers there that I had been asked by Madebras to try to enhance its sales to his company. He confirmed that he had been buying mahogany from Madebras on an irregular basis.

James Latham's hardwood manager told me that his company had sold Brazilian mahogany to Parker-Knoll, Glenisters, G-Plan, Smith and Plumridge, W. H. Ryder, Astolat and many smaller, less celebrated retailers, for the production of furniture, doors, stair fittings and fitted kitchens and bedrooms. He also sold Brazilian mahogany to the furniture restoration departments at the Queen's residences of Buckingham Palace and Sandringham. He sent me an attractive leaflet, which repeated the assurances of the Timber Trade Federation's public relations campaign. The leaflet suggested that James Latham's purchases of wood were good for the global environment, and that the forests would suffer if they were to cease. It claimed that 'Only reputable mills are dealt with by the James Latham Group, thus ensuring not only the quality of the timber, but also that the forest from which it comes is, wherever possible, responsibly managed.'

I was impressed by the frankness of the other British company buying from Imaribo – a smaller timber merchant – which responded to my questions. One of the managers wrote, 'We do our best to ensure that these [wood imports] come from non-destructive producers: however it would be difficult and dishonest to pretend that we could give a categoric guarantee.'

So there is evidence that, by contrast to the reassuring picture of the timber industry promulgated by such bodies as the Timber Trade Federation, mahogany items being sold by well-known retail companies in Great Britain are the product of the most destructive – indeed murderous – timber operation imaginable. It appears that some of the chairs, doors and fitted kitchens being sold in Britain at this moment are, unknown to them, made from wood cut in the Uru Eu Wau Wau reserve.

Aparecido's was one of two companies cutting wood in the Uru Eu Wau Wau territory, and to find out more about the second of them I travelled south, to the town of Jí-Paraná. This settlement was larger and tidier than Jarú, and seemed more self-assured. There were photographic shops, expensive fruit-juice bars and banks from all over Brazil. On the way in I saw posters advertising the campaign of Olavo Pires, a Rondonian senator who was trying to become governor of the state. Pires, who by dint of his spending was almost certain to win, had been foremost amongst those trying to reduce or annul the Indian reserves in Rondônia. The posters advised simply, 'Olavo Pires supports Collor.' In Jí-Paraná I met another member of the network, a man I shall call Eugénio. He told me about the operation of Zé Luís da Costa.

Zé Luís had destroyed even more of the Indian territory than José Aparecido, though his roads had not travelled so far. Within the borders of the reserve he had cut out an area 40 kilometres wide and between 20 and 30 deep. A FUNAI officer trying to protect the Indians had told the network that during the dry season Zé Luís' lorries would pass his post on the edge of the reserve, carrying out several thousand trunks of wood for export. Some of his drivers had also been seen with the bows and arrows of the Uru Eu Wau Wau, which, the officer said, would never be given up alive. As Zé Luís' sister was married to the regional administrator of FUNAI there was little, had they so wished, that any of the officials could do.

Eugénio had been able to find no records of the existence of Zé Luís' timber company. Zé Luís had claimed, when challenged to explain the equipment he owned, that he ran a contracting firm, Costa Terraplenagem; but there was no certification of this, either in the official registers Eugénio had managed to obtain or in the state's income-tax records.

There was no doubt, however, that Zé Luís owned many lorries and bulldozers and that, company or no company, he was using them to cut the trees inside the Uru Eu Wau Wau reserve. He sawed none of the wood he cut himself, but sold the logs directly to other companies. An associate of Zé Luís' had been tricked into revealing that the foremost among these was a sawmill named Madeireira Urupá Ltda. This testimony was all the evidence the network had, but Urupá had itself once possessed one of Jucá's illegal contracts to cut timber in the reserve, and the company was worth examining.

I hired a taxi and had the good fortune to choose a driver who had worked for ten years in a sawmill. As we drove I asked if he could recognize different timbers. He said he could, so I asked him to identify a pile of strangely smooth, orange trunks I had noticed earlier in the yard of a sawmill.

'Brazilnut wood,' he said unhesitatingly as we passed the stack. 'They've taken off the bark so that they don't get caught.'

It was illegal to cut brazilnut trees, as they provided lasting benefits for people and animals. Yet the wood was highly sought, as an important export timber. The taxi-driver said that every sawmill he knew handled it. The logs were quickly debarked and sawn, whereupon the wood became unrecognizable.

In the offices of the Urupá sawmill I mustered all my reserves of innocence and apparent gullibility, expressing astonishment at some commonplace facts. It was a part which needed to be played close to the point of absurdity, so that the antagonist could not imagine that anyone would want to appear such an idiot if he were not like that by nature.

So the charming, crafty owner of the Urupá sawmill and I circled each other behind our two masks: his indifference, my enthusiastic naivety. Each was at first suspicious of the other, worried about how much he had deduced. Who won would be he who could first unmask the other. I had played the game often enough, investigating suspicious institutions, to know that I should always allow the opponent to appear to be leading the conversation, and try to guide it, by my questions, with subtlety and insouciance in the desired direction. I also knew that if once my tone slipped all would be lost, the strings on my opponent's mask would tighten, and I would learn no more than any other clumsy journalist. In Cometa I had lost the game, immediately; in Imaribo I had largely won.

I was again impersonating a trade magazine reporter, expressing the British merchants' worries about diminishing supplies, and offering the possibility of the free advertisement of his goods. His commercial appetite was pricked, and at length he relaxed. He told me he produced 6000 cubic metres of expensive woods each year: mahogany, *cerejeira* and *freijó*, as sawn timber and veneer. The sawn wood was sold to two companies in the far south of Brazil, who made furniture for export to Europe. Some of the plywood he also produced was sold directly to two corporations in the United States, whose names he wrote in my pad, and part of this production was also passed, through a subsidiary of Urupá's, to an importer in England. There were, then, many ways in which timber suspected of coming from the Uru Eu Wau Wau reserve reached the northern hemisphere.

Far from being alone in its exploitation, the territory of the Uru Eu Wau Wau Indians is among the majority of the reserves in Rondônia in which there are illegal timber operations, many of whose earnings come primarily from export. In some of these the Indians, or some of the Indians, have conspired with the loggers to sell their timber, partly for personal profit, but also claiming that FUNAI's failure to supply medicines has forced them to make the money required to treat the tribes' new diseases. In most cases the money has stayed in the hands of the chiefs, and the new division of wealth has caused friction within the Indian communities. The tribes have been badly exploited by the logging companies, who have bought timber from them for only one fifth of the price they pay to other suppliers, and even then have taken far more than they have purchased. In at least one case the Indians have tried to close down the timber operation they had initially agreed to, having found out how little it had to offer them. But the cutters have refused to stop, and have threatened the Indians with death if they try to impede them.

The lives of the Indians have been transformed by the presence of the loggers. The people of the Cinta Larga tribe, for instance, have become dependent for much of their food on handouts from the timber firms. These, evidently, will cease once all the valuable wood has been extracted, leaving the Indians with neither food nor productive forests.

In other Rondonian reserves, like the Uru Eu Wau Wau, the logging takes place without the consent or the involvement of the Indians. Among these is the Guapore biological reserve, one of the most important wildlife conservation areas in Brazil[11]. The small group of uncontacted Indians living there is believed to have been driven from much of its traditional territory by the timber operations. There are now ten logging roads entering the reserve, and the sawmills, astonishingly, have been granted permission to work there by the federal government's Environment Institute. The Rondonian state government is also involved, and has dismissed the reports of the conscientious officials who recorded the illegalities there[12]. Perhaps one of the saddest symbols of the Amazonian Indians' impotence in the face of unconstrained development was the attempt the Guapore Indians made to stop the bulldozers entering their reserve. In the track the machines had made they planted pegs of sharpened wood.

Now that the most valuable woods have been extracted from the regions of Rondônia and Pará most accessible to the sawmills, many of the loggers are moving already to the more distant states of Acre, Roraima and Amazonas, where the forest has so far been least disturbed. Cutting has been restricted in these territories by the lack of paved roads, as the transport of logs over long dirt highways is expensive; but this impediment seems likely soon to be overcome.

Most of the wood cut will continue to serve Brazil's own needs. Wood is still the nation's most important housing material and, as the population is growing rapidly, and houses are soon destroyed by termites and harsh weather, demand will rise for many years. It is partly this need for housing which has completed the deforestation of 17 of Brazil's 25 states. But now that logging has concentrated on the remainder, it is the expensive export timbers whose exploitation is doing most to extend the range of deforestation.

Though by volume such timber represents but a small fraction of production, its high value and distribution through the forest means that it is becoming more important than the domestic market as the crowbar with which the seal of the forest is broken. Chris Uhl described mahogany to me as 'a perfectly designed boardgame for maximum environmental destruction'. No destroying angel could have done better than to scatter thinly, across much of the Basin, trees each worth between $2000 and $5000 to a sawmill.

The extraordinary prices that people are prepared to pay for mahogany in Britain and the United States mean that it compensates a logger to drive a road for many kilometres through the forest in order to reach a single clump of trees. Astonishingly the larger sawmills cutting mahogany are each building 500 kilometres of roads every year, just to reach this one species[13]. The financial incentive to cut valuable timber – mahogany and the woods which are taking its place as it comes close to commercial extinction – has been such that the government has now left much of its Amazonian road-building programme in the hands of unsubsidized private enterprise.

It seems unlikely that there would have been a substantial demand for mahogany in any importing country, were the British market not to have existed. As mahogany has been sold in Britain to build doors, large cabinets, coffins, dining tables and fitted kitchens and bedrooms, and in the United States to manufacture, until recently, mostly smaller items of furniture, the American importers have tended to take only the wood deemed unacceptable to the British.

As the cutting of mahogany and the other rare and expensive woods that British consumers favour is so extraordinarily destructive, it seems to me conceivable that Britain's imports of tropical timber are responsible for as much deforestation as Japan's. Japan, the nation consuming 40 per cent of the developed world's imports of tropical timber, has been repeatedly singled out by environmentalists as the most destructive of wood users. But most of the tropical timber brought into Japan comes from the more consistent forests of South East Asia, where several fine hardwood trees can be found in every hectare. The distribution of mahogany in the Amazon forests is much sparser, so the loggers need to destroy more forest to find the same amount of wood.

Britain is one of the developed world's largest consumers of tropical hardwood[14]. It has until recently closely followed the United States as the second biggest importer from Brazil. The American market has now expanded rapidly, and while it takes $183 million worth of Brazilian wood each year, this consumption satisfies only 3 per cent of its annual appetite for imported timber[8]. Much of North America's Brazilian imports are used for wooden flooring, the expensive alternative to carpets.

Brazil, though it possesses 28 per cent of remaining tropical rainforests, presently has only 6.8 per cent of the world market in sawn tropical timbers. But it has the great advantage of time. As the smaller forests of South East Asia and West Africa disappear, the Brazilian share of the market is rising rapidly. Within a decade or two Brazil is likely to become the world's principal supplier.

All this raises the question of whether or not imports of wood, or some wood, from Brazil should be banned. While conservation groups such as Friends of the Earth have argued for a boycott of much of the tropical timber trade, others, both conservationists and foresters, have suggested that the effect of a boycott would be the opposite to that intended. They have argued that a European refusal to take tropical timber imports would reduce the worldwide price of timber, and so discourage the governments of countries like Brazil from investing in their forests and trying to preserve them. If the forests were of less value for timber production the people living around them would cease to see the trees as a means of making money. Instead they would regard the jungle as potential agricultural land, and so cut it down with impunity.

In the case of Brazil this argument is clearly inapplicable. There it is the export timber industry which first brings deforestation to the virgin rainforest, and provides the roads and the money without which other forms of destruction could not take place. It is exactly because export timbers have such a high value that the forest is being destroyed. Were mahogany trees worth between $20 and $50 each, rather than between $2000 and $5000, no sawmill would invest in building roads to reach them, opening the forest to subsequent clearance by colonists.

Anyone visiting the reserves of Rondônia will see that the export trade, far from protecting the forests there, is the means by which the most precious parts of the rainforest are destroyed. I had investigated only one of the hundreds of big timber operations in the state, yet I had found that, in this case alone, five British and American importers could be strongly suspected of buying timber whose exploitation causes the greatest destruction and human misery. Timber cutters said to be selling their wood abroad have invaded almost every reserve in Rondônia. I would be surprised to find that a single British or American importer of Brazilian mahogany was bringing in wood whose cutting was in every respect legal, let alone sustainable.

Most of the importers of Brazilian wood in Britain claim not to be causing any irreparable damage to the forest. Yet, as I have found, they know little of where the wood they buy comes from and how it is extracted. Their suggestions that the cutters are managing or replacing the forests so that they will continue to produce are risible. Only one eighth of 1 per cent of tropical timber worldwide is produced on a sustainable basis, and not a single commercial full forest management project is yet in operation in Brazil. Our own purchase of fitted kitchens, doors, furniture and coffins made, unnecessarily, from the most valuable and widely spaced of all woods, is one of the most potent causes of deforestation in the Amazon.

I can see little of merit in the additional argument that if we boycott the import of timber from countries such as Brazil we shall lose our influence over the export timber trade there. Foresters have argued that if, for instance, the European Community were to stop buying wood such as mahogany, then less scrupulous purchasers would move in to take their place. I am unconvinced that less scrupulous purchasers exist. It is essential that one nation or group of nations, such as the EC or the United States, take unilateral action and withdraw from the trade. Without such a precedent, it is unlikely that a worldwide boycott could be achieved.

So saying, I do not believe that all imports of tropical, or even Brazilian, timber should be banned. If it can be proved that a particular company is growing or managing its trees with care, then evidently that timber should still be bought. But the claims of such companies must be checked. Those presently announcing that they are replanting mahogany tend indeed to be putting as many seedlings into the ground as they are taking trees from the forest; but the seedlings are being grown in relatively small plantations, while the mature trees are taken from a great expanse of primary rainforest. So while the individual trees the companies fell are being replaced, nothing is done to restore the wider damage caused. Government certificates claiming that the forest is being managed are meaningless.

Regrettably, while a pitifully few private businesses in the developed nations are now making an attempt to regulate the production of the wood they buy, the bodies which might have monitored the timber trade seem to have lost interest. The European Commission was discussing early in 1990 the possibility of restricting timber imports, but now appears to have dropped the idea, and it seems that the General Agreement on Tariffs and Trade, promoting the free flow of commodities, may, if approved, prevent efforts to reawaken it. The proposal put forward by the British Timber Trade Federation, that a levy be imposed on timber imports to help fund sustainable forestry, has been quietly buried, and the Federation seems instead to be spending its money on a public relations campaign, trying to convince consumers that the current trade does not harm the forest.

Whether or not Brazil succeeds in increasing, from zero, its sustainable production of tropical timber, it is clear that if northern consumers are to help conserve the Amazon's forests they will have to look for more imaginative means of building and furnishing their houses and offices. The environmental group Friends of the Earth suggests that we could, with few ill effects, forgo 95 per cent of the tropical timber we import. Much could be substituted by timber produced in existing plantations in temperate countries[14]. The tropical hardwoods we use for many of the doors, floors and much of the furniture we buy could be replaced with pine. Durable temperate woods, such as the European and American oaks, sweet chestnut, false acacia, walnut, cedar and yew, can replace several of the harder tropical timbers we believe we require, and vanity can be satisfied by the excellent textures – supplemented if necessary by staining – of some of these native woods.

Much of the timber we import is used in construction, building the frames of houses and office blocks and mounting windows and doors. Some of this wood can be replaced by native timber, but much would have to be substituted by metal or concrete. Evidently the production of these materials also has an environmental impact, but it is by no means as severe as that of existing tropical forestry.

Northern consumers are becoming more aware of the consequences of using tropical timber. In some places scrap wood is being collected for recycling, and several housing authorities in both Britain and the Netherlands now have a policy of using only temperate lumber. But as the market for wood expands, our imports of rainforest timber continue to increase. There is a desperate need for legislation. The industry has proved incapable of regulating itself, and the fate of some of the Amazon forest is now in the hands of Northern governments.

Whatever we do to restrict our own consumption, logging will continue to spread through the Brazilian Amazon, as domestic demand for timber rises. If, then, the Brazilian government is to control its own industry, the timber companies need to be reformed. Clearly they have first to be kept out of the reserves; but that would solve only a small part of the problem. Sufficient timber could still be produced if the loggers were confined to regions which have already been damaged. The mills could each be given enough of this broken forest to last them for ever if they managed it properly, and were prohibited from moving out of their own concessions.

The use of new species is helping already to ease a little the burden of domestic demand. In the middle of the century 89 per cent of the wood cut in the Amazon came from just six kinds of tree. Now that wood technologists have found the means of using 400 Amazon species, the mills can concentrate on smaller patches of forest. The government should recognize that the highly selective cutting now being practised in the Amazon, unlike selective logging in some managed temperate woodlands, may be no closer than clear-felling to the ideal of sustainable forestry, due to the carelessness with which the few trees are extracted.

The government's efforts to sustain the logged forests of the Amazon have so far concentrated on replanting. This has foundered, as the money raised for this purpose has been either misappropriated or misused. Private reforestation companies the government has hired are, of all the disreputable businesses in Amazonia, perhaps the most corrupt, and as a result replanting in the Amazon has been minimal. It has been argued that attempts to mend the gaps in logged forests are misguided, as trees return naturally when the forest has been cut only once. On the other hand the mass reforestation of pastureland, which is not yet being attempted, could be good for both the economy and the environment.

To delay the deforestation in Brazil would be much in that country's interest. As Chris Uhl has pointed out, if the government were to freeze exports from the forest for a few years, it would soon find that it had a world monopoly. Already one estimate suggests that the Basin's wood, after sawing, could have a value of three trillion dollars[10]. If Brazil used its timber resources wisely it could become one of the richest nations in the world. While the government sat and waited, researchers could devise and begin to implement sustainable ways of harvesting this timber. It is then that the industry could become a means of protecting the forest, rather than destroying it.

IO

THE PROBLEMS I HAVE covered so far are, I believe, the most pressing. If the movement of settlers, the Calha Norte project and the timber industry are not restrained, then there is little hope of saving the Amazon. But several other agents are likely to prove almost as destructive. One which has already commanded much of the world's attention is the construction of hydroelectric dams.

The use of flowing water to drive turbines, much as streams once powered watermills, is a commendable means of generating energy. If well engineered it is clean, sustainable and cheap. It releases neither the air pollutants with which fossil fuels punish the planet, nor the dangerous waste left behind after the generation of nuclear power. In these respects the Brazilian government's determination that hydroelectricity should supply 90 per cent of the needs of the national grid, even while overall energy consumption rises by almost four times[1], seems far-sighted. With regard to the world's impending energy crises it is, but the brave vision has been clouded by the fact that political objectives have been allowed to take precedence over the social, economic and environmental aims which should have guided the energy programme's planning.

The government-funded electricity company, Eletrobras, originally intended to build eighty-one hydroelectric dams in the Brazilian Amazon by the year 2010. Most of the electricity they produced would be transmitted to the south-east of the country, some to the north-east, and a little would stay within the Amazon to supply the industries and settlements developing there. The plans consulted a development fantasy no closer to reality than that which guided the construction of the TransAmazon Highway, or still advises the Calha Norte programme.

That many of the dams are being built with little reference either to their economic potential or to their environmental consequences is evident from the list of those planned. Many of them are designed to flood valleys insufficiently deep and narrow for the rapid water flow required to produce cheap electricity, and have, as the water will spread to cover an area far greater than economics would recommend, an environmental impact out of all proportion to their capacity. Two per cent of the Brazilian Amazon would be flooded were, as now seems unlikely, all the plans of Eletrobras to be realized. This would, by Amazon standards, have only an ordinarily enormous impact, were the 2 per cent distributed randomly around the Basin. But as dams are, of course, designed to flood valleys, they are likely to disrupt the systems upon which much of the rest of the ecology of Amazonia depends. Their positions within the river valleys are also of crucial importance. As a river flows over a plateau, its volume is low but its speed is high. As it crosses the plain on the final stage of its journey, its volume is high but its speed is low. For this reason most of the dams in the Amazon are to be built just where the rivers descend from the plateaus, where both factors are reasonably high. Not only does this mean, if the plans go ahead, that the middle reaches of nearly all the major rivers in the Brazilian part of the Basin will be inundated; but that development will concentrate on just the regions which have to date been least affected. So far settlers, ranchers and industries have concentrated both in the floodplains of the major rivers and on the outer edges of the Amazon plateaus, as these are the most accessible or fertile regions. The inner edges of the plateaus have remained largely unspoilt. It is in these areas that the dams, attracting industries and settlements, are to become new centres of development.

So the environmental impact of the dams could be great, while their economic return could be small or even negative. To see why, in the face of these facts and the outcry they have caused, the Brazilian government intends that many of these concrete fantasies should still be built, it is worth considering the astonishing example of Balbina.

The idea of building the Balbina dam came not from engineers, choosing the rivers which would generate the most electricity, nor from economists studying the country's future energy demands and deciding how they might best be met; but from the office of the president: President Figueiredo, the last of the military rulers of Brazil. In 1982 there were elections, the first since 1961 which could be called fair, to choose congressmen, senators and state governors. The president was concerned about popular support for his allies in Amazonia, so he decided to make a gift to the people of Amazonas, the central state. He would build a dam to supply the largest city, Manaus, with electricity, and to provide the employment and perquisites which any large project brings to its hinterland. He or his advisers saw on the map a river leaving the plateau a few hours' drive north of Manaus, and he announced that the dam would be built there.

The fact that in the dry season the river shrank to a thread was of no concern to the president, nor that the plateau the river crossed was flat, and the river's own valley little more than a dent. Even as engineers and economists demonstrated that the scheme was inviable, and ecologists showed just how destructive it would be, the political momentum to build the dam was gathering. The powerful construction industry and local business groups determined that it should go ahead, however worthless it might prove.

All conceivable measures were taken to ensure that reason would not be allowed to prevail. The plans were kept from the public for as long as possible, obstructive officials were sacked and environmental reports were suppressed. Right up into the final months of construction it would still have been cheaper to abandon the project and find an alternative source of energy than to complete the work. But the builders were not to lose their perquisites, the politicians were not to lose their financial support, and the dam had to be built and the valley drowned.

The river rose into the plateau and is still, as I write, rising. It has crept out of its own valley and into the endless interfingerings of the undulating forest. It has so far flooded 240,000 hectares, and it may not stop until 400,000 have been inundated[2]; though no one at this stage can tell. As the water has climbed it has pushed out the hundreds of families living on the plateau Eletrobras declared to be uninhabited. It has gathered in pools too far from the river's flow ever to be emptied, and there the vegetation it has killed rots, releasing hydrogen sulphide and methane gases. The dam has stopped the upstream migration of the turtles which the last of the Waimiri-Atroari Indians eat, and has cut these people off from some of the hunting and fishing grounds which helped to sustain them.

The acidity of the water, caused by the rotting trees, is likely to eat through the turbines of the dam every few years, adding to its financial costs. Already the electricity it produces is four times as expensive as that which can be bought on the world market. As the average annual flow is just one quarter of the dam's capacity, and falls in the dry season to 0.4 per cent, Eletrobras might now divert a second river into the reservoir, thus compounding the damage it has so far inflicted, while still failing to make the dam pay.

While none seems to have been conceived in a womb quite as dark as that which bore Balbina, dams in the Amazon continue to be installed for the benefit not of the users but of the builders. Eletrobras, attempting to exclude competing companies, has staked claims in most of the valleys of the Amazon, however unsuitable they may be, and in order not to forfeit them has felt compelled to build. Twenty-five are now under construction. Of these projects only five appear to have taken serious account of the social and environmental impact. These twenty-five alone will displace 91,000 people, many of them Indians, from their homes. All eighty-one, if built, will unseat 500,000. In only four cases have the people to be moved been consulted about their resettlement, or even seen the plans.

A faint voice of reason has begun to whisper in the padded cells of the planners, and most of the construction projects initially destined for completion by 2010 have been postponed, though there is as yet no guarantee that the most destructive of the dams are not to be built. As their future is being considered in secret, not only have the residents of the Amazon valleys no hints as to what their fate might be; but Eletrobras is itself deprived of the advice and discussion which could have reformed some of its less promising projects.

What has not at any length been considered is to what extent the intended supply is a response to the projected demand, or the demand a response to supply. Five per cent of all the electricity now being generated in the Amazon is used by the big aluminium smelters constructed by foreign companies just to the south-east of the Basin. They were installed there because of the cheap energy the Brazilian government guaranteed; otherwise they might have remained in the countries whose corporations built them. The smelters are of slight value to Brazil. They employ few people and leave little money behind in the country. The guaranteed price of the energy they receive means that for much of the time the Brazilian taxpayer is subsidizing the Japanese conglomerate[2], and the assured supply means that the citizens and Brazilian industries of the area are often blacked out.

The deals were made between the corporations and the unscrupulous politicians of the military government; but President Collor, far from cancelling them, has singled out the subsidy these foreign firms receive as one of the only two incentives to private industry to survive his austerity programme. If the new dams being built in Amazonia are to supply a similarly artificial demand, then the money they cost and the forest they consume are wasted indeed.

Change in the south-east of Amazonia is being supervised and financed through a project with which foreign governments are closely connected. In 1982 work began on a mine at Carajás, in the far south of the Basin, exploiting the biggest known deposit of high-grade iron ore in the world. This enterprise, with a railway carrying iron ore to smelters on the coast of Maranhão, received 32 per cent of its finance from foreign countries. The European Community provided 600 million dollars, Japan 450 and the World Bank 305. Brazil became the supplier of 50 per cent of the EEC's iron ore.

Soon after the onset of the Carajás programme, the government decided that the mine would become the centre of a development scheme involving 18 per cent of the Brazilian Amazon, an area of ninety million hectares. Charcoal-fuelled smelters would convert the iron ore into pig iron; other industries would use energy both from the trees and from the dams being built; and investors would be encouraged to cut ranches or factory farms from the forest, raising cows, eucalyptus, oilpalm, rice and soya.

While the mine itself and the railway which serves it are models of environmentally sensitive planning, the projects which have sprung from them are as destructive as any yet inflicted on the Amazon. Around the Carajás railway the mining company has carefully preserved a strip of forest 80 metres wide. Beyond that most has been damaged or destroyed for 300 kilometres[3]. Settlers, encouraged to move in by the government, are now raging through the forest, unchecked by any but the ranchers seeking to monopolize the destruction. Sawmills and charcoal burners have established themselves along the roads and railway, and garimpeiros have poured in to exploit the gold which accompanies the iron ore.

Of the twenty-seven Indian reserves in the region, only eleven had been formally protected by the time the major infrastructure was installed[4]. Already some of the 13,000 Indians of the area have been expelled from their lands. Some of the colonists who settled there are now amongst the poorest people in Brazil, and while their demand for food rises, agricultural lands in the shadow of Carajás continue to be converted into unproductive cattle pastures. Were this enormous project to proceed as the government has planned, it would double the area of forest damaged in the Brazilian Amazon by 1995. But Brazilian pressure groups have now succeeded in closing down some of the iron smelters, having convinced the courts that the smelting companies were not fulfilling their legal obligations to protect the environment.

The foreign investors who helped to build the mine and the railway which have become the core of the wider scheme have denied any responsibility for the developments they did not directly fund. But as the European Parliament's environment committee said, referring to the European Commission's investment, 'the EC would need to be blindingly stupid not to be aware of the crucial role played by the mining project in the larger programme.'[5] The foreign funders could not have been oblivious to the implications of what they were doing; but it seems that the access their investment afforded them to iron ore at banana prices overrode any finer feelings for the environment and its people.

Development in the Amazon cannot be contained unless road building is restricted. By giving settlers and ranchers access to the forest, the big trunk highways can cast a shadow several hundred kilometres in width. Of these the most criticized has been and remains the BR364, which has cut into the west of the Brazilian Amazon.

The 364 was extended and paved as far as the Rondônian capital of Porto Velho in the 1980s, with financial help from the World Bank. It became the means by which most of those settling in Rondônia entered the state, and thereby perhaps the single most destructive piece of engineering in the world. As the settlers and ranchers moved up it, the wealth of the state – its timber and minerals – now flows down, towards the ports and cities in the south of Brazil. It has become, moreover, the gateway to other parts of Amazonia, and settlers are moving from there into Acre, western Amazonas and Roraima.

Now, with the help of the InterAmerican Development Bank, an organization similar in principle to the World Bank, the next section of the road is being paved, linking Porto Velho to Rio Branco, the capital of Acre, the most vulnerable of the undeveloped states. Already the unpaved road into Acre has led to explosive deforestation, and it has brought epidemics of polio, yellow fever, whooping cough, typhoid and measles to the Indians there. When the paving is complete Acre can expect devastation of the sort Rondônia experienced in the 1980s.

The InterAmerican Development Bank suspended its loan to help pave the road for several months in 1989, as the government had taken inadequate measures to protect the Indian reserves in Acre. But in July 1989, though the Brazilians had in no tangible way improved the situation, it resumed funding. It claims that the loan is being used as a stick and carrot to encourage the government to protect the forests; but though the carrot is much in evidence, and is being happily consumed by the donkeys administering the project, there is little sign of the stick.

The governments of both Brazil and Peru have ratified the further extension of the BR364, to the western end of Acre, where it can join the Peruvian network. Of all the stages of the road, this has attracted the most attention. Conservationists fear that not only will this last link open the remotest part of the state to exploitation; but that the road will serve as a channel for the flow of the Amazon's wood, minerals and agricultural products to the expanding markets in East Asia.

The extension is planned as a means of shortening the route from Brazil to the Pacific. At present freight bound for Japan or South Korea has to pass through the Panama Canal or circumnavigate the Horn; an extended 364, guerrillas and chaos permitting, could allow traffic to reach the ports on the Peruvian coast four days after leaving Rio.

The Japanese government was invited to submit funds to the road extension project but has so far declined. There is no doubt, however, that the Japanese are anxious to amplify their commerce with Brazil, a country becoming one of their major suppliers of raw materials. President Collor pledged in his election campaign to build the road; his Environment Secretary, José Lutzemberger, has pledged to fight it. A solution which might save both face and money would be the construction of a shorter link to the Pacific, from central Brazil through Bolivia to Chile or Peru. This may indeed, if environmental pressure is maintained, take the place of the BR364 extension.

Another road opening up the western forests is the BR429, leaving the 364 in the middle of Rondônia and cutting westwards through the Guaporé valley to the Bolivian border. A depressing but by no means unusual feature of this highway is that, though it was planned to give access to settlers, not a pocket of the lands it passes through is fertile. Already it has proved to be among the most destructive of the Rondônian ventures, and now there are plans to pave it.

One of the longest established lunacies in the Amazon is the Jarí project, an ill-considered attempt by an American shipping billionaire to convert 1.6 million hectares of primary forest in the Amazon's mouth to plantations of paperpulp trees. Poor soil, fungus and insect attacks stunted his crop, and in 1982 he sold the project at a loss to a Brazilian consortium. This claims to be profiting from its purchase; but in truth the money it makes comes largely from the china-clay mines it has opened among the plantations. The troubles of the scheme seem not to have been instructive: the Carajás programme is now planning to plant eucalyptus under the same conditions as those which foiled the shipping magnate.

Amnesia is the muse of Amazon planning. Just as in Brazil the future comes quickly, and projects which take a year to yield are considered to be long-term investments; so does the past recede, and lessons taught by the failure of one project are forgotten by the time the next comes to be planned. The disasters of the TransAmazon Highway somehow failed to suggest to the developers that the construction of the 364 in Rondônia could cause similar environmental problems, and the lessons of the Rondônian road do not seem significantly to have informed the planning of its extension into Acre. The catastrophe of cattle-ranching, subsidized with such losses by the Amazon Development Superintendency, did nothing to prevent the Carajás programme from disbursing similar incentives.

One of the Brazilian Amazon's latest means of self-destruction is the oil and gas it has recently revealed to prospectors in the west. A substantial gas field has been found close to the Juruá river in western Amazonas state, while oil has been struck in the basin of the nearby Rio Urucú. There is less there than was originally thought, but the reservoir could be part of a larger structure. Intensive road networks are already being installed to serve the exploitation of these deposits. If, as seems likely, a road is built from the Juruá field to supply gas to Rondônia, the western forests will receive in return a flood of settlers.

As the forest goes the troubles of the human beings there multiply, for colonists as much as for Indians. One of the less attractive aspects of the Amazon's diversity is the number of diseases persecuting the people working there. Some of the illnesses fatal to man are those which customarily afflict monkeys. Under normal circumstances humans are unlikely to come into contact with them, as the monkeys live in the trees and man lives on the ground. But as the trees are brought down and the game is killed, so the pathogens turn to the nearest available hosts. As people, unlike monkeys, have no natural resistance to these afflictions, they may quickly develop fatal or crippling symptoms, like the hideous disfigurations of Amazonian leishmaniasis, or the deadly flushes of the mysterious scarlet fire. As I write, vampire bats deprived of their natural prey in Mato Grosso state are responsible for a rabies outbreak among the goldminers there. To suggest that the jungle is biting back at its aggressors is to invoke a mortal justice which seems singularly lacking on the Amazon frontier: rabid bats keep out of air-conditioned offices.

Some of the living systems of the Amazon are especially vulnerable. The foodwebs of the valleys, for instance, are being unravelled more rapidly than those of the upland forest. As the trees of the floodplains are cut, the life of both white- and blackwater rivers is deprived of its sustaining nutrients. This problem is exacerbated by the scarcely restrained commercial fishing fleets. On some tributaries thousands of tonnes of piranhas are being netted to make fishmeal, which is used as animal feed or fertilizer. The bigger boats pursuing food fish have a policy of discarding their first catch if they take a better second one, simply dumping the dead fish overboard. This wastage means that some of the most important commercial species in the Amazon, those that have supplied the people there with their cheapest source of animal protein, seem destined for economic extinction.

Among the rarest of habitats in the central Amazon plateau are islands of rock. Perhaps as many as 15 or 20 per cent of the plants growing on each one of these may be found on no other[6]. Rock in the Amazon is in considerable demand, and some of the islands have already been levelled to build roads or, close to Manaus, hotels.

The scrublands – or *cerrado* as they are called in Brazil – to the south of the Amazon are also of great biological importance. Like the forests, they support an extraordinary diversity of wildlife, and they are the principal refuge of such wonders as the maned wolf and giant armadillo. Some of the settlement schemes planned for the Basin are to be diverted to the cerrado; and soyabeans are being grown there to feed European cattle, to help build the Common Agricultural Policy's beef mountains.

In the Amazon itself it is some of the most striking of the large animals which are threatened with extinction, often because they are remarkable. The giant otter and black caiman, for instance, are hunted for their skins, while rare parrots such as the hyacinth macaw – almost twice the size of the familiar blue or scarlet macaws – and the golden-winged parakeet are being overexploited for sale to collectors.

The export of live animals and animal skins from the Amazon has become one of its major industries, especially in Bolivia, Surinam, Guyana and Paraguay, through which much of the produce is transported. The trade is largely illegal, but as the traffic of the rarer species can be as lucrative as the movement of drugs, it is attended by similar levels of corruption. Parrots are sold to enthusiasts in the United States, monkeys to research laboratories, skins to the manufacturers of shoes, bags, belts and coats. Driven perhaps by an urge to advertise their appreciation of the forest, tourists in the Amazon still buy decorations made from the wings of butterflies or the feathers of rare birds, destructive as the trade is.

Hunted game remains one of the major sources of meat in the Brazilian Amazon, and to serve the growing population an estimated fourteen million wild mammals are killed each year[7]. The forest cannot support these hunting levels, and when the game populations collapse they tend to bring down important parts of the foodwebs to which they are tied. The exploitation extends into the forest canopy – where monkeys are among the easiest animals to shoot – and into the river systems, where manatees and giant turtles may now be in danger of extinction.

The impact of both the direct exploitation of animals and, of much more importance, deforestation, means that the Amazon forests are likely to be losing some tens of species every day. Due in large part to the destruction of tropical rainforests, it seems that the world may be deprived of one half of all its species in the next fifty or one hundred years. This would mean that man, having come into being when there were more species on earth than ever before, will have presided over the return to a lower global diversity than there has been since the great extinctions of sixty-five million years ago. It has been suggested that we may not be able to identify 5 per cent of the unknown species on earth before 80 per cent of them become extinct. Nowhere is there as much to lose as in the Amazon.

While many species are being removed from the Amazon ecosystems, others, to no lesser effect, are being introduced. Of all the Sarney government's schemes for producing food in the Basin, few have been pursued with such enthusiasm as buffalo-ranching. The feet of water buffalo, unlike those of cattle, do not rot when the animals are grazed on deforested floodplains. This observation suggested to the government that the buffalo could become the efficient beef producer the Amazon lacked. This it may be, though not on Amazon soils. Regrettably it is also, in the words of one scientist, 'the most environmentally destructive of all domesticated animals'. Buffalo have little respect for fences or the other conventions usually restraining grazing animals. They swim well and tend to commute among the islands of the floodplains, ever, it seems, in search of undisturbed habitats. On arrival they destroy the bankside plants among which many of the animals helping to sustain the river ecosystems live. As President Collor's Agriculture Minister is one of the pioneers of buffalo farming in Brazil, the animal is likely to become a significant cause of the Amazon's destruction.

So there are developments planned or being executed on every side of the Brazilian Amazon. The Carajás programme in the south east and the logging and burning around such centres as Paragominas and Tailândia further to the north are likely to ensure that by the year 2000 there will be no substantial forests left between the Rio Tocantins and the Atlantic. If development proceeds as expected the forest will be fragmented up to the Rio Tapajós by 2015[8]. As it is these eastern forests which first recycle much of the water sustaining the remainder of the Amazon, the westward forests might not survive for long beyond that date.

Assuming for the sake of argument that they do, they will by then have been much reduced by other means. There are now settlements and ranching projects along much of the southern frontier. As the timber industry finances a new wave of colonization, development will advance rapidly along new roads, cutting into the hearts of the states of Amazonas and Pará, and possibly soon linking the southern or central frontiers to the new colonization projects slowly being established in the north by Calha Norte. Timber may provide the money required to realize the armed forces' plans, and open the entire northern border to exploitation. Garimpeiros establishing themselves in Indian reserves are likely to attract further developments, such as service towns.

In the west the flow of both colonists and logging companies from the damaged forests of Rondônia into the pristine lands of Acre and western Amazonas is now turning from a trickle into a flood, likely to be augmented by the implementation of Calha Norte's western extension. The central core of the Amazon is in danger of fragmentation by roads built by the oil and gas companies[9] and the mining firms now prospecting in the region. On the central floodplains farming and the developments associated with the growing towns threaten to spread to engulf most of the flooded forest. It is hard to see how the Brazilian Amazon could, by the year 2030, be other than a series of forest fragments surrounded by expanding frontiers.

Around 11 or 12 per cent of the forest in the Brazilian Amazon has now been cut, most of it in the last twenty years. The remaining forest is disappearing at the advanced rate of approximately five million hectares, or 2.3 per cent, each year. Most importantly the infrastructure has already been established which renders the desolation of 50 per cent an inevitability, in the absence of social and economic changes affecting the whole of Brazil. When – possibly between the years 2030 and 2040 - the forests have been reduced to a manageable size, perhaps 10 per cent of their original area, then the world might begin to make a serious attempt to save them. There may be no chance of preserving more than that.

None of this is to suggest that all developments in the Amazon are negative; rather that the measures required to reverse the damage are beyond the scope of present Brazilian or international plans to protect the environment. The appointment of the fiery campaigner José Lutzemberger as the government's Environment Secretary was an excellent decision of President Collor's, though it is hard to see how Lutzemberger can do much to halt what is happening in the Amazon when men like Antônio Cabrera, Bernardo Cabral and General Tinoco Ribeiro occupy the crucial Agriculture, Justice and Army ministries. There is indeed evidence that, though Collor is backing him on many issues, other government departments are successfully impeding Lutzemberger's conservation strategy.

While none but José Lutzemberger seem eager to identify the causes of deforestation in the Amazon, there is no shortage of measures designed to address the symptoms. Some may even have significant, if ephemeral, effects. In June 1990 President Collor launched his 'Operation Amazonia'. This increases the number of forest guards, who are empowered to catch and punish people burning or mining illegally or trawling for fish. According to Mr Collor these guards will be supported by the armed forces and advised by a joint commission of government and non-governmental organizations. These are excellent though limited developments.

José Lutzemberger has promised that President Sarney's unconstitutional decrees reducing the reserves of several Indian tribes will be revoked, though whether or not this lies within his power has yet to be demonstrated. The government has put forward good proposals for how the Amazon should be used, determining where the forests are to be preserved, where they are to be used in such a way that they are not destroyed and where they are to be replaced by farms or other developments. But the maps and strategies it has drafted so far are no more than a theory of management; the social and economic implications of these plans have yet to be acknowledged.

The new government's attitude to research in the Amazon is in timely contrast to President Sarney's. It was said that Sarney's personal advertising budget was bigger than the amount of money he authorized for Amazon research. Not only would his government not pay for the scientific work itself; but he forbade the researchers to accept funds from abroad. So while foreign organizations and governments were trying to pour money into research in the Amazon, work there was shrivelling through want of funds. Much of what remained, even student grants, was embezzled by corrupt bureaucrats or misspent by the nodding dogs the government appointed to run the research institutes. Many brilliant scientists lost heart in their work. Those who remained were able to do so only by dedicating all they possessed to science: several I knew were paying for their research from their own meagre salaries.

This policy, which bore the brand of blind stupidity associated with the National Security Council, was doubly destructive. Not only is scientific work crucial to efforts to save the Amazon; but from the little the researchers managed to complete have come theoretical advances as exciting as any the natural world has inspired in the late decades of this century. The true pioneers of the Amazon, which is as receptive to interpretation as it is little known, are the scientists.

Collor has now welcomed the foreign funding of Amazon research, and this is perhaps his most significant advance on Sarney's Amazon policies. Regrettably it has come too late for many projects, and some of the conservation battles the scientists were fighting have already been lost.

While some fine ecologists have been invited to join the civil service, in some cases to be promptly sacked by the irascible Mr Lutzemberger, the bureaucratic institutions supposed to be administering change remain moribund. Much was made of the many millions of dollars of fines imposed by the Environment Institute on people burning the forest without authorization in 1989; but scarcely a clipped centavo was collected. Many administrators know that if they fulfil the duties the law demands of them they do so at the cost of either their careers or their lives.

Events in the other Amazon nations give cause for both optimism and pessimism. Some of the greatest hopes for the forests are vested in the Indian organizations now well-established in countries such as Bolivia, Peru and Ecuador. In 1990 800 Bolivian Indians demonstrated the growing power of protest in the Amazon when they marched the 700 kilometres from their territory in the lowlands to the Andean capital La Paz. There the popular support they secured persuaded the President to accept their demands that their landrights be recognized and timber cutters be expelled from a forest reserve. This triumph may serve to reduce the annual rate of deforestation in the Bolivian Amazon, recently estimated as 2.1 per cent[10]. Much of this is due to population pressure and economic changes in the Bolivian highlands. As the world price of tin fell sharply in 1985, the government turned to timber-cutting as a means of raising foreign capital, and to colonization as a means of resettling redundant miners.

The Bolivian Amazon is also blighted by favours granted to

businessmen and political supporters. Seventy-five big companies have been awarded twenty-three million hectares by the government. Rivers feeding the Amazon are poisoned not only by the mercury liberated by garimpeiros, but also by the acid used in the manufacture of cocaine. There is no sign of a reduction in the illegal traffic of animals: in one consignment recently intercepted by inspectors there were 375,000 skins; but as government employees at most levels are involved in the trade, no company has yet been prosecuted[11]. More positively the Bolivian government declared early in 1990 that it would stop all new economic activity in the Amazon.

The Indians of the Peruvian Amazon have persuaded their government to allow them to take much of the responsibility for their own development. The biggest of their organizations is now mapping and demarcating the lands of the people it represents and promoting schemes intended to enhance their self-reliance. Some groups have succeeded in expelling the colonists, missionaries or guerrillas in their territories. But the government remains committed to change in the Amazon. In December 1988 the Peruvian Congress passed a law which was designed to relieve overcrowding in the Andes, by promoting settlement in the forests. Its opponents have described it as 'the coca law', because, they say, the peasants moving to the Amazon will have no economic option but the cultivation of cocaine. The lands being colonized fastest are those of the eastern Andes. Here the rainforest is particularly diverse, and protects the fountain-heads of many of the rivers which cross the Amazon Basin.

Ecuador is proportionately the most destructive of the Amazon nations. Four per cent of its Amazon forests are disappearing each year, and development projects are already being implemented which will hasten the obliteration of what remains. Foremost among these is oil exploitation. The work of some of the Northern companies operating there is one of the most disreputable examples of multinational misrule anywhere in the world.

Among the twenty foreign oil companies now working in Ecuador are some of the best known names of the garage forecourt. The environmental record of some of these firms is striking. First, without any effective controls, they have laid down a network of roads and trails for prospecting. Their own employees and other colonists settle along these, as they open up forest lands which were previously inaccessible. Around these tracks is laid a grid of seismic lines: trails of explosives, the echoes of whose detonations are used to chart the structure of the underground rocks. These are discharged without regard to the lands through which they run, destroying Indian crops and river ecosystems.

Having begun to drill for oil, some of the firms have invested in no meaningful provisions either to prevent accidental spillage or to dispose safely of the pollutive chemicals used in the process of separating oil from water. These are hot, caustic and contain chlorides, sulphates, cyanides and arsenic. They are flushed directly into the rivers the Indians use for drinking, cooking and fishing, which run eastwards into the remainder of the Basin. Fish are already extinct in several parts of the watershed.

By 1989 the Ecuadorean government had not considered itself obliged to fit the principal piping systems with any valves other than those used for pumping purposes. So when a pipe ruptures, oil may spill for days until the section between the nearest pumping valves has emptied itself. Thirty major oil spills have been reported from one pipeline alone, and slicks hundreds of kilometres long have smothered the forest rivers. Behind the veil of the jungle Northern companies, some of whom spend many millions of dollars advertising their environmental concerns at home, seem to be free to do as they please.

Much of the forest the oil companies are destroying lies within Indian territories and wildlife reserves. Of the Indian groups whose lands are being ruined, the Waorani, some of whom have no contact with the outside world, are the most vulnerable. The Ecuadorean government has granted them title to some of their ancestral lands, on condition that they do not interfere with the oil firms. The World Bank is considering a $100 million loan to pay for the infrastructure the companies might use in exploiting their territory. The British government owns a decisive 'golden share' in a corporation prospecting one of the last intact forest regions in Ecuador. This could, if the government chose, be used to restrict the firm's potentially destructive activities.

Ecuador's forests carry the additional burden of the country's outmoded land laws. These rule that primary forest lands are unproductive, and can therefore be appropriated for land reform. The private owners of forest land feel constrained to clear it, so that it is not redistributed to peasants. In an attempt to establish sovereignty over a boundary region it claims from Peru, the Ecuadorean government is filling the disputed lands with colonists.

Road-building and oilpalm-planting help draw an ever-rising tide of settlers into the lowlands.

Colombia has received more praise for its environmental policies than any of the other Amazon nations, and most of it is deserved. In 1989 Colombian Indians were granted control of 18 million hectares of forest. Their rights to follow their own traditions and customary laws were endorsed, and they were made responsible for the conservation of their territories. There is some concern that the Indians' jurisdiction in these lands does not extend to minerals rights. But the government's new policies have encouraged tribes to reawaken their traditions, and malocas are now replacing some of the individual houses the people were once coerced into building.

Elsewhere, however, Indian leaders are still being killed by ranchers and the gunmen they hire. Around the most southerly part of their common border, both Colombia and Brazil are implanting settlements. There has been heavy colonization of the uplands of the Colombian Amazon since the 1960s, and cattle ranching has been proliferating throughout the 1980s. Coca plantations and the associated influx of peasants account for a significant proportion of the 2.2 per cent of forest Colombia loses each year.

Venezuela had spent little until recently on development in the Amazon. But the low oil prices and debt bills of the 1980s persuaded the administration to look to the forests as a source of income. Important new roads have facilitated logging, mining and the opening of agricultural lands. Rising oil prices in 1990 may, by contrast to their effects in Brazil and Ecuador, help to preserve the forests in Venezuela, whose oilfields lie outside the Amazon.

The forty-one million hectares of Amazon forest in the Guyanas – Guyana, French Guiana and Suriname – have until now remained largely undisturbed, with little penetration or settlement, and exploitation only of distinct resources such as greenheart timber. In Guyana this is changing rapidly. The Brazilian government is paying the ill-famed mining company ParanaPanema to build a road from northern Brazil to the Guyanan coast. The road gives ParanaPanema access to an opencast goldmine it is developing in Guyana; allows Brazilian garimpeiros to reach the goldbearing rivers of the southern Guyanan Amazon; and provides Guyanan colonists with an opportunity to exploit the country's pristine savannahs and rainforests. Timber companies are said to have been granted concessions to cut throughout the forest lands the road crosses.

Guyana has already absorbed many of the Brazilian miners whose future in Roraima was uncertain, and the Guyanan government is encouraging more to enter, in return for a percentage of their earnings, as the country is short of labour and has difficulty in exploiting its own mineral deposits. Goldmining there is particularly destructive. The garimpeiros work in the rivers with machines known as missile dredges[12]. These uproot the vegetation on the banks, then spray the bared sediments until they collapse into the water, whereupon pumps attached to barges suck up the material and grade it. The process stirs so much mud into the rivers that the water sixty kilometres downstream cannot be used for washing. Rivers whose beauty earned the Guyanan government a considerable proportion of its tourist revenues have been reduced to muddy gutters.

But the deep afflictions of the Amazon are not to be found among these troubles. Settlement, mining, military installations, ranching, timber-cutting, dam construction and road-building are merely symptoms of the disease the Amazon is suffering. If one of these factors is suppressed, others will take its place, and efforts to resolve these problems without addressing the situation which gave rise to them are like working to clean up an oilspill while the pipe remains uncapped. Nothing of substance will change in the Amazon until the troubles are traced to their sources. The sources may be the very institutions Northern governments and others who claim to be fighting for the forest are in fact defending.

The forest's persistent problems are a lack of democracy and the concentration of wealth. The fight to save the environment is necessarily a fight for better representation and a better distribution of resources; without these things there is nothing to restrain either the adventurism of the super-rich or the destructive desperation of the poor, and nothing to force the region's leaders to protect its people and the places they inhabit. It is striking that Ecuador and Brazil, the two Amazonian nations with the worst distribution of wealth, are also those two, in corresponding order, with the highest rates of deforestation.

Brazil has since its foundation suffered from both unaccountable power and an extreme inequality of riches. But in the second half of this century, after halting improvements, the situation became markedly worse, when a coup replaced a democratically elected government with a caucus of military leaders and their allies. This is the event from which Brazil is still recovering, and whose consequences continue to afflict the forests of the Amazon.

The civilian government of João Goulart was in many ways imperfect, especially as the president had taken to bypassing some of the restraints Congress might have imposed, using misleading populist messages to stimulate demand for the changes he wished to introduce. But much of what he fought for was development of the sort which might have protected both the people and the forests from the injustices endemic to Brazil. His development programme was based upon agrarian reform, educational improvements and housing for the poor: an attempt to generate economic growth by means of greater equality. He also tried to impose tighter controls on foreign companies, which, he claimed with some justice, were draining the economy and restricting the growth of Brazilian businesses.

The leaders of the armed forces, defenders of the traditional order in Brazil, saw these plans as a threat to their long-established privileges, and a means by which the intellectuals, priests, unionists and peasants they feared might become more powerful. The industrialized nations with which Brazil traded were affronted by Goulart's revocation of the exceedingly lucrative deals they had struck with friends in previous Brazilian governments.

In 1964, with the support of the United States, the army generals seized power[13], and quickly rounded up the people they felt threatened by, torturing and executing those who had worked hardest to replace the traditional hierarchy. The United States president, Lyndon Johnson, sent the coup leaders a message congratulating them on the success of their operation, saying that he was pleased the Brazilians were solving their problems 'within the framework of constitutional democracy'. As the generals, with the help of his administration, had ousted a democratically elected government and suspended or overruled all inconvenient constitutional provisions, the message might have surprised them.

As a mark of confidence in the new government and by means of support, the United States Treasury, the World Bank and the International Monetary Fund began to disburse money liberally, funding developments which helped to rescind Goulart's intended reforms. Massive projects of prestige to the leaders but little benefit to the people began to be financed, and the policies were established which would later guide development in the Amazon. American tax dollars were channelled through the United States Agency for International Development to train and equip the security forces, among whom were the torturers being used to maintain what the government considered to be order. There are allegations that United States police advisers themselves participated in some of the most prodigious brutalities.

By comparison to the administrations which followed, the government established by the coup leaders and led by General Castello Branco was moderate. As, in 1969, control passed to General Costa e Silva, civil liberties were further restricted, the media were heavily censored, and development moved further from any semblance of helping the people who needed it most. The economy, with the help of foreign loans, boomed; but one of the greatest indictments of military rule is that even when annual growth reached 11 per cent, the gap between rich and poor continued to expand. This growth was sustained by heavy borrowing and the extraction of money from sectors such as education and poverty relief, to finance incentives and special favours for big business. The policies pursued with apparent success in the 1960s and 1970s are in large part responsible for Brazil's current economic crisis.

Rather than social and economic reform, the government gave the people public relations. Brazilians were given money with which to buy televisions, and the Globo network, securing a hold on Brazil which has yet to be relieved, broadcast to the people a pleasing image of the presidents who administered the nation's darkest days. Because of the implacability with which he projected his own image, boosted short-term economic growth and blamed the problems which the government had engineered on the enemies of the state, even the third and most repressive of the military rulers, General Emilio Médici, was, like many of the world's most abhorrent dictators, admired by the people he governed. But as Médici trumpeted his virtues, the Brazilians themselves fell silent, as his agents worked to extinguish dissent.

Every wave of torture, state terrorism and extrajudicial execution was preceded by the invention of enemies with which to justify the repression. With the help of doctors and psychoanalysts new methods of torture were devised to extract information about largely imaginary forces of guerrillas and communists. The torturers, who were members of the police and armed forces, were given presents by big businessmen. Throughout this period the United States gave unconditional support to the Brazilian government. The American administration, like the Brazilian generals, claimed that communist subversion was a danger to the nation, and that the military government was indispensable in suppressing it.

For all its horrors, the Brazilian government never exercised the total repression once visited upon the citizens of the Soviet Union or Romania, or still suffered by the people of Burma or Guatemala. The tyranny was erratic. People were imprisoned, tortured or killed as their existence or liberty was inconvenient; but the administration bore few grudges. A celebrated scientist I met had been jailed by the military government for his political beliefs. Soon after his release by the same government he was appointed, without any renunciation of his views, director of one of Brazil's most prestigious research institutes.

Brazil was thrall, as one commentator has suggested, to an authoritarian situation, not an authoritarian regime[14]. Congress and a parliamentary opposition, though manacled, survived; some of the military courts the government established to try subversives were just; newspapers could fill the empty gaps left by the censors with recipes for inedible dishes. The incomplete nature of the dictatorship kept the hopes of reformers alive, and these were stoked by the work of the church in Brazil and foreign pressure groups, such as Amnesty International.

Throughout the period of military rule, Amazonia came to be used as a dustbin for the government's economic and political refuse. The peasants whose land had been appropriated by investors and politicians were encouraged to move there; the businessmen favoured by the administration were invited to make money there. The image of Brazil the governments' public relations campaigns made such use of – the pioneer state, ever pushing forward the frontiers of development – was cast in Amazonia.

In 1974 General Ernesto Geisel was manoeuvred into power by some of the more moderate commanders of the armed forces. He began, erratically, to soften the administration. While he felt constrained to appease the extremists in the armed forces by continuing to imprison or eliminate dissidents, he presided over congressional elections which were freer than those his predecessors had permitted. As a result the opponents of the military government began to gather strength. Liberation theologians became a pivot of the opposition, and they were helped by lawyers and a less restricted press. In response to this, members of the armed forces established vigilante groups, threatening or killing the campaigners.

Though President Geisel allowed unions to organize and reintroduced the right of habeas corpus, he left Congress effectively powerless, and the internal security organizations, responsible for the terror and the eradication of dissent, intact. President Carter's administration criticized Brazil's human rights record and substantially reduced United States support; but Geisel used the opportunity to rally approval for his government in the name of nationalism. As the sharp rise in the oil price in 1973 and 1974 had retarded Brazil's economic growth, the government borrowed heavily from Northern banks. The bankers, eager to unload the money the Middle Eastern oil producers had invested, lent to projects and economic programmes which in calmer periods would have horrified them.

As, in 1979, General João Batista Figueiredo came to power, it became evident that the excesses of military rule were coming to an end. The opposition began to organize with some freedom. Political prisoners were released and exiles allowed to return. New political parties emerged, the most radical of which was the Workers' Party, gathering around the union movement. But while the prospects for democracy improved, wealth continued to move to the rich from the poor. Government policies which encouraged big landowners to increase the size of their properties led to a sharp rise in the numbers of landless peasants, people who had no option but to flee to the shanty towns or the Amazon. While the small-scale farming producing most of Brazil's food was allowed to wither, the landlords received incentives to divert their production from staple to export crops. Even the Agriculture Minister was driven at length to complain that the nation was exporting food 'while thirty million of us are starving'.

In the late 1970s the country began to pay for the profligacy of the earlier military leaders, whose effects had been compounded by the oil crises of 1974 and 1979; the loss of demand for Brazilian exports caused by a world recession; and rising foreign interest rates. Inflation rose like a tidal wave, at the same time as the economy sank into recession. Debt became a crippling incubus, as interest rates in the creditor nations rose from 6.5 per cent in 1976 to 21.5 per cent in the 1980s.

A campaign for direct presidential elections began to accelerate after reasonably fair congressional elections were held in 1982. Congress decided to vote on the issue, and rallies of up to one million people gathered in the cities to demand a plebiscite. The campaigners were narrowly defeated, and the deputies decided instead that they themselves should select the next president. This was, however, a significant advance, as previous presidents had been chosen by army generals. The extremists in the military leadership seemed to be preparing for a coup; but the opposition's choice of the conciliatory Tancredo Neves as its candidate calmed them and won support from some members of the ruling party. To secure the votes of these dissidents, the opposition chose José Sarney, a long-serving but comparatively moderate senator in the governing party, as its candidate for vice-president.

Tancredo Neves won convincingly and prepared to become, in 1985, the first civilian president of Brazil since João Goulart was overthrown in 1964. For the frustrated electorate he became a messianic figure. The day before he was inaugurated he was taken to hospital, where he remained until he died, never having entered office. José Sarney, the compromise candidate and faithful servant of the military government, became the civilian president.

Sarney was a man divided between his old loyalties to the traditional system of arbitrary rule and the concentration of wealth, and his new responsibilities to change that order. His government was largely composed of people from the privileged minority which had ruled Brazil for the preceding twenty-one years, many of whom were or had been members of the armed forces. Yet he had been authorized to abolish censorship, plan sweeping land reforms and poverty relief, and summon an assembly to prepare a modern constitution upholding citizens' rights to full democracy.

In some respects Sarney made a real if confused attempt during his first year or two in office to improve the distribution of wealth and power. But much of what the military government had achieved through legislation and repression, the political and economic élite it had favoured now sustained by private means. Many of the press empires which had blossomed during the days of censorship and government propaganda still spoke for the government and against its detractors. The Globo television network remained, and remains, one of the minority's most penetrative means of frustrating social reform. The landowners retained, with the help of the Ranchers' Union they established, the power to enlist politicians and terrorize their opponents. Business conglomerates had secured such a share of the nation's wealth that their grip on the political establishment could have been relieved only by a government of considerably more commitment than President Sarney's.

In 1986 the government engineered a small economic boom. Like the boom of the early 1970s it was little more than a populist palliative, spending the future to pay for the present. Like his military predecessors President Sarney became a master of short-termism, *imediatismo* as it is known in Brazil. For this the forests as well as the future of the country suffered, as rapid exploitation rather than sustainability was the favoured mode of development.

Sarney's poor economic management and the debts and distortions his predecessors had bequeathed led, when his attempts at price control collapsed, to explosive inflation, capital flight, strikes and the abandonment of the social and agrarian reforms the government had promised. Trying to please all sides, unduly susceptible to the influence of lobby groups, attempting to maintain control by using the military government's weapon of the presidential decree, Sarney came to the end of his term compromised to the extent of paralysis. To please powerful business groups he had maintained support for the most inequitable and destructive of Brazil's development projects, and had failed to enforce most of the environmental protection policies he had promised. In the last twelve months of his government prices rose by 4,600 per cent.

President Sarney lost control before he had even begun to address the troubles which were the legacy of twenty-one years of military rule. The old confederation of businessmen and politicians had managed to resist his pale efforts to replace the traditional power structure with anything but a nominal democracy. Military leaders still held some of the most important administrative posts, and had achieved perhaps more influence over the planning of the country's future than they had preserved during the last years of formal military rule. Torture continues today as one of the principal means the police use for securing convictions or restraining peasant activists.

There has been no amelioration of debt, unemployment, violence or the concentration of wealth. Educational standards, deliberately reduced by the armed forces, remain abysmal. Though literacy is improving, 18.5 per cent of adult Brazilians are still incapable of signing their names, a rate said to be worse than Ethiopia's[15]. Regional elections remain largely internal affairs, with power passing between members of the age-old élite, while much of the electorate, being ill-informed, stands by and does what it is advised. Far from being, as the military government's propaganda suggested, a land of opportunity, Brazil is among the most stratified nations in the world.

In December 1989 the second round of the first free presidential elections since military rule began were fought between Luís Ignacio da Silva, or Lula, the roughcut radical union leader who had been one of the most industrious opponents of the military government, and Fernando Collor de Mello, the rich, suave son of the owner of a television station, who had served the military rulers as a federal congressman. Fernando Collor's expensive campaign, backed by the Globo network and other organs of the once official press, helped him to a narrow victory.

President Collor, when he took power in March 1990, launched an ambitious austerity programme, which now seems regrettably to have foundered. In the first hundred days of Collor's term, the new government's popularity rating fell from 71 per cent to 36 per cent. Inflation, having been markedly reduced, is again climbing; the president's privatization programme has run into trouble; and attempts to reduce the deficit and the number of public sector employees are both taking far longer than planned. Brazil's economic troubles appear destined to persist.

President Collor truly seems to have good intentions towards the rainforests; but his own system disarms him. While his government continues to represent the interests of the old confederation which has for so long governed Brazil, he cannot be an effective defender of the Amazon. As development still favours the developers and not those being developed, as the armed forces and powerful lobby groups retain their influence in government, there is little that can be done to address the causes of deforestation. There is no better environmental preservative than democracy.

While, like its political distortions, Brazil's economic inequalities were exacerbated by military rule, the system from which these spring is as old as the European colonization of Latin America. The writer Eduardo Galeano has suggested that Latin America is so poor because it was once so rich[16]. As the continent was abundant in precious metals and stones, forest products and new crops, the pioneers there dedicated themselves to draining it. In North America by contrast wealth needed to be built. There the settlers worked on making the land itself rich, rather than on increasing the wealth of the people supervising its exploitation. In this way they laid a solid foundation, on which an economy could grow without, initially at least, consuming itself.

Latin America's history is, since the Conquista, the story of exploiters and exploited. When the tribal people of the Amazon that the colonists made use of died out, the caboclos and a new underclass of Portuguese Brazilian peasants took their place. When these proved insufficient, no social reorganization was required to admit imported slaves. It was in the days of the conquistadores that the great divisions between rich and poor were first established. They have persisted to the extent that 29 per cent of workers now earn less than the minimum salary, while some Brazilian businessmen are among the highest earners in the world.

It is this pattern of colonization and exploitation from which the Amazon still suffers. Amazonia is now used by the south of Brazil much as Brazil was once used by Portugal. It is in many respects an internal colony, from which wealth is drained by the rich and to which the undesirables of the nation – the poor whose problems must be swept out of sight if they are not to upset the established order – are sent. The Amazon's future is not a choice between development and deprivation; by contrast the developments in the Amazon have deprived Brazilians of their livelihoods.

It is easy and comforting to label individuals in the Brazilian government corrupt, and to ascribe its problems to their failings. But in truth the country's troubles seem to be not the abuse of its system, but the system itself. There is in fact little of what we in the North would immediately recognise as high-level corruption. Money is seldom exchanged for favours within the top echelons, as there is no need: the caucus of politicians, soldiers and businessmen governing Brazil support each other through legislation, public expenditure and political campaigning. If the traditional institutions of Brazilian government were working more efficiently the problems of the nation would be exacerbated, not mitigated; indeed it is its inconsistencies which are among the political model's few saving graces.

While it is evident that Latin America's peculiar and distorted version of capitalism is inimical to equitable development and environmental conservation there, some observers believe that the orthodox capitalism advocated by nations such as the United States and Britain may also be inappropriate for developing countries like Brazil. The wealth and power of Britain and North America were established under conditions which cannot be repeated. These nations were lucky enough to be entering their important development phases when there was access to cheap fuel, colonies and imported slaves, and they could resort to widespread protectionism to establish their domestic industries. None of these options is available to the nations trying to develop today. Yet the economic theories we in the North encourage and in many cases oblige these countries to apply are products of those special conditions in which we developed. Adam Smith told a conquering nation how, in the eighteenth and nineteenth centuries, it could enhance its global prosperity. He has less to say to the people of modern Brazil.

Our impositions of such developments as the International Monetary Fund's economic reforms and Green Revolutionary farming techniques have shown in many cases that what might have worked for us may not work for nations whose circumstances are different. If development does not emerge from the needs of undeveloped people, but instead springs from the theories of the developers, it is likely to administer only misery.

Northern nations have made the mistake of equating success in the developing world with raw economic growth. As the growing inequality, repression and misery of the years in which Brazil achieved a growth rate of 11 per cent show, growth may be of benefit only to the few. Unless development in Third World nations is based to some extent upon bringing the bottom levels closer to the top, it will necessarily be unsustainable. That we should regard rapid growth as necessarily right, and comparative stasis as wrong, seems to show a lack of concern for the future both of the global environment and of the people who are to inhabit it. The communities which have survived in the Amazon – of Indians, caboclos or canny colonists – are those which have achieved a degree of stasis in their lives and in the way in which they use the forest. It is their concern for the resources of the future which we in the North have sometimes had the gall to call stagnation.

The distortions of the Brazilian system allow the government to resist attempts to call it to account. Civil servants have several strategies for avoiding responsibility for unravelling the chaos they cause. The commonest is to blame somebody else, even another member of the same department. Another resort is to suggest that the department is incompetent: it would like to amend the situation, but is too disorganized or impoverished to do so. There often seems to be ample evidence to support such claims, but they become less credible when the officials are called upon to implement a policy their superiors truly wish to effect. A further strategy is to announce, with a thunderclap of publicity, an important programme of reform, taking the initiative from the critics; then to work inchmeal to undo it, in such a way that no single retraction attracts the attention of the press. This was what happened, for instance, to the last government's environmental legislation package, called 'Our Nature'.

During President Sarney's term a favourite trick was to call upon the patriotism of the people whenever the government received either internal or foreign criticisms. The critics, he claimed, were part of an international conspiracy to destabilize Brazil and take control of its resources, being run by the comunistas or the americano gringos as convenience dictated. In truth, any economic drainage or political deformation for which foreigners are responsible in Brazil is effected with the collusion of the administration. All of these strategies enable Brazil's traditional leaders – landlords, businessmen or generals – to avoid the reforms Brazil and its rainforests need.

It may then seem strange that the Brazilians continue to vote their oppressors back into power. The electorate has so far had few unimpeded opportunities to choose its leaders; but on these rare occasions most of the mayors, congressmen, senators and governors the people have voted into office have been members of the privileged minority responsible for their misery. There is in fact nothing unusual about this. In Brazil as in Romania and Bulgaria – where the people freed themselves from communism only to vote it back in – an infrastructure of thought has been laid down by the administration which helps to ensure compliance with the will of the minority. The great irony attending attempts to dislodge a demagogy is that the more repressive it has been, the harder it is for people to abandon their belief in it. Release a long-caged bird and it returns to its cage.

To institutionalize a population's way of thinking there need be no conspiracy, no thought-control. It simply has to be taught to be indifferent. People around the world tend to do as they are told. They are told on the whole not by goose-stepping lunatics, but by slick men and women with money to spend on advertising. To follow unthinkingly the seductive path lit by those who can afford to broadcast their messages is tempting even to the people of Western Europe. In Brazil institutionalized passivity is well established. Into the first half of this century the peasants working on a landowner's estates were loyal subjects. He would provide their clothes, their medicine, perhaps their housing; he would be godfather to their children; and in return and as there was no choice they would devote their lives to his service. It bred in Brazil a culture of acceptance: people accepted their social position unquestioningly, were it of master or of slave. Even now, though in many places people work hard to defend their rights, there are parts of the countryside in which it is hard for a peasant to accept that he could be anything but a peasant.

Once a traditional Brazilian politician is voted into a position of trust he can then use the placement to divert the funds of the state and its petitioners into his hands. One of the ironies of Brazilian political campaigns is that the successful candidates are often those who use the money they have stolen from the population to persuade the population to vote for them. The mark of a good confidence trickster is that his victims are grateful for the services – be they free meals or transport to the polling booth – which he seems to have rendered.

But it is above all through education that the problem becomes systemic. The military government is said to have deliberately reduced the educational standards in Brazil, and it is perhaps this which is the poison hardest to purge. Not only are the teachers of the new generations those who were ill educated by the old; but the whole educational establishment is sick to the point of paralysis. In Maranhão I met teachers being paid four dollars a month for their work, as bureaucrats at every level were pocketing money the federal government had provided. As a result the teachers were forced to spend more of their time growing crops than working in the classroom. Many of them had received no training, moving into school having just come out of school.

The military government knew, as dictatorships elsewhere have discovered, that power is other people's ignorance. In both schools and universities there are still informal networks of agents, passing facts about their colleagues to the National Information Service and its successor. Creativity and excellence were objects of suspicion when the armed forces were in power. As 43 per cent of adults in Brazil have never finished primary school, 43 per cent are likely to vote back the people responsible for that miserable state of affairs, as they know no better. Democracy is meaningless in the absence of education.

Education of course is the key to a successful and careful society. Without it there is little hope of the growth with social equality and environmental preservation which may be the only means of sustaining a developing economy. By denying the people access to knowledge and understanding, successive governments have unintentionally rendered them incapable of pulling Brazil out of the mess in which it flounders. Having hobbled the goose so that it cannot get away, they can do nothing to stop it being caught by the fox.

In some respects the North has itself to blame for the worrying situation in the Amazon. The United States assisted the coup bringing the military leaders to power, and subsequently contributed, in the face of popular opposition in Brazil, to the survival of the governments most responsible for the destruction of the forests. The hawks have come home to roost.

One of the most persistent problems throughout Latin America, which rebounds onto its environment as well as its people, is United States support for governments which are neither representative nor progressive. Throughout this century North American administrations have shown that they are prepared to assist their political allies whatever the cost to the continent's people or states. Though its beliefs about how nations should develop may be of no relevance to the situation in Latin America, the United States has isolated and even eliminated those governments which do not share them. Were a government to be elected in Brazil which was truly committed to agrarian reform and a better distribution of wealth, it would not, in view of recent Latin American history, be surprising if the United States were to pull it down. Such an administration would be unlikely to grant the United States the extravagant terms of the trade it now enjoys with most of Latin America.

In May 1990 President Bush told a meeting of business leaders in Washington that Cuba was the only nation in Central or South America in which people were not living under a freely elected government. His acceptance of the purely nominal democratic situations of El Salvador, Guatemala and Paraguay, where the repression is worse than that of Cuba, is unremarkable to those who have studied United States policy in the region. It is partly because of the interference of the United States, backed by the other developed nations of the North, that the reforms the Latin American countries and their rainforests need most are never allowed to begin.

What the American government enforces politically, the World Bank and International Monetary Fund achieve economically. Their single economic doctrine seems to be applied as rigidly as was the economic model in communist Eastern Europe, often with equally disastrous effects. Their reform packages have served to add to the strength of the plutocracies of many nations, while exacerbating the poverty of the poorest. In some countries IMF strategies have been among the most pervasive causes of deforestation. Yet if Third World states do not accept IMF or World Bank programmes, they may find themselves subject to an informal embargo on foreign investment or a formal refusal to renegotiate their debts. President Bush has recently made it clear that debt reduction in Latin American nations will depend on their acceptance of IMF and World Bank terms.

Debt is itself one of Brazil's most serious constraints on reform and sustainable development. The government can meet its interest payments only by depleting the resources of the nation. The recessions the debt repayments have contributed to have helped to drive Brazilians into the forests; and the government has been unable to devote sufficient money to nature conservation. The size of the debt has tempted Brazilian planners to look for solutions of a similar scale. One of the incentives to invest in fabulously destructive schemes such as the Carajás programme and the hydroelectricity plan is a mistaken belief that such big projects will rapidly generate the big money the government needs.

Worldwide it is inconceivable that Third World countries could meet their debts as the North demands[17]. In 1988 the Third World delivered $51 billion more to the First World in debt payments than it received in foreign aid. UNICEF figures show that in the same year the deaths of at least 500,000 children were caused by cuts in healthcare forced by attempts to pay back international loans. The Sarney government alone paid out $56 billion in interest on Brazil's $115 billion debt, without reducing the capital owed by one cent.

Yet the validity of these loans, especially in the case of Brazil, is dubious. It has been estimated that a serious audit would show that around two-thirds of Brazil's debt is illegitimate. The Brazilian Bar Association goes further, in claiming that all the original loan contracts were unconstitutional, as the military government which agreed them did not submit them to Congress for approval. Borrowing was a largely private affair, arranged between members of the government and unscrupulous foreign banks, in many cases to sponsor programmes of no benefit to any but the privileged minority. Many of the loans were disbursed for projects which a good banker would have dismissed as insane, such as the construction of the Balbina dam.

Yet these appalling investment decisions are still being visited upon the people and environment of Brazil, with little hope of remission. The injustice is compounded by, for instance, the fact that banks in Great Britain have already made provisions against debts they do not believe they will be able to reclaim, and will receive as a result more money in tax relief on their 1989 accounts – £1.5 billion – than Britain gives in international aid. But even this debt, which the British taxpayer will pay the banks so handsomely to set aside, will still be held against the Third World nations which incurred it.

The United States has agreed, subject to compliance with IMF reforms, to write off a proportion of the $7 billion Latin America owes the American administration. This has been welcomed, but is of course a trifling proportion of the $420 billion the region owes. It seems unlikely that much more of the debt, crippling, unjust and destructive as it is, will be forgiven. In the United States at least it is politically inviable to be seen to give too much to foreigners. The 'debt for nature' swaps which some people in the North are proposing regrettably seem unlikely either to make a substantial impact on the debt, or, as they stand, to be viable means of protecting the forest.

Our attempts to defend the environment in Brazil are also seriously compromised by the fact that we in the North set such a bad example. Not only does our hypocrisy about environmental protection reduce our credibility in the eyes of the Brazilians; but it also suggests that if we, with our vocal pressure groups, our learning and our development, cannot look after our habitat, there is little chance that Brazil can reform its own behaviour. This demoralizes the Brazilians trying to defend the Amazon and encourages the Brazilians hoping to continue destroying it.

Soon after the last British Prime Minister called for a massive international effort to avert global warming, she announced that Britain itself was to do nothing to reduce its emissions of greenhouse gases, and would seek instead only to stabilize their output. President Bush performed a similar feat of contortionism when, having exhorted developing nations to look after the world, he announced that the United States would refuse to countenance any permanent limit to its own gas emissions, on the mistaken grounds that this would restrict economic growth. Governments in the North have done almost nothing to address the major problems their countries inflict upon the environment. They have chosen instead to convince their electorates of their concern with such minor and inexpensive measures as reducing the cost of lead-free petrol.

Though we find it easy to criticize Brazil for short-termism – imediatismo – we are in fact guilty of precisely the same mismanagement. The question of why, when everyone in Brazil knows that ranching is of no use to the people, the environment or the economy, it is allowed to continue, is the same as the question of why, when everyone in Britain knows that public transport is good for the people, the environment and the economy, it is allowed to disintegrate. The answer too is in both cases the same: it is a matter of using the resources of the future to stoke the boiler of the present, and of changing the physical and mental infrastructure of the nation to favour the incumbent government.

When the administration of the United States, which is responsible for one fifth of the world's greenhouse gas production, announces that it will do nothing to limit this pollution, and proposes instead such adaptive measures as building seawalls – which of course Third World nations cannot afford – and tying bags to the ends of cows to catch the methane they produce, it demonstrates that it has no interest whatsoever in the long-term survival of the planet, and every interest in its immediate re-election.

Our hypocrisy is compounded by the freedom with which we allow our corporations to operate abroad. Were oil companies to behave in the North with one tenth of the disregard for the environment they demonstrate in Ecuador, it would cause a scandal of unprecedented proportions. Yet Lynda Chalker, the British Minister for Overseas Development, had the gall to suggest at a recent conference in London that if the British government knew about such things it would stop them. If the information is freely available to the public, I cannot see how it can fail to be accessible to the government, which retains shares in some of the oil companies operating there.

I have had to concentrate on the negative aspects of the Brazilian system, as it is these which are responsible for much of the Amazon's deforestation. But beyond the government and the bureaucracy, Brazil can be an engaging and uplifting place. It was the Brazilians who showed me that the disease we suffer most acutely in Britain and possibly other Northern nations is self-consciousness. It is this trait, so easy to see from abroad, so difficult to recognize at home, which denies us the ease with which friendships are struck among strangers in Brazil, and gives rise to the vanity and isolation which drive us to scorn the people we do not know.

In Brazil, by contrast, people live at peace with human imperfection. There is a reluctance to punish or to expose the faults of others. This tolerance serves both to detract from and to add to some of the miseries of the nation. People may tolerate the injustices others suffer just as they might accept their own bad fortune.

There are, however, some excellent and busy pressure groups and associations of peasants, urban workers, and forest people working for change, and it is their activities, if any, which might still be able to halt the destruction in the Amazon. Among the most important provisions of the new Constitution were those guaranteeing the independence of public prosecution. Conservation groups have been making use of this, suing companies or administrators failing to discharge their environmental obligations. In the south-east of Brazil, though not in Amazonia, there is an ecology movement just as visible as those in developed nations, with campaign material on the sides of buses, on shopfronts, even in bars. But most of the concerns of the environmentalists there are, understandably, regional. It is common to meet middle-class Brazilians who have toured Europe and the United States but have never visited the Amazon, and the events there may appear just as remote from Rio as they do from Britain. Concerns about the nearby Atlantic forest or the pollution by heavy industries in the south and south-east tend to overshadow fears for the future of the Amazon. The movement is most vigorous too amongst a prosperous and well-educated minority. For most people the insecurity of life – the troubles of inflation, unemployment, homelessness and urban violence – is of more concern than the calamity which may or may not fall upon Brazil when in a few decades the Amazon has gone.

What Brazil lacks in justice and prosperity seems to me to be partially compensated by what it possesses in terms of humanity. Even in the most miserable slums there is a kindness, a tendency towards self-sacrifice, which in Europe was once considered to be an aspect of nobility. It is a nation both selfish and selfless. People may climb from the mires of absolute poverty by treading on the heads of their fellows; but it is also notable that it is the poor who truly help the poor. In tourist areas it is the Brazilians who give to the beggars.

Brazil is a bad place to work in and a good place to relax in, and it is indeed true that much of the great energy of the Brazilians is expended on pleasure. It is a place in which a frustratingly obstructive system is staffed by people who are often open and helpful. Sometimes to one's delight, sometimes to one's annoyance, the nation is free from the ethic of customer service. One can wait a long time for attention in a cafe or a shop and when it comes it may be graceless; but it arrives without the false smiles and technical courtesies taught on training courses in the North. Allied to this is a refreshing lack of subtlety on the part of public figures. Corruption and the abuse of power, while not necessarily much more pervasive than in the northern hemisphere, are much easier to detect.

Brazil is a place in which things will be done, but done, in all likelihood, raggedly. If the exhaust falls off a car it will be reattached with a piece of string. If the string breaks, wire will be used. Cars will not, if they break down, be abandoned on the roadside, as they may be in Africa; but in repairing them their drivers are unlikely to trace the problem to its source. There is a term for this idiosyncrasy, of which the Brazilians themselves are well aware. When faced with a problem you *da um jeito,* or give it a throw. It is this which is both the hope and the despair of the defenders of the Amazon.

11

Solutions to the crises of the Amazon are necessarily solutions to the crises of its people. The biggest ecosystem on the earth's surface cannot be protected unless the people living within its borders are kept alive by sustainable means. The notion of the absolute preservation of the Amazon, as if it were a gigantic nature reserve, is evidently absurd. There are sixteen million people in the Brazilian part of the Basin; it covers altogether an area three times the size of Western Europe; and there are some ways in which the forests can be used by the Amazon nations without suffering serious damage. Not only must our concern for humanity not be overridden by our concern for nature; but the two interests are in many senses one. Turning the Amazon's destroyers into the Amazon's conservationists, hard as it is, is easier than turning the inhabited Amazon back into a wilderness.

Clearly in order to align the sustenance of the Amazonians with the conservation of their resources, their livelihoods must no longer be dependent on such lunatic developments – ultimately bad for them as well as for the environment – as uncontrolled timber logging, ranching or freelance mining. It is also clear that planning in the Amazon must turn away from the grand ideas generated by governments to small ideas generated by the people being developed, who have the best understanding of their own needs and the most immediate interest in making the changes work.

This is not to say that all big projects are by nature destructive: a well-planned hydroelectric dam can be more sustainable and less damaging than the million home fires it replaces; a big mine, confined to its borders, can be less disruptive than uncontrolled digging by garimpeiros. But each of these big projects has a small part to play in the benign use of the Amazon, as does every reasonable development. The solution to the Amazon's destruction is many solutions; to each of the Basin's different demands there must be a different response.

The simplest and most popular response to the Amazon's troubles in the last few years has been the suggestion that its own resources should be used to ensure its preservation. The idea that the harvesting of forest products, such as rubber, brazilnuts, new fruits, resins and medicines, could become the profitable alternative to destruction is appealingly tidy: the forest provides its own economic justification. But it now seems that we might be making the same mistake about the Amazon's potential to support the collectors of its natural bounty as our forebears once made about its potential for agriculture. The harvesting of forest products will sustain some livelihoods, and will help to conserve some forest; but as a means of saving much of the Amazon or employing a high proportion of its inhabitants it is unserviceable.

While international enthusiasm about the Amazon's potential to provide for itself continues to build up, the harvest of wild forest products is in fact declining. Most of the extracts – resins, oils, fruits and nuts – that the forest once supplied to the world have been replaced, either by synthetic substitutes or by plantations in other tropical countries. The small proportion of the rubber, chewing-gum, essential oil, cord and other products still extracted from the forest is more expensive to produce and of a less consistent quality than the mass-produced majority. There is an excellent chance that the forest will provide us with some of the medicines and new industrial products we seek, and a low probability that any of the benefits of these discoveries will be returned to the forest.

The world's optimism about the forest's capacity to pay for its own conservation began with the triumphs of the rubber-tappers' movement. In 1985, while peacefully confronting organized violence as intense as that of Maranhão, the men and women extracting rubber from the trees of the western Amazon won the right to protect their forests from the developers. At the eventual cost of the murders of several of their leaders, Chico Mendes among them, the rubber-tappers persuaded the government to rule that the ranchers be kept from their territories for ever, by declaring the land to lie within extractive reserves, in which only the tappers could work. Some of those who have applauded their successes would be surprised to learn that the rubber-tappers are not, as they have often been portrayed, conservationists defending the forests for the good of the world, but peasant trades unionists, trying to secure their constitutional rights. It is this which makes their movement a significant one in Amazonia.

But despite their courage and their resultant victories, the lives of the rubber-tappers are no example for other Amazon peasants to follow. In a survey of one of the fifteen extractive reserves so far ratified by the government, each family of rubber-tappers was found to make less than $900 a year[1], despite being entitled to take rubber from between 300 and 500 hectares of forest. Much of this money comes from government subsidies; but as the people the subsidies were designed to support – the rich rubber barons who in some places still enslave the tappers – are declining in number, the government money is likely soon to stop. Because rubber is being mass-produced both in chemicals factories and in plantations in other parts of the world, Brazil can import it for one third of the price that it costs to extract from the Amazon. The nation which once supplied the world with rubber now produces only one half of what it needs for itself.

The rubber-tappers are still under pressure from ranchers, colonists and loggers, because of the large amount of land each family needs to survive. In the east of the Amazon the Jarí Company, administering the disastrous paperpulp plantations started by the American shipping billionaire, is said to have been forcing the nearby rubber-tappers to sell their land, by cutting down their rubber and brazilnut trees. The battles between landlords and tappers are still being fought, and political pressure in the west is such that Chico Mendes' successors remain poorly defended from the ranchers attempting to eliminate them.

The forest in which the rubber-tappers live is by no means intact. Each family makes a small clearing in which to grow staple crops, and where they have particular economic difficulties these clearings have been extended to produce crops the people can sell, destructive as these are. In one extractive reserve in the state of Acre, 15 per cent of the forest is said to have been spoilt in this way[2]. The remaining trees still recycle water and store carbon; but the diversity of animals is lower than that of forest from which the rubber-tappers are absent.

But though rubber-tapping is not the Amazon's salvation, the social movements it has given rise to are of great importance. The tappers are peasants who have taken control of their own destinies, and done what is within their power to sustain their fragile livelihoods. And this by necessity has involved the conservation of many of their resources. As they are now responsible for their own development, they are likely to survive economically where many of the settlers still doing as the government has suggested will fail. With the help of the schools, the rubber and brazilnut factories and the research into new forest products they are commissioning, they should be able to withstand the ranchers and the markets which seem to be ever on the point of ruining them.

But the enthusiasm of conservationists for harvesting from the forest is not confined to securing the livelihood of the rubber-tappers. While 70,000 people in the Brazilian Amazon are registered as professional rubber, nut and essence collectors, and they occupy perhaps 4 to 7 per cent of the forest area, some environmentalists would like to encourage many more of the Amazon's inhabitants to turn from farming to forest harvesting, becoming 'treekeepers', as I feel the forest product collectors should be called. It seems to me that in some cases it might be more viable to do the opposite.

Much of the environmentalists' enthusiasm came from a report published by some American scientists in 1989[3]. It described their study of the economic potential of part of the Peruvian Amazon. They calculated that if all the fruits, nuts, oils and resins there were extracted by treekeepers, they could earn over $400 from each hectare of forest each year, rendering the forest itself far more valuable than the wood it could produce or the farmland it could give way to.

There are regrettably many reasons why their figures bear little relation to reality. They presumed that treekeepers working in the forest could viably collect as many products as were to be found. In truth the separate harvesting, storage and marketing of more than one or two forest crops at a time is impossible for most of the peasant families in the Amazon[4]. Their calculations also assumed that the demand for what the forests can provide is infinite, while in reality it is already met or exceeded by the existing supply. If any more of most products were collected the surplus would remain unsold or the price would drop, and the treekeepers would be no more prosperous than before. Most parts of the Amazon, moreover, are too far from the towns for their forest extracts to survive the journey to the market. When I asked the scientist Anthony Anderson, one of the foremost thinkers on treekeeping in the Amazon, how much of the Basin could viably be used for commercial forest harvesting, he told me 'possibly less than is used today'.

There are several known and doubtless many unknown commodities in the Amazon which could be of great use to the world; but how their exploitation could benefit the forests, or even the Amazon nations, is hard to see. As soon as an international market develops for any forest product, businessmen around the world start looking for ways either to substitute it synthetically or to grow it in plantations. Because the places in which plants grow in the wild are also the places in which their special diseases are found, these are, paradoxically, the least suitable areas for growing those species in plantations. Rubber cannot be cultivated in the Amazon because of the leaf fungus which has evolved there to attack it; when many trees are planted close together the spores of the fungus build up in the air until every plant is infected. As rubber is not native to Malaysia, no special diseases have evolved to destroy it there, which is why Brazilian rubber in Malaysia has outmatched Brazilian rubber in Brazil. People promoting new forest products from the Amazon may find that they are doing nothing but developing markets for other countries to exploit.

There may, however, be some potential for forest products as new crops for Amazonian smallholders to grow. If only a few trees of each species are cultivated together their diseases can be controlled, and the more diverse are the crops a peasant depends on for subsistence, the less likely the loss of his entire harvest becomes. The plants of the Amazon have evolved to cope with its peculiar soils and water regime, so they could readily replace, in small quantities, the temperate crops which have proved so unsuitable. The *pupunha* palm, for instance, producing oil, animal feed and a sustainable source of starch and protein, could become a staple; also the tucumã, which can rapidly reforest degraded land and produce proteinous fruits; the urucūm bush – from which we get annatto colouring, but whose seed could also become an excellent substitute for rice or wheat – thrives on atrocious soils; the chicken nut can be easily harvested as it grows on long strings; and newly discovered manioc varieties grow faster and yield better than those the colonists now use[5].

There are possibly hundreds of species of marketable fruits and nuts peculiar to the Amazon – some of which are just beginning to find an external market – and some interesting varieties of fruits we already know of, such as pineapples weighing fifteen kilograms. *Timbo*, the fish poison some Indians use, could become a degradable pesticide of little danger to humans; trees are being tested for new resins, paint substrates, industrial gums and edible oils. But if markets for these products do develop they are, again, likely to be of little benefit to Amazonians. Perhaps the best hope for treekeepers, like the rubber-tappers, is to keep finding and developing new forest products, constantly replacing those which are taken from them by plantations or laboratories. They will doubtless discover, as many pioneers have done before them, that there are greater rewards for the scavengers than there are for the hunters.

For small groups of treekeepers the money such organizations as Cultural Survival in the United States and the British company Bodyshop raise by marketing their products abroad will be indispensable; but the export of treekeepers' produce may not be the large-scale development solution its advocates have suggested. The international market, especially one which depends upon the consumer's interest in the environment, is fickle. People prepared to pay high prices for environmentally sound brazilnuts while ecology is in the headlines may rapidly return to cheaper brazilnuts when they are allowed to forget what is happening to the planet. If treekeepers become dependent on the market's expansion they may be destroyed by its contraction.

Nevertheless, Cultural Survival's sale of fruit and nuts produced by some groups of rubber-tappers and Indians has both raised the awareness of the consumers in the United States and financed the installation of a brazilnut processing factory which is helping to support the rubber-tappers. If the range of exported forest products is wide enough to buffer the collapse of the market for one or two of them, and new species are regularly added to the selection, then these international sales could become an important part of the treekeepers' subsistence. There seems to be some potential for selling in Europe or the United States the oils on which soaps and cosmetics are based, fragrances for perfume manufacture, hair dye, and flours and fibres for wholefoods, extracted from plants in the Amazon[6].

*

Of all unlikely forest products, perhaps the most profitable is *açaí*. Açaí is a dark purple, oily drink, rather like a thick, sweet, non-alcoholic stout, which revolts on the first encounter. With persistence it becomes tolerable, even pleasant, and it appears to be craved by the people of the Amazon estuary, who consume up to two litres a day. In the rivermouth city of Belém there are red tin flags projecting from houses along most of the mean streets and rickety jetties of the waterfront, and in the shade of the açaí stalls they advertise, the fruits of a palmtree – dusty black and the size of sloes or blueberries – are pulped in water. One kilometre across the Rio Guamá is the forest the palmfruit comes from.

Belém, like some of the other towns of the Amazon, is remarkable for its proximity to the forest. A city vulture flying over its refuse heaps can see into the eye of a jungle vulture flying across lands which have never been cleared since the Conquista. Taking a boat from the tottering shacks of the jetties, the knotted telegraph wires strung with the skeletons of kites, the noise of traffic, ice-cream sellers and police sirens, onto the incoming tide, I returned in a sigh's breadth to the natural world of the Amazon. Clusters of flowers slid past in the flotsam; fish swirled or flung themselves clear of the river. Within twenty minutes I was entering a channel between two of the marshy islands of the far bank, where the greatest commotions were the squabbles of the parrots.

I had come, in October 1989, to see a project perhaps unique in Latin America, a combination of ecological research and practical development work, simultaneously assessing the use of the trees and suggesting how it might be improved. The forest, as I could see from the boat, was, in terms of its structure, largely intact, and overhung the stilted houses on the riverbanks. The value of the fruit it produced clearly outweighed any returns from agriculture, in a place flooded by the highest tides.

In the project's field station I met Oscar, one of the islanders, who took me out into the forest to see the trees he had been labelling, to show the researchers which of them were valuable. Oscar's family, like those of the other inhabitants, had lived on the Ilha de Combu for several generations, his forebears being among the caboclos who had supplied much of the world's rubber, resins, cocoa, essential oils and gums, when the Amazon was the repository of such things. Like the others, Oscar knew the trees close to his house just as anyone in Britain or the United States might know the shops and bars of the surrounding streets. He could immediately tell me not only which tree species grew near by, but how many of each there were.

The forest canopy was less dense than that of the jungle I knew from the central plateau, but still kept the ground cool and dark. Most of the biggest trees were of occasional use to the islanders, not commercially, but as reserves of the resins, fruits and medicines they used themselves. Oscar cut into the bark of the *breu branco* tree, and the air was immediately imbued with perfume. He told me that the sap repelled mosquitoes, and when I spread it on one arm and not on the other I found it to be effective. The inner bark of the *araticú* tree he showed me was used as an antidote to snake venom. The sap of the *acaçú* was a deadly poison used for killing fish, while that of the *caxinguara* tree, which looked identical to me, was to be drunk to purge intestinal worms. Amongst the freshwater crabs scuttering through puddles were the fallen fruits of the *taperebá*, sharp and sweet, and under the trees on the river channel was cocoa, whose developing pods broke rudely from the trunks and branches.

But much the most important of the forest trees was the açaí, a slender palmtree with feathery leaves. In the wet soils of the Amazon estuary the açaí grows naturally in great abundance; but close to their houses the islanders had also favoured it, killing some of the other trees which interfered with its growth[7]. But since many of the other species had their own uses, and served to shade the young palms, and, as one woman told me, 'because we make enough money anyway', açaí was not allowed to exclude all others. Further from their homes the forest, though they still gathered from it, remained unmanaged.

I went to collect the fruit with Gilberto, who lived on the other side of the channel. He was a young man of great agility, with ridges on his back and thighs which might have been inexplicable had he not been seen at work. To gather the açaí fruit he made a belt from the tough sheaf of a palm frond, which he held taut between his feet. He knitted his fingers behind the trunk of an açaí palm and leapt up the stem, using the rough surface of the belt as a treefrog might use the suckers on its feet. In this way he was in the canopy, fifteen metres from the ground, in twenty seconds.

There he slit the stalks of the fruit bunches with a knife from the belt of his trousers, and slid down again, one hand full, a moment after he had reached the top. The fruits grew in clusters like the twisted strands of a bead curtain, and on the ground Gilberto rapidly stripped them from their strings into a basket. Where a trunk was too slim to bear his weight, Gilberto slid up an adjoining one, and swung the crown he perched in back and forth until he could reach the neighbouring leaves, whereupon he could pull himself close to the bunches of fruit. By eleven o'clock in the morning – we had started at dawn – the most arduous of his day's work was done. By comparison to the rubber-tappers, or for that matter to many of the workers in the town across the river, the açaí islanders were prosperous, each taking around $2500 a year from 30 or 40 hectares. They had the advantage of being able to gather many of their daily requirements freely, though they had to buy from Belém the staple foods their marshy soils would not bear. They were disadvantaged by their distance from hospitals and secondary schools.

The people on the Ilha de Combu trade little besides açaí, shrimps, cocoa and rubber. Sometimes a basket of fallen fruit is gathered for the market, or fibres are cut from which hats can be woven. There are two fulltime herbalists on the island collecting medicinal bark, leaves and seeds; but on the whole the treekeepers there, like any others, use their time to exploit what is most profitable. If the great abundance of the Amazon is not used to capacity, there are good reasons.

Even so, the research project's American field manager was experimenting with new tree species, or improved varieties of the species they already exploited, to help the people guard against the day when the market for açaí, like the markets for so many forest products before it, collapsed. The boom in demand for wild açaí, which resulted from the growth of the Amazon's urban population, seemed to be leading inevitably to the market's eventual collapse, as businessmen saw that the healthy trade would justify the establishment of plantations, which would be easier to manage and harvest. So John Rombold, who lived on the island, had started a nursery, and was consulting the people on what they considered to be the best alternatives.

On my third day on the Ilha de Combu I borrowed a canoe and paddled down the channel between the islands. Throughout the forest there were birds. White-breasted toucans fed on the palmfruit, parrots and parakeets chattered among the taller trees. Squirrel monkeys were common, little men collecting their own açaí. In the river I saw a four-eyed fish, an animal which swims half in and half out of the water, its eyes partitioned so that it can see both above and below. Oscar had told me that in the forests of the island there were boa constrictors and anacondas, otters, caiman, armadillos, turtles and pacas. There had once been tapirs and jaguars, but hunters from Belém had killed them. All these existed or had existed despite one of the highest human population densities in any part of the Amazon forest. As I returned to Belém in a fruit-collector's launch, I was amazed to see the skyscrapers approaching through the trees.

I returned to the Ilha de Combu during the cocoa season, in February 1990, with my friend Roselis. Rain was now falling steadily, the sky was dusty with it, and we crossed and recrossed the channel in clinging clothes, watching the cocoa being harvested. The cocoa trees are descendants of those the Portuguese planted, two centuries before, though the crop itself is native to Amazonia. The islanders harvest it in the wet season as few of the açaí trees are fruiting then; but at the beginning of 1990 the price was so low that, as John Rombold said, it would have been sensible to feed it to the pigs, as it was cheaper than bran. All the world's cocoa growers had suffered from a glut; but the Amazonian producers had also been struck by the classification of their crop as refuse, suitable only for producing soap. It was certainly of variable quality; but apparently the powerful cocoa producers of the central Brazilian state of Bahía had succeeded in relegating the entire crop, so that they could buy it at soap prices and sell the best of it to produce good chocolate.

Of all the forest products of the Amazon, medicines appear to have the highest unrealized potential. But there is an astonishing contrast between the excitement generated about the medicinal possibilities of forest products and the lack of interest in finding out whether this excitement might be justified. Either pharmaceutical companies are successfully keeping their work secret or, as perhaps seems more likely, they are waiting for non-commercial researchers to do the expensive work of testing. A few Amazonian extracts have, however, begun to find their way onto the markets. The *jaborandi* shrub is used to cure glaucoma, and has already saved thousands from blindness. Regrettably it is now being overharvested by the company which produces the drug. Among other examples is the world's most powerful emetic, which can be grown only under a closed canopy forest; with a friend I have started an agency to handle extracts being produced by Indians in Rondônia. But the great potential of the

Amazon to cure many of the world's ills remains largely unexploited.

The medicinal qualities of plants are due to the means by which they try to defend themselves from animals and diseases. Plants produce chemicals designed to make them inedible, by interfering with the inner workings of the organisms consuming them. What may be fatal or repulsive to one animal might, when used correctly, destroy the diseases affecting another.

While most plants have some defence against predators, in the Amazon they are particularly well armed. Not only is the diversity of pests they have to overcome much greater than elsewhere, but the regularity of the environment means that they can be attacked at all times of the year. The high humidity means that destructive fungi can flourish; and the fact that the trees have to struggle so hard for minerals or light encourages them to defend what they secure with particular vehemence[8]. As a result there are in the leaves of every tree of the mature forest over fifty different defensive compounds, many of which will be unique to a species. It is also because of their defences that tropical trees produce such resistant wood. Its hardness protects them against boring insects and its natural preservatives against rot.

Some scientists have doubted whether the Indians, in the 12,000 years or so they have spent in the Amazon, using only trial and error, could indeed know as much of the medicinal properties of plants as they claim to. They have suggested that many of the different extracts each tribe describes as cures may in fact be placebos. But as information, as well as merchandise, was likely to have been exchanged across the Amazon, and as there were once many millions of Indians living there, it seems to me that the probabilities of such knowledge having accumulated through trial and error and dissemination are good. The many poisons the Indians use for different purposes; the hundreds of manioc varieties they have developed; their ability, with the use of herbal unctions, to make parrots grow feathers of new colours, suggest that a precise understanding of plant medicines would not be anomalous.

There is certainly much circumstantial evidence to suggest that Indian and caboclo medicine works. Researchers collecting reputedly therapeutic plants in the Amazon claim to have used them to cure themselves of many of their own afflictions; when I had suffered from intense stomach pains for two days in Belém I visited one of the city's medicine markets and bought, on a stallkeeper's advice, the seedpod *boldo* and the leaf *juca*. Half an hour after drinking the tea I brewed from these I found that the pains had been, despite my scepticism, relieved; and when they recurred a second dose was sufficient to put an end to them.

The medicine markets in Belém are perhaps the finest in the Amazon. In the stalls at Ver-o-Peso, on the waterfront, there are at any one time over 40 species of medicinal plants, and across the year more than 100[9]. As well as reputed cures for arthritis, bronchitis, kidney disease, dysentery, high blood pressure, gastric ulcers, tumours, epilepsy, eczema, menstrual problems, syphilis and neurosis, there are herbal potions for attracting women or men, for rubbing on a hunter's gun to improve his aim, and for guarding against other people's ill-feelings. There is a leaf which you put in your pocket to avoid getting lost. And the many sloth's heads, snakeskins, skulls of waterbirds, eyeballs of dolphins, seahorses, stingray tails and bottles of tortoise fat, which are sold to cure everything from impotence to bad luck, are a reminder that the extraction of forest products is not always good for the Amazon.

In view of this profusion of reputed cures it is amazing that so little is being done in Brazil to see whether or not they work. In 1989 I could find only three laboratories in the country attempting to find out what was in the plants and whether it was effective. Of this work the most exciting was that being supervised by the great enthusiast Professor Walter Mors in Rio de Janeiro. He had been collecting plants from all over the world, some of them from the Amazon, which were reputed to counteract the effects of snake venom. One, he told me, had been carried by the ancestral Indians all the way from China; and both there and throughout the Americas it is still used by traditional healers for the same purpose. He was trying to find a substitute for serums, which are both difficult to handle and involve the painful poisoning of horses in order to produce antibodies. Walter claimed already to have positive results.

He had neutralized the venom of the South American rattlesnake, and was now working on what he hoped would become a cure for all snakebites, by mixing extracts of the many plants he was testing. He was hoping, simultaneously, to find drugs which could be used in the treatment of other disorders. As snake venoms cause nerve destruction, muscle wasting, heart attacks or internal bleeding, the discovery of antidotes could lead to cures for other causes of these conditions, and a possible revolution in the treatment of hitherto intractable diseases.

Another of Walter's lines of research, even more exciting than the first, is his quest for an anti-viral agent. Virus infections can be prevented by inoculation, but they cannot as yet be cured once they have become established. The drugs we take when we contract a viral disease are to prevent secondary infections by bacteria; I am told that viruses themselves in the human body have so far proved indestructible by medicines, and we must use our own antibodies to fight them. But Walter Mors has taken an extract from an Amazon tree which he has used to kill herpes, swine disease and foot and mouth viruses. A few months after I watched him at work the story broke that his extract could be a cure for AIDS, though his testing has not yet confirmed this.

In view of these great advances his laboratory was making I found it astonishing that he and his team were, when I met them, debilitated by a lack of funds and support. Researchers in his department had to pay their technicians' salaries from their own pockets, after their own wages had been reduced by more than half: they survived with the help of their friends. While they struggled, in the darkness of penury, to make discoveries which could transform the condition of the human race, the corporations and governments of the world merely watched and waited, like vultures, ready to carry off the prizes for their own use when the work was complete.

A similarly scandalous negligence was starving research in the University of Rondônia. There the scientists I visited had been working with the plants the Karitiana Indians use to regulate their reproduction. The Karitiana use leaves which they claim can determine the sex of their children: one they take produces boys, another girls. They have drugs to prevent conception, drugs to encourage conception and drugs to cause spontaneous abortions or permanent sterility. But when I met the researchers at the beginning of 1990, despite their love and enthusiasm for the work, they were closing the laboratory, as their money had been cut short.

Funding for research on medicinal plants now seems to be about to improve, and the developed world can expect to start enjoying the side effects of Amazon plant defences before long. The United States' National Cancer Institute will be testing 1500 plant samples each year for the next five years. But the benefits are unlikely to reach back to the people who first discovered the properties of such plants, the Indians and caboclos of Amazonia. At a recent conference, the UN Food and Agriculture Organization discussed the rights of traditional farmers and indigenous people arising from other people's use of the plants they had developed. While the delegates agreed that traditional farmers should be encouraged to continue to provide benefits to the rest of the world, no specific means were proposed by which they themselves might profit from this service.[10]

The damage such omissions do to the fight to save the forests is evident from what is happening in Madagascar. It was there that the rosy periwinkle was found, the plant now saving thousands of children from death through leukaemia and the example used most commonly by journalists for demonstrating the value of the forests. Yet because not one cent of the considerable financial rewards of this discovery has found its way back to the forests, they are every day becoming less capable of yielding new medicines, as plant species there are becoming extinct as fast as any in the world.

Paradoxically it appears that the product most likely to protect the forests and provide the people there with a sustainable livelihood is timber. Work is just beginning in the Amazon which, by complete contrast to the depredations of the sawmills now plundering the Basin, could show that timber can be taken commercially from the forest without inflicting lasting damage.

Of the sustainable timber projects there the most exciting are the two schemes producing wood for the Ecological Trading Company in Britain. In both Peru and Ecuador the ETC is working with Indian communities to help them protect themselves against the traditional loggers – deforesting their lands for little but a token payment – and to ensure that their forests never degenerate. By dispensing with middlemen and accepting a smaller cut, the ETC is able to pay the Indians around 25 per cent of the eventual price of the wood it sells, while the sawmills, in the case of mahogany, pay less than 0.2 per cent. As Chris Cox of the Ecological Trading Company points out, this means that the Indians need to sell more than one hundred trees to the traditional loggers to make the money his company will pay for one.

The first of the projects, in Peru, is being hampered by the government and Sendero Luminoso guerrillas; but were it allowed to operate in peace it could prove an excellent means of preserving the forest. The trees are cut in long narrow strips, following the contours of the hills around which the Yanesha Indians live. All the trees from each strip are taken, and the buyers are encouraged to accept what is produced, rather than demanding a certain type of wood which, to destructive effect, the cutters would then drive into the forest to find. The logs are pulled away by oxen, which cause no damage either to the soil or to the trees. As the cleared strips are bordered on each side by forest and neither fire nor cultivation is allowed to follow the cutting, they are rapidly recolonized by trees. In each of forty years a different strip is cut, and at the end of that period the loggers can return to the first strip, which should by then have become indistinguishable from the rest of the forest. A machine which forces preservative into the logs unsuitable for sawing allows poles and posts to add to the value of the harvest.

The Ecuadorean project ranges over a much greater forest area and involves a remarkable new mobile sawmill. This can be broken down into components to be dragged by horses and, using none but the existing forest tracks and waterchannels, can be brought to the valuable trees selected for cutting. In this way, after careful felling, the tree can be sawn on the spot, and the planks dragged out by the horses, causing none of the damage associated with the tractors hauling away whole trunks. The small gaps left by the single trees being cut are no more disruptive than the holes left in the canopy when a tree falls naturally.

In both cases the projects have been discussed at every stage with the Indian communities, and it was the Chachi Indians of Ecuador who approached the ETC, rather than the other way round[11]. Part of the money returned to the Indians will be used by the communities themselves to build schools and provide healthcare, helping them to achieve the political and economic self-sufficiency necessary if they are to defend themselves against their many threats. Both projects could save the Indian groups from their impending economic disasters.

In such cases it is clear that the timber industry can help to save the forests. This is because it is the people who own and inhabit them who are responsible for their management. The arguments of the people who oppose a boycott of tropical timber – that higher timber prices will encourage people to look after their forests – are invalid if those valuing the forests as a lasting resource are being disregarded by those profiting from their immediate destruction. As the welfare of the sawmills, unlike that of the forest people, does not depend on the continued existence of a particular part of the forest, high prices encourage them to range freely in search of valuable timber.

While the great majority of companies using Amazonian timber in Britain and the United States are either unaware of how that timber is produced or are lying to their customers, there are some making active efforts to see that the extraction of the wood they use does not damage the forest. One of the Ecological Trading Company's customers, the British furniture maker Lucinda Leech, has written that she would 'much rather pay higher prices now for quality timber, if that helps to encourage responsible producers and secure my supplies for the future'. A poll has demonstrated a similar preparedness to pay more among consumers; it is just that most of the big manufacturers in Britain have failed so far to respond to this concern with anything other than public relations campaigns.

In Brazil two potentially sustainable timber projects are materializing, an enterprise in Acre being funded by the International Tropical Timber Organization and the Brazilian government, and a largely experimental scheme in the Tapajós forest in the central Amazon. In both cases the extraction techniques have been carefully planned, but there is a possible danger that the people living in or near these chosen forests may not be sufficiently involved. If local people become simply the employees of a project, rather than its decisive participants, they are less likely to be interested in the preservation of its resources.

While these schemes might be of benefit to the forest, those proposed by some Brazilian and multinational sawmills are likely to be neither sustainable nor restorative. The companies claiming to replace the trees they take are generally either confining their replanting to plantations, while continuing to cut throughout the primary forest, or growing mahogany seedlings in the forest gaps they have left. Not only is neither of these plans likely to be viable – as plantations in the Amazon suffer from disease and soil constraints, and gaps in the forest canopy are likely to close before mahogany seedlings can mature – but neither of them does anything to make good the damage inflicted in the process of extraction.

There is little point in trying to restore much of the forest being cut today, as it is likely to grow back without the help of man. The forest itself, by contrast to the delicate relationships between some of the animals and plants living there, is more robust than was once imagined. The shoots sprouting from the cut stumps of trees and the seeds left in the soil mean that if it is cleared only once it will quickly regenerate, returning to its original size after perhaps 200 years. Many of the original tree species will not exist in such a forest, and it will be able to support a much smaller diversity of animals; but it is likely to store carbon and recycle water as efficiently as the virgin jungle.

But if the land is repeatedly cleared, the shoots burnt and the seeds in the soil poisoned, then it will be almost impossible for forest to return without help. This situation is becoming increasingly common, as cattle-ranchers keep their pastures open for longer, trying to extract some money from them before they become permanently barren. It is here that treeplanting can be of benefit both locally and globally. And the restoration of such degraded land has been shown to be much easier than scientists had previously imagined.

It had long been assumed that trees which had adapted to the shade and humidity of the primary forest could never be cultivated in the harsh and arid scrublands of degraded ranches. But Chris Uhl and his research team – the people also assessing the damage caused by the timber industry – have found that even the valuable species of the densest forest, such as brazilnut and mahogany trees, grow swiftly in the ranchlands. The reason they fail to do so without human help is that the seeds of such trees do not reach the pasture.

Like those of candidates for the American presidency, the qualities seeds need to reach degraded lands are just the opposite to those required once they get there. It is only the smallest seeds, which can float on the wind or be digested and defecated by birds, which are likely to find their way to the pastures, and these are either eaten immediately by ants or mice or smothered by the coarse grass left behind when cattle can no longer be grazed. Only seeds with a coat hard enough to resist being eaten and an energy store big enough to produce shoots and roots which can break through the mats of grass are likely to survive, and these are too big and heavy to reach the land without assistance[12].

So Chris Uhl and his team have been testing the heavier seeds, with astonishing results. When I stayed on the ranch in Paragominas where they were working, I walked with Chris across a blasted land of sharpgrass, bare soil and thorny weeds. In the middle of this desolation were rows of seedlings he had planted as little more than sprouts just eight months before. Some of them, mahogany included, were now nearly two metres tall.

All the seedlings required was a hole made with a stake, a little weeding and, for those which might have been burnt by the sun, the shade of a palmleaf. Some had been provided with manure, though this seemed to be dispensable. Chris suggested that the scattering of large seeds around the pasture, without planting, might also be reasonably effective, or horses and cows could be induced to swallow them and left to wander around in the fields, scattering seeds prepackaged in the fertilizer which could help them to establish. It was not necessary to plant the entire pasture in order to restore the forest. Small clumps of trees, especially as they attracted the birds which might bring in seeds which could establish among trees but not among grasses, would rapidly spread, fusing together in time to form a continuous forest.

Trees grow well in pastures, despite the impoverished soils there, because all their resources are initially devoted to establishment, unlike crop plants which are designed for production. As their roots burrow far into the soil, they can find the nutrients washed by the rain beyond the reach of other plants.

As growing trees, unlike the mature forest, absorb atmospheric carbon dioxide, turning it into the carbon which builds their trunks and leaves, reforestation in the tropics could be the cheapest and most effective means of counteracting greenhouse warming. If 400 million hectares of degraded lands in the tropics were reforested today, the developing trees would absorb all of the carbon dioxide the world is likely to release in the next few decades[13]. The cost of this restoration has been calculated at approximately $16 billion each year for ten years, making reforestation, though apparently expensive, many times cheaper than the likely damage caused by global warming. The cost could be considerably lower if Chris Uhl's suggestion of planting forest islands and letting them fuse were adopted. It would then be likely to fall within the range of the annual expense of the United States space programme, with the advantage of addressing the ills of this planet, rather than trying to introduce them to others. As the principal exponent of the reforestation idea has pointed out, if international resources were devoted to replanting on this scale, the trend of forest use around the world would change completely.

*

Clearly forestry of this type would be an excellent source of employment for the people of regions like Amazonia. But failing the imagination and farsightedness required of world leaders to implement it, other means of supporting the people now living there desperately need to be found, if the Amazonians are not to destroy the remainder of the rainforest. It has been argued that the priority of Amazon research must be to work on settling and employing the colonists, rather than finding means of supporting the existing treekeepers, excellent as that objective is. For if the colonists are not stabilized, and continue to be driven, by crop failures, ranchers and unemployment, from one part of the Amazon to another, then they will destroy any efforts to preserve the forest by other means.

Either the colonists must be encouraged to leave the land for the Amazon's cities, which would cause even greater urban disruption than already exists, and draw in people from outside Amazonia, or they must be introduced to agricultural techniques likely to sustain both themselves and the places they work in.

The options for effective agriculture in Amazonia are limited. The continued production of annual crops like rice, beans and maize is possible only with the use of fertilizers and pesticides which neither the peasants nor Brazil can afford. The alternative to annual crops is of course perennial crops: trees and shrubs which live and produce for longer than one year. Their cultivation is perhaps more promising in Amazonia, as they make better use of the poor soils, require less work to maintain, and provide the stability which might help the colonists to combat other people's attempts to expel them from their land. But they are not by any means a panacea.

There are several ways of growing perennial crops in the Amazon, none of which is without problems. The colonists could be introduced to some of the subtle means of managing regenerating forest used by the Kayapó and other tribes; but as even the scientists working with the Indians do not claim to understand their techniques well, they are likely to be hard to transfer. Indeed, by means of the perverse criteria by which the government judges development to be taking place, it is the Indians who are being encouraged to copy the colonists.

Plantations of greater than a few hectares clearly do not work in Amazonia. Plant diseases in the Amazon are so diverse that they soon destroy species brought in from other continents, even though they have not evolved to infect them, as oilpalm and coconut growers have recently been discovering to their cost. The most promising resort seems to be the comparatively new discipline known as agroforestry, though even in this case the potential is not proven.

Informal agroforestry has been practised for centuries by the Indians and caboclos of Amazonia; but it has only recently been recognized by scientists as a skilled means of producing food. It involves at its simplest a mixture of treegrowing and crop production, but some of the models now being designed by scientists are, in theory, cleverly integrated. One of the most popular ideas is the cultivation of annual crops in the spaces between rows of planted trees. The trees draw nutrients out of the soil and nitrogen out of the air, and the branches cut from them can be used to provide these minerals to the crops growing in between. But new research[14] suggests that the trees might in fact make a minimal contribution to the productivity of annual crops, and that the farmers will still need to use liberal applications of fertilizers and pesticides.

Another scheme, designed by researchers in Manaus, involves the integration of the two processes of treegrowing and food production, with the development of a food forest. Here it is the trees themselves, such as breadfruit, jackfruit, the pupunha palm, bananas and beantrees, which produce the starch, protein and fats the settlers need. Underneath them can be raised anything the people lack, such as pigs, or fodder leaves for sheep. It does seem to be a sustainable system, especially with such innovative means of fertilization as a shifting toilet one of the researchers has designed, which hygienically provides each tree with just the quantity of manure it requires[15]. But the problem with this model is that the settlers are conservative in their habits, and reluctant to change their diets from rice and black beans to palmfruits and treepods.

What might be the best model of all is Anthony Anderson's suggestion of a system incorporating three distinct means of farming the forest. Close to their homes the settlers could be encouraged to manage intensive treegardens, such as – if they could be persuaded to change their habits – the food forest. A little further from their houses the forest could be loosely managed, perhaps like that of the people on the Ilha de Combu, who cut some of the trees interfering with the açaí they favour. Beyond that the settlers could gather products from the unaltered forest, much as the rubber-tappers do today. This scheme is also, of course, difficult to implement, and requires careful training. In the face of these difficulties it is clear that the first concern of anyone attempting to save the forest and improve the welfare of the people there must be to stop the flow of new colonists to Amazonia.

Some of the existing colonists in the Amazon do farm effectively, despite all the difficulties of the region. Perhaps the most successful are the Japanese settlers at Tomé-Açú, 120 kilometres to the south of Belém. Soon before watching the cocoa being harvested on the Ilha de Combu, my friend Roselis and I travelled by bus to visit these least probable of all Amazonians.

The first Japanese arrived in Tomé-Açú in 1929, when their government was trying to reduce unemployment by redistributing its population. It had agreed with the Brazilian administration that a colony be founded in the forest where Japanese peasants could farm. The settlers, like many others, soon found that the soil would not support the rice they tried to grow. The cocoa they planted died and they failed to sell the vegetables they cultivated to the other Amazonians, most of whom still seem to regard leafy plants as food for animals. As yellow fever and malaria killed many of the immigrants, others fled, and by 1942 only 98 of the 350 families who had settled there remained. But it was then that the colony became an internment centre for enemy aliens. Immediately after the war the replenished Japanese population of Tomé-Açú discovered the great potential of pepper.

By 1956 the Japanese colonists had substituted domestic produce for all of Brazil's imported pepper, and were beginning to export. By 1961 the 500 farms were producing 5 per cent of the world's supply. But in the early 1960s the world price of pepper fell, and fungus began to ravage the Amazonian plantations. Some farmers were bankrupted and again the colony began to empty. But those who stayed had learnt that to depend on a single crop was to be exposed to the vicissitudes of commerce and nature; while to cultivate many different species was both to provide themselves with financial stability and to make better use of the natural conditions. Without consciously attempting to do so they began to replicate in some small way the forest their farms had replaced.

By 1990 the people of Tomé-Açú were selling fifty-five crop products[16] and were still diversifying. Through the cooperative they managed they created new markets, added value to their products and ensured that they were paid fair prices. As a result they had achieved not unbounded wealth, but what seemed to be both a reasonably steady income and a means of staying on their land without destroying it.

We walked into the cooperative headquarters in Quatro Bocas, a settlement a few kilometres from the town of Tomé-Açú. The establishment was plain and well organized. Nearly everyone walking or cycling through the gates of the compound was Japanese. They moved with a briskness alien to the other parts of Brazil I had visited. I had trouble convincing myself that we were still in the middle of the Amazon jungle.

We were taken to the office of Toshihiko Takamatsu, the cooperative's director, a curt, pleasant, open man, who after sixteen years in Brazil still had difficulty with his Portuguese. In his telephone conversations he would ask '*Ah só? ... er, é sim?*.' He took us around the factories the cooperative had built for smoking rubber and sifting peppercorns. The technology was simple, inventive and easily maintained. He began to tell us about the other work of the cooperative, which was helping the farmers to develop new crops and techniques and providing cheap credit and equipment, when a siren sounded.

'*Ah – er tudo bem*. We shall then continue in one hour and one half.'

As we watched the people promptly leaving their offices, Roselis said that it was this which had brought the Japanese success, in the midst of so much chaos.

After lunch we were introduced to Getúlio Kazuyuki Sasaki, the half-Japanese, half-Brazilian agronomist employed by the cooperative to advise the farmers, a lively, humorous man. We went with him to visit the new agricultural systems the farmers had devised.

Most of the Japanese families owned between 100 and 150 hectares, of which 20 would at any one time be under cultivation. The first farm we visited specialized in rubber, pepper and passion fruit, but grew a great variety of minor crops. There were *acerola* bushes whose berries were to be processed for fruit juice, *guaraná* trees for the manufacture of a fizzy drink, coffee, cocoa, vanilla vines and several Amazonian fruit species. There were small stands of timber trees which would not mature for thirty years, testimony to the farmer's preparedness to invest.

The different crops were integrated to use the land and its

resources as efficiently as possible. While the young rubber trees developed, pepper was grown in the alleys which had to be left between them. Cuttings from the pepper bushes were believed to keep pests away from the rubber. As the rubber trees matured they would shade out the spice bushes; but by then the trees themselves would be producing. When the canopy closed the pepper would be replaced by crops requiring shadow, such as cocoa and the Amazonian fruit *cupuaçú*.

While other Amazonians had been deceived by the size of the lands they had been given – and the size of the Amazon itself – into farming loosely over many hectares, the Japanese had come to understand that they needed to apply their efforts intensively to just a few. By contrast to some of the other forms of farming in the Amazon, the agroforestry at Tomé-Açú brought people onto the land rather than throwing them off, as each Japanese farmer employed several Brazilians. This and the heavy fertilization and use of pesticides required made their farming expensive, and on the farms themselves there was no conservation of primary rainforest. But as they were careful to prevent the degradation of the soil, the colonists there would never have to leave and move further into the jungle.

We were led around the farmyard by the farmer's wife, whose name to my shame I was unable to transcribe. She had a pond where both fish and geese were raised for sale and an orchard which again made me stop for a second to assure myself of where I was. All the best fruiting trees of South East Asia were growing there: mangosteen, rambutan, lychee, langsa, new varieties of starfruit, nutmeg, aniseed and, to my amazement, trees which were to bear the stinking durian, the greatest delicacy in Asia.

Around the house were bonsai trees and ornamental shrubs the farmer had found in the jungle. Inside, amid her Japanese prints and Brazilian furniture, the farmer's wife told us how her family had come from Japan fifty-two years before. Now that Japan was trying to attract labour rather than to shed it, her children had returned there to work.

Getúlio took us to the factory the cooperative had built with the help of a World Bank loan. There the many fruits the farmers had grown were being processed to make juices, frozen pulp or iced lollies. A cocoa-processing unit was soon to be installed, separating the pulp for human consumption, the pods for fertilizer and the beans for fermenting and drying. The produce would be trucked to Belém and shipped by the cooperative from there to São Paulo, eliminating all middlemen.

Marketing was a key to the success of the farmers at Tomé-Açú, and the reason for the failure of many others in the Amazon. Because the cooperative acted for the whole community it was big enough both to negotiate good prices for its established products and to create markets for new crops. The farmers each brought in around $10,000 a year, of which around $2000 was left when their expenses had been paid. They agreed that without the cooperative they could not have made money.

Perhaps the best products of Japanese agriculture in the Amazon are the two restaurants close to the cooperative at Quatro Bocas. There the most excellent Japanese food is sold at Brazilian prices: I would hazard that these are the cheapest Japanese restaurants in the world. We met Getúlio with several friends of his, joking rapidly in Japanese. Among them was Noburu Sakaguchi, the shaven-headed old man who owned the first farm we had visited. When I complimented him on his orchard, and told him how surprised I was to see trees such as durians, he grinned until his eyes disappeared into his laughter lines.

'No, don't talk to me about dulian. All day I think about dulian and only get hungrier and hungrier.'

He told us he had decided to bring back the seeds from Malaysia, where he had been staying on his way back from a visit to Japan. In the foyer of his hotel was a notice forbidding people to enter with durians, because of the appalling smell of sewers which attends them. He smuggled two into his room in a bag, ate the pulp and then began cleaning the seeds so that they could be sneaked through customs, for the export of vegetable matter was forbidden. In scrubbing them he used up all the toilet paper in his bathroom and rang down for some more. When the porter arrived he gagged, and told Noburu he could have as much toilet paper as he needed, and a doctor too if that would help.

After two hours of scrubbing Noburu was satisfied that he had exorcized the smell, and that day he went to the airport to leave for Brazil. He could not help noticing the stares of the other people in the queues, and when he reached the x-ray machine an official drew him aside and asked, 'You've got durian, haven't you?' Noburu admitted that he had, he was searched and all but two of the seeds were found and confiscated. While people changed seats on the aeroplane to avoid him and the stewardess suggested he might like to sit beside the toilet, he succeeded in smuggling his precious germplasm into Brazil inside a packet of cigarettes. He planted them with care, and for twenty years nurtured and encouraged them, all the time thinking of the fruit he had not tasted since the hotel room in Malaysia. At last they flowered.

'The fruit?' He shook his head in resignation. '*Senhor*, they are both males.'

Farming of the type the people at Tomé-Açú have developed would be difficult for other Amazonians to copy. Most have neither the capital nor the coordination they would need. But the work of a peasant syndicate on the other side of the Amazon, in the settlement schemes of Rondônia, shows that the colonists can break the circle of destruction and desolation many feel condemned to tread.

The people of Ouro Prêto d'Oueste, on the BR364 in the middle of Rondônia, were part of the first wave of colonists to have been encouraged by the government to move to the state. Until the end of 1988 they had, like most of the other migrants, simply cut, burnt and watched their soils crumble away from them, not through want of effort but through want of expertise. Indeed, the harder they worked the more destructive and less sustainable their agriculture became.

Many had left, moving to the new frontiers of Acre, Amazonas and Roraima. Others had been forced to sell part of their land, to make up for bad harvests or to buy the medicines they needed. Those who stayed lived at the mercy of soils which sometimes failed to yield, crop prices which might not compensate the costs of cultivation, and advice from government scientists which served only to make their situation worse. But among them was a body of people who became determined to confront these problems, rather than to flee them. They examined the markets, looked for products which could be grown for less labour and more reward, and began to consider means of farming the forest soils without permanently damaging them. They won funding from the Canadian Embassy[17], and by the time I visited them early in 1990 they had already installed their first experimental farming systems.

At the syndicate headquarters in Ouro Prêto I met one of several colonists for whom I was to evolve a great respect. Matilde Oliveira de Araujo was the daughter of a peasant who had migrated from the southern state of Minas Gerais when his crops failed and he was forced to sell most of his land. His family had travelled for five days on the back of a truck, and bought some of the cheaper land the government was offering in Rondônia. Life had become if anything worse than the stringy subsistence they had achieved in Minas Gerais. Selling to middlemen, they were paid even less than the low market price for their crops. Matilde, though she had scarcely been educated, had developed a profound comprehension of the Brazilian political system. She was acute and startlingly persuasive, and had taught herself to administer the syndicate's accounts.

The peasants' union was establishing several experimental farms, through which the members hoped to discover the means of sustainable cultivation. It was building a meeting house and dormitory, to help bring the peasants together, as they had come from all parts of Brazil and so differed in experience. The union was trying to improve the collection and marketing of the farmers' crops. This involved lobbying the state government for better roads and transport services, and this lobbying, as Matilde explained, had exposed the peasants to death threats from the ranchers. Because they were trying to free themselves from the support and control of the state, they were regarded as a menace.

The syndicate had purchased a flatbed truck, in which Matilde took me for an hour across the ranchlands and failed farms of the earliest Rondônian settlements. There was scarcely any cultivation visible amid the wreckage we passed. For tens of kilometres the land was deserted, and succoured just the bleached and knotted scrub of a landscape prematurely aged. Then we came to groves of green trees, and among them, overrun with chickens and children, a neat wooden house.

Valmir de Souza, the farmer, was a confident, fatherly man, as bright and optimistic as Matilde, and an enthusiast for the crops he tested on the syndicate's behalf. His passion was bees, and he spoke of them as if describing his vision of a new world order, bringing down the flat of his hand onto his table. He was testing the viability of honey production, and though he had received no formal training and had learnt all he knew by the light of a paraffin lamp from the books he had borrowed, it was already clear that his optimism was not misplaced. After just a year his thirty hives were producing 500 kilograms of honey for the syndicate, and had the potential to offer much more. And the honey, unlike the adulterated dregs brought to the state from São Paulo, had the flavours of the forest trees the bees tapped. We ate it with manioc cakes still warm from the griddle, hot milk and bowls of the many fruits Valmir had planted around his house. Unlike most of the colonists he had achieved something close to self-sufficiency, producing his own coffee, sugar, sawn wood and staple crops.

Valmir used his hives to demonstrate to the other peasants the art and the rewards of beekeeping. One litre of honey sold for the same price as one sack of rice, and each farm could produce many more litres than sacks. The market was unlikely to become saturated, as the honey was replacing the imports from the south. One attraction was self-evident: when we went to see the hives Valmir simply pointed at the stream of bees and told us, 'My workforce does it all for me.' He said that few of the peasants had come to learn, however, as they had been frightened by stories of killer bees.

Valmir also wanted to experiment with fish-keeping and new agroforestry systems. He was growing some of the plants the Indians had used, such as a shrub whose leaves lather like soap when rubbed in water, and trees which produced both fruit and new flavours of honey. He was careful to keep the soil on his farm covered by vegetation at all times to avoid leaching.

'If you conserve the forest you have a better life,' he told me. 'But we need finance and technical assistance to do it. We want to preserve the forest, we don't want to spend all our lives fruitlessly cutting and burning; but the government is not helping us to do it.'

Matilde and I drove away again across the wasted lands, until we arrived at the experimental garden the unionists had established. Here the peasants had demonstrated that they could produce on just half a hectare more income than could be squeezed from the five normally cut each year to grow rice and beans. The garden's manager, Mauro dos Reis Custôdia, a man of perception and curiosity, like the others teaching himself his new tasks as they confronted him, led us around the rows of vegetables he had learnt to cultivate. The soil had been mixed with coffee husks and cows' manure to provide nutrients, and covered in rice husks to keep it moist. Mauro had installed a system of hoses and sprinklers for irrigation, and had studied the crop rotation necessary to avoid the recurrence of plant disease. The market, he told me, was for the moment safe, as Amazonians were just beginning to recognize the virtues of eating animal food, and this garden sold all it could produce.

Mauro said that other peasants were already beginning to garden, and found that they needed to work less, suffer less, destroy less to produce more. The union was inviting agronomists to Ouro Prêto to teach its members new techniques in agroforestry, the use of native Amazonian trees and the construction of firebreaks and hedges. Matilde hoped that the syndicate would soon be able to start a nursery, growing the seedlings of the trees which could secure their long-term subsistence. They could then start to replace the forest cover they had, in their ignorance, destroyed. As we stood in the syndicate's garden the sun came through the clouds which had been threatening to break over us since we had arrived. In the midst of the desolation left by two decades of greed, of politics, of negligence, it lit upon half a hectare of hope.

With the dawn of the following day I left the boarding house I had been staying in and walked through the backstreets of a nation's broken dreams. Shops and bars were pulling up their blinds as I passed them. When I reached the bus station, ragged children were already shouting and pushing fruit and sausages on sticks through the windows of the stationary buses. I noticed that some of them were blond and blue-eyed, descendants of the German immigrants whose hereditary trek, still uncompleted, had served to carry them ever further from prosperity.

I watched for a moment the uneven pantomime I had first witnessed at the beginning of my journey, in a bus station in Maranhão: some years, it seemed to me, before. Men in straw stetsons jostled near the doors of the buses, or stood on the pavement in loose descriptions of the jackets of cowboy thrillers in the station's news stands. Mulecarts passed by; a one-legged man brandished a crutch at the children who were teasing him; peasants with faded eyes sat and watched all and nothing of the evanescent world around them. There ticked through the blood of all, who bustled, shouted, watched and waited, the strange quick–slow metronome of energy, the jagged heartbeat of Brazil. I turned around once, to memorize the scene, then I stepped into a bus, and out of the story of the Amazon.

257

12

WE MUST ESCAPE FROM the outmoded idea that destruction is regrettably necessary if development is to take place. Ludicrous as it seems in this age of environmental enlightenment, such thinking still pervades the offices of some of the ministries in the Brazilian government and such wardens of tradition as the International Monetary Fund. The fossil policies of these institutions suggest that a nation must absorb its wilderness in order to develop, forcing each particle of land to contribute to the national economy. All the evidence from the Amazon suggests, by contrast, that its destruction is costing Brazil money, retarding the country's development, and threatening the future of its inhabitants.

Development and conservation are necessarily one, if development is to be of benefit to any but the tiny political and economic caucus now controlling it, and to lead to more than the most ephemeral social and economic improvements. Were development decisions devolved to the people being affected it would soon become clear from the choices they made that their own interests coincide with the conservation of the environment. The peasants of Ouro Preto told me they knew that the destruction of the forest brought them nothing but ill; but that while they had been allowed no influence over the course of their own lives they had been without the power to prevent it.

Not only are the needs of the people controlling development at odds with the needs of those they are developing; but the requirements of the state itself may be distinct from what is good for some of its people. All around the tropics there are two states in every nation, capitalist and communalist: the big business state, which generates national income and promotes economic growth, and the peasants who work not for profits but for subsistence. If, as is repeatedly happening, the one is allowed to crush the other, then the solid floor of the nation crumbles: bereft of their communities and their traditional livelihoods, the once communalist peasants become the rejects of the capitalist society, and fall into the trough of dispossession, poverty and the loss of identity. It is then that they become not the defenders but the destroyers of the environment, like those who were once the subsistence farmers of Maranhão and are now the colonists of Amazonia.

I am not suggesting that the different states should be decoupled, but that they be allowed to coexist. The small must be able to survive alongside the large; not every life should be subordinated to the raw national goals of producing exports and generating growth. This means that the absolute faith in the orthodox model of capitalism followed thus far by developers in and out of Brazil must be renounced, and not only because it is historically inappropriate. Adam Smith believed that each worker should concentrate on a single task, contributing directly to the national economy. This model conflicts with the solutions that people such as the peasants of Ouro Preto, the Japanese of Tomé-Açú or the Kayapó have evolved for themselves: they have found that their survival depends upon diversity, not upon specialization. It is in part the government's attempt to encourage, as the orthodox capitalists advocate, every member of the nation to become a functioning and discrete part of the national economy which has sent the settlers of the Amazon over the precipice of desolation.

While foreign development agencies, such as the World Bank, the InterAmerican Development Bank and government departments in the Northern nations are beginning, albeit erratically, to wake up to the new demands of development, they are still capable of inflicting damage, even when their intentions are good. One reason for this is that their funding structure is such that it is sometimes more difficult to raise the $10,000 which might be required to finance a small sustainable development, than the $10 million which may be needed to implement a big and ultimately destructive scheme. In all of the biggest funding agencies there are people whose jobs are to disburse money. These people each have a certain amount of money that they have to give or lend to other countries every year; if they fail to spend that amount they are considered not to be working hard enough. As they have to check the projects they administer at each stage of implementation, they do not have the time to give money to more than perhaps ten new initiatives each year. This means that if their annual budget is $100 million – and it can often be more – then their average disbursement must be $10 million.

As small organizations, representing the people to be developed – such as the syndicate at Ouro Preto, or the Tukano people's association at Taracuá – would have no use for this sort of money, it must inevitably go not to them, but to the grandiose schemes of governments and big businessmen. When it reaches the governments of states such as Rondônia, Amazonas or Pará, it serves not, as it was intended, to smooth out the differences between rich and poor, powerful and powerless, but to exacerbate them. State politicians use the disbursement of these funds to secure their own positions: in Rondônia agricultural technicians are hired on the basis that they will encourage the farmers to vote for their employers, and the farmers are rewarded with money taken from a World Bank loan in exchange for their support.

As a result of such distortions the $25,000 given so far by the Canadian Embassy to the 4000 peasants of the syndicate in Ouro Preto has brought more good to the state of Rondônia than the hundreds of millions of dollars the World Bank has spent there. The $12,000 the Tukano association is asking for is likely to do more to avert one of the greatest of the Amazon's impending disasters than all the huge sums the German government or the World Bank have been thinking of lending to the Brazilian government's Environment Institute. But as the environmental charities who might have been able to provide such smaller funds are now themselves fighting for survival – because green enthusiasm worldwide seems not to have been matched by green munificence – it is the small amounts which are the hardest to secure. Raising such money, while the development banks unload their billions, is a matter of street collections and sponsored walks.

By no means all the disbursements and initiatives of the big foreign agencies have been misdirected; some of the money they have provided has been crucial to the survival of groups helping to defend the Amazon. The Canadian International Development Agency is working with rubber-tappers in the state of Acre to help them use the forest profitably and sustainably[1]; and the researchers advising the açaí collectors on the Ilha de Combu are funded by Britain's Overseas Development Agency, as are several important conservation research projects in the Amazon. Some of the Basin's most promising initiatives are being financed by the German and Swedish governments, as well as some regional authorities, such as the government of the German state of Hessen. The International Tropical Timber Organization has been careful to plan what may be the sustainable use of some of the forest in Acre[2]. The American-based Ford Foundation is helping Brazil to investigate the potential for agroforestry; and the G7 group of powerful industrialized nations is considering a global forest convention[3], which, if it works, should slow down deforestation worldwide.

But the good some agencies are doing is equilibrated by the harm which either others or even they themselves are causing through the funding of destructive projects. Though its administrators have now promised to reform it, the Tropical Forestry Action Programme – run by the Food and Agriculture Organization, the World Bank, United Nations Development Programme and World Resources Institute – has reportedly been responsible for more, not less, deforestation worldwide, by pouring money into the corrupt and destructive timber industries controlling the forests of many nations. The TFAP has helped to exclude forest people from their homes, and turn primary forest into plantations.

The World Bank, astonishingly, is still funding logging in virgin rainforests. Though the Bank has trumpeted its new commitment to preserving the environment, the pressure group the Environmental Defense Fund has reported that 'for every case where there appear to be promising changes we can identify two or three ecological débâcles of equal or greater scale where the Bank refuses to act even when apprised of the facts.'[4] The World Bank's attempts to repair some of the damage caused by its disastrous lending to the settlement projects in Rondônia expose the rot which still infects even its well-intentioned projects.

Though its new lending to Rondônia has been designed to protect the remaining forests there, the Bank's use of the corrupt institutions of the state to disburse the money and its inadequate consultation with local people appear to condemn this new funding to do nothing but add to the damage already inflicted. It has emerged that none of the local groups with whom the World Bank claimed to have discussed the project even exists[5]. It has failed to consider some of the most serious problems afflicting the state, such as the concentration of landownership, the invasions of Indian reserves, uncontrolled mining and urban poverty. The Brazilian scientists supposed to be implementing its plans have decamped to the south of the country for lack of funds. As it still fails to accept full responsibility for the chaos its earlier development work has caused[6], it is hard to see how the Bank can justify its claims to have truly reformed.

While the World Bank is at least attempting to change, the International Monetary Fund still seems to be unconcerned about the environmental impact of its policies, and its economic restructuring packages remain among the world's most persistent reasons for deforestation. Neither is the United States government likely to improve the situation it has helped to precipitate in the Amazon: discounting the money for drugs control, it is giving progressively less aid to Latin America, just as the needs of the people there are growing. Its money is instead going to countries which are richer, but more politically useful.

If the Brazilian government is to prevent the final destruction of the Amazon forests, there are certain policies which must be priorities. The first of these is agrarian reform, and with it the granting of secure title to the land owned by peasants all over Brazil. In this way not only is the movement of people to the Amazon likely to be reduced, but the colonists already settled there will not be forced by the ranchers and sawmills to move further into the forest. All over Brazil there must be support, in the form of credit and infrastructure, for the small farmer, and agricultural policies sensitive enough to take account of the fact that different people, and different places, have different requirements.

Development planning in the Amazon should be the preserve of the people living there, not the privilege of people who do not have to suffer its effects. Decisions should be made by plebiscite and consultation, not by those with the most land, the most money or the most guns. The armed forces must be entirely removed from development in the Amazon. The size, the powers and the prestige of the agencies supposed to be guarding the forests against unauthorized destruction must be increased, and it would seem sensible to privatize them, freeing them to act with the self-interest of the other private enterprises in the forest. The budgets for scientific and agricultural research need to be greatly increased, and the researchers released from political obligations to their employers: for without

this there will be no means of assessing the suitability of new developments.

Large-scale timber-cutting and any future exploitation which
requires the removal of forest should be confined to areas which
have already been damaged, and all sawmills failing to follow strict
conservation guidelines must be closed down. Roads of any nature
should be built only with the approval of the federal government,
and then must be confined to regions which are already degraded.
Colonists in Amazonia, having been assured that the ranchers will
not be able to expel them from their lands, must be shown ways of
improving their lives sustainably. Extensive clearance in the Amazon,
for speculation or cattlefarming, must be made illegal.

But none of this will happen without a change of attitude
throughout the institutional structures of Brazil and the other
Amazon nations. While democracy remains a sham and development
a means of promoting the interests of an elevated minority, such
lesser improvements as agricultural extension will be ineffective.
The campaigning power of money, state-owned or private, must be
limited; the media empires which established their hegemony under
military rule must be broken down; political patronage and the
influence of industrial and proprietorial lobby groups must be
ruthlessly restrained. Above all there needs to be a massive investment in and reform of the education system, without which the
people are but the supplicants of the powerful minority. And unless
the power of the wealthiest individuals and corporations of the
nation is curtailed, then the people of Brazil are condemned to
destroy all that they might have left to their descendants.

Some of the measures required to save the Amazon will be
expensive, just as some of the means of destroying it are lucrative.
The future of the forests must not be assessed, as many are tempted
to assess it, only in economic terms. It is more remunerative to
cut a patch of forest for timber and then invest the money in
another business than to harvest in perpetuity the lesser amount
that the trees there can produce sustainably. But while the profits
from cutting are evident, the costs may at first be invisible, and
will be borne when they arise by people other than those who
benefited.

As it is their heritage too which is threatened by the destruction of
the Amazon, and their mistakes as well which are responsible for
much of what is happening there, foreign governments must also do

more to forestall the greatest ecological catastrophe in human history. They must extend their development aid to reach the people who can do most to help: the Indians, the treekeepers, the colonists who should be the allies, not the enemies of the Amazon. It is they who must be allowed to build the car of progress and to steer it, and we in the North who should be the humble passengers of their development, paying for some of the petrol but keeping our hands from the wheel.

Above all the Northern nations must abandon their neurotic suppression of all but the economic systems modelled on their own. Now that the enmity between East and West is coming to an end, it is time to allow a new tolerance to guide our foreign policy. Nations must be allowed to adopt the systems which suit them, not forced to adapt to the systems which suit the North. We cannot help the Amazon countries while we support the oppressive, the destructive and the greedy. The money, the work, the rhetoric we expend in trying to protect the Amazon are swept aside while the storm of geopolitics still blows.

As individuals we in the North would be surprised to find how powerful we are. The governments of Brazil and the other Amazon nations are remarkably sensitive to foreign pressure. I was at first surprised to see that campaigns in Britain against environmental abuses in Brazil receive more coverage there than they do here. It is such demonstrations of concern in the Northern nations which have repeatedly been used by Brazilian pressure groups to persuade their own government to act. The campaigning organizations I have encountered in Brazil, though autonomous, all stress their dependence on the support of individuals abroad.

It is also striking, as I have shown, how little money is required to fund the developments which can do most to help. It is the charities and pressure groups in the North which are best placed to administer development funds, as it is they that have the closest links to the people's organizations in the Amazon, and the truest commitment to positive change. As these, remarkably, are now beleaguered by shrinking incomes, the importance of small donations becomes enormous. But all of the forest's defenders must have the patience to acknowledge that no means of saving the Amazon will be easy to effect, either by governments or by independent organizations. The depth of the problems is such that the implementation of sensible solutions will be complex, protracted and controversial. But the sensitivity of the development planning required should not defuse the vigour with which it is pursued.

The 1990s will be the watershed of Amazon development. If the Amazon is to be saved the crucial decisions need to be taken in these years. If the remainder is to be destroyed it is in these years that the framework of destruction will be laid down. In the sixteen weeks this book has taken to write I have watched the solidification of the paradox, both in Brazil and at home, which might become the model of our neglect for the remainder of the decade. As our concern for the environment develops and its place in the political agenda becomes assured, our inaction remains as comprehensive as before. We are prepared to deal with minor issues, politically safe and economically painless to address; but the responses of both politicians and their electorates to the troubles which could threaten the welfare of mankind – global warming and tropical deforestation being first among them – have been pitiable.

There is no need for further deliberation in the northern hemisphere. We know what the choices are. Either we take the painful decisions now, to revise our political and economic influence abroad, forgive much of the debt we hold against nations such as Brazil, and restrict our own companies and consumers; or we continue, as we are doing now, not to address the diseases of the rootstock, but to paint the yellow spots on the leaves of the forest green. Our indifference, if it persists, will buy us seats as spectators of the world's greatest environmental tragedy.

Unless there is a drastic renunciation of our current complacence and hypocrisy, the Amazon will not survive. The policies required are beyond the imagination of governments which have repeatedly shown themselves unsuited to the tasks of planning for the future of the planet and its people. It falls to those who have awoken to the consequences of what is happening to fight to protect the Amazon. It is upon the outcome of this fight that our era will be judged.

REFERENCES

Regrettably there is only space to refer to a few of the publications which have been been invaluable in the compilation of this book. I hope to have listed the sources of the most unusual information, as well as the texts which might be most useful to anyone wanting to learn more.

CHAPTER 1

1. Extracted from Erwin, T.L. 1988. The tropical forest canopy: the heart of biotic diversity. In E.O.Wilson, (Editor) *Biodiversity*. National Academy of Sciences.
2. David Arkcoll, personal communication.
3. Nepstad, D. et al. 1989. Deep roots and nutrients of an Amazonian forest and abandoned pasture. Manuscript.
4. Walker, I. 1987. The biology of streams as part of Amazonian forest ecology. *Experientia* Vol 43(3).
5. From figures compiled by Irving Foster Brown.
6. Salati, E. et al. 1989. Solos, agua e clima na Amazônia. MS.
7. Leopaldi, P.R. et al. 1987. Towards a water balance in the Central Amazon region. *Experientia* Vol 43(3).
8. Salati, E. and Vose, P.B. 1984. Amazon Basin: a system in equilibrium. *Science* 225.
9. Bruce Nelson, pers comm.

CHAPTER 2

1. Roosevelt, A. 1989. Resource management in Amazonia before the Conquest: beyond ethnographic projection. *Advances in Economic Botany Vol* 7. The New York Botanical Garden.
2. Posey, D.A. 1987. *Alternatives to destruction – science of the Mebengokre*. Museu Paraense Goeldi.
3. Hecht, S.B. and Posey, D.A. 1989. Preliminary results on soil management techniques of the Kayapó indians. *Advances in Economic Botany* 7.
4. Anderson, A.B. and Posey, D.A. 1989. Management of a tropical scrub savannah by the Gorotire Kayapó of Brazil. *Advances in Economic Botany* 7.
5. See also Dubois, J.C.L. 1990. Secondary forests as a land-use resource in frontier zones of Amazonia. In A.B. Anderson (ed.) *Alternatives to*

266

deforestation: steps toward sustainable use of the Amazon rain forest. Columbia University Press. New York.
6. E.g. Posey, D.A. 1985. Native and indigenous guidelines for new Amazonian development strategies: understanding biological diversity through ethnoecology. In J. Hemming (ed.) *Change in the Amazon Basin* Vol 1. Manchester University Press.
7. Bruce Nelson, pers comm.
8. Anthony Anderson, pers comm.

CHAPTER 3
1. Animação Cristãos no Meio Rural. 1989. Terror polícial no campo – MA. Open Letter.
2. Temme, Frei A. 1989. O que acontece no Aguiar, 6.89; O que esta acontecendo no Aguiar, 9.89. Animação Cristãos no Meio Rural. Secretariado Regional.
3. Amnesty International. 1988. *Brazil: authorized violence in rural areas.* Amnesty International Publications.
4. Movimento dos Sem Terra. 1985. Relatório dos Sem Terra no Maranhão. Assembléia Geral 28-30 Junho 1985, Buriticupú.
5. *Jornal do Brasil.* 1.4.90.
6. Seitz, J.L. 1988. *The politics of development.* Basil Blackwell Ltd, Oxford.

CHAPTER 5
1. Lourenço, A. 1989. Amazônia é um grande garimpo. *Tempo e Presença* Vol 244 & 245. CEDI.
2. Lacerda, L.D. et al. 1989. Mercury contamination in the Madeira River, Amazon – Hg inputs to the environment. *Biotropica* 21(1).
3. Bruce Forsberg, pers comm.
4. Claudia Andujar, pers comm.
5. Ação Pela Cidadânia. 1989. *Roraima: o aviso da morte.* CCPY/CEDI/ CIMI.
6. Francisco Bezerra, pers comm.
7. Kopenawa Yanomami, D. 1989. A todos os povos da terra. Open letter to President Sarney, 1.8.89.
8. *Porantim.* December 1989. CIMI.
9. *A Crítica.* 26.6.89.
10. *Porantim.* January/February 1990. CIMI.
11. Comissão pela criação do Parque Yanomami. 1990. *Yanomami Updates.*

CHAPTER 6
1. Smole, W.J. 1989. Yanoama horticulture in the Parima Highlands of Venezuela and Brazil. *Advances in Economic Botany* 7. The New York Botanical Garden.
2. *Porantim.* December 1989. CIMI.
3. Ramos, A.R. 1987. Reflecting on the Yanomami: ethnographic images and the pursuit of the exotic. *Cultural Anthropology* 2(3).

CHAPTER 7

1. Phillipe Lena, pers comm.
2. CEPAMI. 1988. Realidade das famílias de migrantes no estado de Rondônia – 1987. Cadernos do CEAS no 119.
3. Lena, P. 1989. Estrategias camponesas de capitalização no PIC Ouro Preto (Rondônia). Paper presented to the Seminario Internacional dos Americanistas, Amsterdam, July 1988.
4. Fearnside, P.M. 1990. Human Carrying Capacity Estimation in Rainforest Areas. MS for *Trends in Ecology and Evolution*.
5. E.g. Mitschein, T.A. et al. 1989. *Urbanização, selvagem e proletarização pássiva na Amazônia*. CEJUP, Belém.
6. Browder, J.O. 1988. Public policy and deforestation in the Brazilian Amazon. In R. Repetto and M. Gillis (eds) *Public policies and the misuse of forest resources*. World Resources Institute. Cambridge University Press.

CHAPTER 8

1. Ninck, D. 1989. *Imagens de uma viagem, que Theodor Koch-Grunberg fez entre 1903 e 1905 aos povos do Alto Rio Negro*. COIAB.
2. Chernela, J.M. 1989. Managing rivers of hunger: the Tukano of Brazil. *Advances in Economic Botany* 7. The New York Botanical Garden.
3. Chernela, J.M. 1985. Indigenous fishing in the Neotropics: the Tukanoan Uanano of the blackwater Uaupés River basin in Brazil and Colombia. *Interciencia* 10(2).
4. Folha de São Paulo. 16.11.86.
5. See e.g. Nobre, A.D. 1988: Projeto Calha Norte. Transcript of speech by Coronel Aviador Antônio Nascimento. ISEA, Manaus, 6.1.88; Santilli M., 1987. The Calha Norte project: military guardianship and frontier policy. *Cultural Survival Quarterly* 13(1), from *Tempo e Presença* 23.
6. International Institute of Strategic Studies. 1990. *The Military Balance 1989–1990*. Brassey's Defence Publishers, London.
7. *Jornal do Brasília*. 8.3.89; *Jornal do Brasil*. 31.10.86.
8. See Chaves Fernandes, F.R. ?1986. *Quem é quem no subsolo brasileiro*. MCT CNPq, Brazil.
9. E.g. Bayma Denys, General R. 1989. Governo e Meio Ambiente. *Horizonte*, September.
10. *Porantim*. January/February 1990. CIMI.
11. Nobre, A. D. 1988. Projeto Calha Norte. Transcript of speech by Coronel Aviador Antônio Nascimento. ISEA, Manaus, 6.1.88.
12. E.g. FUNAI. 6.9.88. Portaria do Presidente PP No 1098/88.
13. Buchillet, D. 1989. Pari-Cachoeira: o laboratório Tukano do Projeto Calha Norte. MS for CIMI.
14. Buchillet, D. 1990. Notas sobre a expulsão de índios de seu território. MS for Survival International.
15. Ação Pela Cidadania. 1989. *Roraima: o aviso da morte*. CCPY/CEDI/CIMI.
16. *Constituição, República Federativa do Brasil*. 1988. Article 231.
17. UN Economic and Social Council. 25.8.89. First revised text of the

draft universal declaration on the rights of indigenous peoples. Commission on Human Rights. E/CN4/Sub2/1989/36.

CHAPTER 9

1. Uhl, C. 1989. Cattle-raising in Pará – evaluation and alternatives. MS.
2. Uhl, C. and Boone Kauffman, J. 1990. Deforestation effects on fire susceptibility and the potential response of tree species to fire in the eastern Amazon. *Ecology* 71(2).
3. Browder, J.O. 1988. The social cost of rainforest destruction: a critique and economic analysis of the 'hamburger debate'. *Interciencia* 13(3).
4. Browder, J.O. 1988. Public Policy and Deforestation in the Brazilian Amazon. In: R. Repetto and M. Gillis (Eds). *Public policies and the misuse of forest resources*. World Resources Institute. Cambridge University Press.
5. Philip Fearnside, pers comm.
6. E.g. Binswanger, H.P. 1989. Brazilian policies that encourage deforestation in the Amazon. World Bank Environment Department Working Paper No.16.
7. Mauro Victor, pers comm.
8. Plowden, C. and Kusuda, Y. 1989. Logging in the Brazilian rainforest. MS for Rainforest Alliance Network, New York.
9. Uhl, C. and Guimaraes Viera, I.C. 1989. Ecological impacts of selective logging in the Brazilian Amazon: a case study from the Paragominas region of the state of Para. *Biotropica* 21(2).
10. Uhl, C. et al 1990. Wood as an economic catalyst to ecological change in Amazonia. MS.
11. E.g. Rasmusson, U. 1989. Travel report from visits to the state of Rondônia, Brazil. MS for Friends of the Earth.
12. Rasmusson, U. 1989. Comments vis-à-vis the World Bank loan for 'Rondônia Natural Resource Management.' MS for Friends of the Earth.
13. Chris Uhl, pers comm.
14. Counsell, S. 1990. *The Good Wood Guide*. Friends of the Earth.

CHAPTER 10

1. Ministério das Minas e Energia and Eletrobras. 1987. Plano Nacional de Energia Elétrica 1987/2010. Relatôrio Geral.
2. Fearnside, P.M. 1989. Brazil's Balbina dam: environment versus the legacy of the pharaohs in Amazonia. *Environmental Management* Vol 13(4).
3. Anderson, A.B. 1989. Smokestacks in the rainforest: Industrial development and deforestation in the Amazon basin. MS for World Development.
4. Treece, D. 1988: Brutality and Brazil: The Human Cost of Cheap Steel. *Multinational Monitor*. February.
5. European Parliament Committee on the Environment, Public Health and Consumer Protection. 1988. The environmental problems of the Amazon region. Draft report.
6. Anthony Anderson, pers comm.

7. Redford, K. 1990. Paper presented at the Rainforest Harvest Conference. Friends of the Earth/Media Natura. London 17–18 May 1990.

8. Johns, A. D. 1988. Economic development and wildlife conservation in Brazilian Amazonia. *Ambio* 17(5).

9. E.g. Fearnside, P.M. 1989. Deforestation in Brazilian Amazonia: the rates and causes of forest destruction. *The Ecologist* 19(6).

10. Myers, N. 1990. *Deforestation rates in tropical forests and their climatic implications.* Friends of the Earth, London. *Many of the figures in this section come from this report.*

11. Painter, J. 1989. Bolivian Ecology. MS for *Index on Censorship*.

12. *Catholic Standard* of Guyana. 17.9.89.

13. *I am indebted for much of this material on the history of the military government to the fine work of* Skidmore, T.E. 1988. *The Politics of Military Rule in Brazil 1964-1985.* Oxford University Press. New York, Oxford.

14. Linz, J. cited in Skidmore, T.E. above.

15. Folha De São Paulo 2.11.89

16. Galeano E. H., 1973. *The open veins of Latin America: five centuries of the pillage of a continent.* Monthly Review Press. New York.

17. Cartwright, J. 1989. Conserving Nature, Decreasing Debt. *Third World Quarterly* 11(2).

CHAPTER 11

1. Schartzmann, S. 1989. Extractive Reserves: The Rubber Tappers' strategy for Sustainable Use of the Amazon Rainforest. In Browder, J. (Ed): *Fragile lands in Latin America: the search for sustainable uses.* Westview Press, Boulder, Colorado.

2. Anderson, A.B. 1990. Land-use strategies for successful extractive economies. Paper presented at the Rainforest Harvest Conference. Friends of the Earth/Media Natura. London 17–18 May 1990.

3. Peters, C. et al. 1989. Valuation of an Amazonian Rainforest. *Nature* 339(6627) 26.6.89.

4. John Rombold, pers comm.

5. E.g. Arkcoll, D.B. and Clement, C.R. 1989. Potential new food crops from the Amazon. In G.E. Wickens *et al* (Ed.). *New crops for food and industry.* Chapman and Hall, London.

6. Baker, L. 1989. Marketing non-timber forest products: prospects and promise. Consultative Group on Biological Diversity/Cultural Survival workshop report. 7 November 1989.

7. Anderson, A.B. and Jardim, M.A.G. 1989. Costs and benefits of floodplain forests management by rural inhabitants in the Amazon Estuary. A case study of açaí palm production. In J. Browder (Ed.). *Fragile lands of Latin America: the search for sustainable uses.* Westview Press. Boulder, Colorado.

8. E.g. Gottleib, O.R. and Kaplan, M.A.C. 1990. Amazônia: tesouro química a preservar. *Ciência Hoje* 11(61).

9. van der Berg, M.E. 1984. Ver-o-Peso, The ethnobotany of an

Amazonian market. *Advances in Economic Botany*, Vol 1. The New York Botanical Garden.

10. FAO. 1989. Report of the Commission on Plant Genetic Resources, 3rd Session. 17-21 April 1989, Rome.

11. Cox, C. 1989. Developing sustainable sources of tropical timber from indigenous territories in Ecuador. Ecological Trading Company.

12. Nepstad, D., Uhl, C., and Adilson Serrão, E. 1990. Surmounting barriers to forest regeneration in abandoned, highly degraded pastures: a case study from Paragominas, Pará, Brazil. In A.B. Anderson (Ed.) *Alternatives to deforestation: steps toward sustainable use of the Amazon rain forest*. Columbia University Press. New York.

13. Myers, N. 1990. *Deforestation Rates in Tropical Forests and their Climatic Implications*. Friends of the Earth.

14. E.g. Lal, R. 1989. Potential of Agroforestry as a sustainable alternative to shifting cultivation: concluding remarks. *Agroforestry Systems* 8(3).

15. David Arkcoll, pers comm.

16. Subler, S. and Uhl, C. 1990. Japanese agroforestry in Amazonia: a case study in Tomé-Açú, Brazil. In A.B. Anderson (Ed.) *Alternatives to deforestation: steps toward sustainable use of the Amazon rain forest*. Columbia University Press. New York.

17. Canadian Embassy Agroforestry Advisory Group, Brasília. ?1989. Projeto de desenvolvimento agroflorestal em comunidades de pequenos agricultores, Região Ouro Preto-Jarú, Rondônia. Project Document.

CHAPTER 12

1. Canadian International Development Agency. 1989. Sustainable development of Acrean Forest resources. Project No. 204/16379. Draft plan of operation.

2. ITTO 1988. Integration of forest-based development in the western Amazon – phase I: forest management to promote policies for sustainable development. Project Document.

3. G7 Communiqué 11.7.90.

4. Rich, B.M. 1989. Statement concerning the environmental performance of the World Bank, before subcommittees of the US House of Representatives, 26.9.89. Environmental Defense Fund.

5. E.g. Letter from the Environmental Defense Fund to the World Bank, 22.2.90.

6. See World Bank Country Department 1, 1990. Brazil: Rondônia Natural Resource Management Project.

INDEX

açaí fruit, 236–8
Acre state, 201
Adolfo, Frei, 25–6, 35
agrarian reform, 41–3, 262
agriculture, experiments, 250–7;
  problems for, 126–7, 248–9,
  257
agroforestry, 249–50, 256–7
Altino, José, 65–6, 102, 105
Amazon river system, 4–5
Aparecido da Silva, José, 179–80
army, Brazilian, and Calha Norte,
  2, 149–52; landownership, 156,
  262; in Tukano lands, 142–4,
  162–4

Bacabal, Maranhão, 25–7
Balbina dam, 196–8
Barbosa, Adelino, 25, 31–3
Barbosa, Manoel, 27, 32–3, 46,
  49–53, 59
Bayma Denys, General Rubens,
  149, 151, 152
beekeeping, 255
Belém, 236, 240–1
Bezerra, Francisco, 118–19
Boa Vista, Roraima, 64
Bolivia, 208–9
Brazil, 3, 35, 150, 151, 228;
  international debt, 225–6;
  military government, 213–17
Brazil, government, 23–4, 130–2,

212–24, 258–9; corruption, 172–
  173, 220; policies for future,
  244–5, 262–5
buffalo ranching, 205

caboclos, 20
Cabrera, Antônio, 41, 42
Calha Norte project, 131–2, 137,
  145, 149–52, 154
Canada, 254, 260
capitalism, 221–2, 258–9
Carajás iron mine, 199–200
cattle-ranchers and ranching, 41,
  156–7, 262–3; cause of
  deforestation, 167–9; in
  Maranhão, 24–5, 27; organized
  crime, 31–2, 39, 58
Centro dos Aguiar, 24–5, 31–3
Chimarão airstrip, 74, 103–5
climate, 7–11
coca and cocaine, 209, 211
cocoa, 239
Collor de Mello, President
  Fernando, 41, 101, 207,
  219
Colombia, 211
colonization *see* settlement
Cometa Madeiras timber company,
  179, 181–82, 184
conquistadores, 14, 220
Cultural Survival, 235
culture, imposition of alien, 114–16

dams, 195–6, 197–8
debt, international, 216, 225–6
deforestation, 205–6, 208–9; by
    cattle-ranching, 167–8; by
    settlers, 123–5; and misdirected
    investment, 260–1, see also
    forest; timber trade
democracy, in developing
    countries, 222–4
development, prospects for,
    259–61, 263–5
diseases, 14–15, 83, 142–3; among
    Yanomami, 63, 96, 110–11;
    endemic, 203
Dog's Head region, and Calha
    Norte project, 132–5
durian fruit, 253–4

Ecological Trading Company,
    243, 244–5
Ecuador, 208–10, 244–5
education, 218–19, 223–4, 263;
    missionary school, 145
Eletrobras electricity company,
    195–6, 197–8
European Community, 191, 192,
    199–200

Figueiredo, President João Batista,
    216
fire, effect on rainforest, 8, 9,
    173–5
fish, 128, 137, 139, 160; poisons,
    235, 237
foreign investment, 199–200, 207–8,
    213–214; imbalance of, 259–61
forest, life cycle of trees, 7, 8–11;
    regeneration, 245–8
forest management, 15–17, 190–4,
    243–5
forest products, harvesting, 231,
    233–4; medicines, 239–43;
    potential, 234–5
Friends of the Earth, 190, 192, 222
FUNAI (Brazilian Indian

protection agency), 137, 151–2,
    177, 178–80; and Tukano, 147–9;
    and Yanomami, 63, 96–8,
    101–2, 118

garimpeiros (miners) see mining
gas fields, 202–3
Geisel, President Ernesto, 215–
    16
General Agreement on Tariffs and
    Trade (GATT), 192
Germany, 260–1
global warming, 7, 10–11, 227
gold see mining
Goulart, President João, 213
Great Britain, 227, 228, 260–1;
    timber imports, 175–6, 183,
    184–5, 186–7, 189–90
Guyana, 211–12

health care, among Tukano, 145–6
hydroelectricity, 195–9, 230–1

Ilha de Combu, 236–9
Imaribo timber company, 183,
    184
Indians, in Colombia, 211;
    origins, 12–13, 18–20; rights of
    156–7; use of rainforest, 15–22,
    156–7, 240, see also Kayapó;
    Tukano; Yanomami
InterAmerican Development Bank,
    129, 200–1
International Monetary Fund, 225
    227, 258, 262
International Tropical Timber
    Organization, 245, 261
Ipanaré, 161–2, 163, 164
iron mining, 199, 201

Japan, investment, 191, 201
Japanese settlers at Tomé-Açú,
    250–54

Jari project, 202, 232
Jarú, Rondônia, sawmills, 178–9
Jeremias airstrip, 68, 71–2, 104, 106
Jí-Paraná, Rondônia, 185–6
Jucá, Romero, 98–9, 121–2, 177, 179

Karitiana Indians, 242
Kayapó Indians, 15–18

landownership, 21–3, 40–1, 124–5, 156–7
liberation theology, 35–6, 215–16
Luís da Costa, Zé, 186
Lutzemberger, José, 201–2, 206–7

Macarão airstrip, 87, 91–4, 103–4
Madeireira Nacional timber company, 156–7
Madeireira Urupá timber company, 186–7
mahogany trees and timber, 173, 181–5, 188–9
Manaus, 8, 128
manioc, 16
Mann, Barbara, 64, 65–6, 106–8
Maranhão, 24–5, 37–9, 40–1, 43–58; land disputes, 24–31; miners from 69–71, 75
marketing, importance of, 252–3
medicines, development of, 239–43
mercury poisoning, 77–8
miners, 62–6, 69–71; attitudes to Indians, 84–5; expulsion from Indian lands, 99–100, 101–2, 104–6, 119–22; life in camps, 74–5, 79, 82–4, 86
mining, 61–102; description of, 68–9, 75–8; in Dog's Head region, 153–4; and Yanomami, 63–4, 96–7

missionaries, Salesian, at Taracuá, 144–7
Monteiro, Milton, 29–31, 34
Mors, Professor Walter, 241–2
murder, 37–9; among miners, 80, 81–2, 83, 92–3, 103–4

National Forests, development in, 153
nature, man's relationship with, 158–9
Negro, Rio, 5–7, 132, 134–6

oil fields, 202, 209–10
Ouro Preto d'Oueste, 254–7

Pará state, 173, 175
Paragominas, 171–5
ParanaPanema mining company, 154, 211
Pau Santo, 28–31, 48, 53–4
pepper, as crop, 250–1
peripona see Tukano Indians
Peru, 208–9, 243
police, brutality, 27–8, 30, 32–4, 39–40; corruption, 45–7
Porto Velho, Rondônia, 176–7

rainfall, 8–11
rainforest see forest
Ranchers' Union, 27, 39, 41, 218
research, government funding, 207–8; into medicines, 239–43
reserves, 125, 187–8, 199
roads, 129, 161–2, 200–2
Rondônia, 125, 175–8; roads through, 129, 200–2; University, 242; see also Uru Eu Wau Wau reserve
Roosevelt, Anna, 13
Roraima province, 62–4
rubber, 234–5, 251
rubber-tappers' movement, 231–3

São Gabriel da Cachoeira, 132–4
São Luís, 44–5
Sarney, President José, 40–1,
    180–1, 207, 217–19
settlers, 2, 125–9, 205–6;
    agricultural experiments, 255–7;
    reasons for migration, 21–4
Siqueira, Captain, 135, 137, 140–2,
    143
smuggling, 82–3
soil, fertility, 5, 16–17, 125–6

Taracuá, 143–9, 154, 157–8
television (Globo) network, 214–15,
    217–18
timber trade, companies, 156–7,
    179–87; effect on Indians, 188;
    export, 172–3, 175–6, 180–94,
    188–92; need for control of,
    193, 262, 263; sawmills, 170–3,
    177–9; sustainable projects,
    191–2, 193–4, 243–5; threat to
    rainforest, 2, 168–9, 173–5,
    190–1
Timber Trade Federation, 185,
    192
Tomé-Açú, Japanese in, 250–3
torture, 39, 41, 214
towns, growth of, 128
TransAmazon Highway, 129
'treekeepers', 233–4, 235
Tropical Forestry Action
    Programme, 261–2
Tukano Indians, and army, 142–
    3, 162–4; and Calha Norte
    project, 131–2, 133, 152–5;
    fishing, 18, 137, 139, 160;
    peripona people, 159, 163–4;
    and Salesian missionaries, 144–
    7; traditions, 135–6, 138, 157–
    8, 159–61

Uaupés, Rio, 136, 154
Uhl, Chris, 174–5, 189, 246–7
United Nations, Food and
    Agriculture Organization, 127,
    243, 261
United States of America, 189–90,
    191, 224–5, 226, 262; and
    environmental pollution, 227,
    228; foreign policy, 213–15,
    224–5
Uru Eu Wau Wau reserve, 176–84,
    185–8
Urubuquara, village, 162–4

Venezuela, 150, 152, 211
Vidal da Costa, Sgt, 32–4, 46–7,
    54–5, 59

wealth, distribution of, 212–13,
    219–20
wildlife, threatened, 6, 203–5
women, in mining camps, 79–80;
    and Tukano organization, 149
World Bank, 129, 199, 201, 225,
    260–1

Xâvier, Capt Moises, 50–3, 56–7,
    58–9
Xâvier, Col Francisco, 45–6, 50

Yanomami Indians, 63–4, 88–91,
    118–19, 156–7; cultivation by,
    112–13; and FUNAI, 96–8;
    infanticide, 15, 130; life among,
    108–14, 116–17; and miners, 62–4,
    72–4, 83–5, 95–102

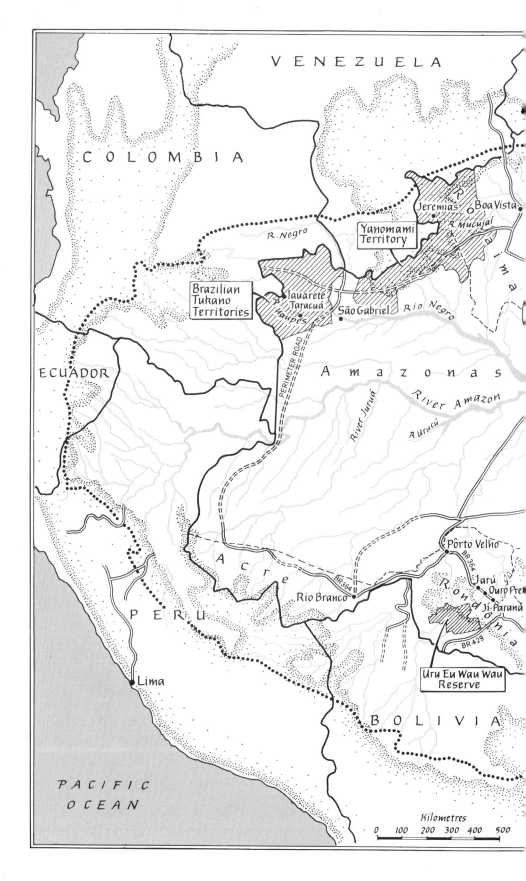